Evelyn Findlater's
WHOLEFOOD
COOKERY SCHOOL

OPTIMA

—— Evelyn Findlater's ——

WHOLEFOOD
◆ COOKERY SCHOOL ◆

ILLUSTRATED BY PETER BAILEY

An OPTIMA book

© Evelyn Findlater 1988

First published in 1988 by
Macdonald Optima, a division of
Macdonald & Co. (Publishers) Ltd

A member of Maxwell Pergamon Publishing Corporation plc

British Library Cataloguing in Publication Data

Findlater, Evelyn
    Evelyn Findlater's Wholefood cookery school.
    1. Food: Dishes using natural food –
    Recipes
    I. Title   II. Findlater, Evelyn. Evelyn
    Findlater's Wholefood cookery course
    641.5′637

    ISBN 0-356-15449-1

Macdonald & Co. (Publishers) Ltd
3rd Floor
Greater London House
Hampstead Road
London NW1 7QX

Printed and bound in Great Britain by
Richard Clay Ltd
Chichester

Cover photograph by Gerrit Buntrock
c/o Anthony Blake Studios
54 Hill Rise
Richmond
Surrey

CONTENTS

INTRODUCTION

This book is a course of cookery lessons and is the result of teaching many students the art of vegetarian wholefood cookery. The classes were originally instigated by my customers in the wholefood shop and cafe I ran for three years. Much to the customers' surprise, and mine sometimes, the food tasted delicious and I spent most of my time during that period giving recipes and advice to keen and interested people who wished to change their existing diet to a healthier one.

The book is not just a conglomeration of healthy recipes but is designed to introduce wholefoods gradually into the daily diet in a way that is easy on the purse as well as the digestion. I spent years trying out random recipes, which added strange ingredients to my store cupboard – some were successful to taste but played havoc with my digestion, while others were downright disastrous. I won through in a hit and miss way.

In devising my course I had to find an easy beginning that had a familiarity about it and would encourage people to succeed – producing not only healthy meals but also food that was deliciously acceptable to *all* the family. Having had four children and fed hundreds of their friends through the years my advice is don't despair. Most children are a pain to feed at some stage in their lives no matter what diet you happen to be on, so you might as well give them a healthy one with the occasional gooey indulgence thrown in.

Throughout the course I also try to point out

as simply as possible the nutritional value of the foods which, if gradually incorporated into the diet in a balanced way, will help the body to function more efficiently within a very short time.

Many people are under the misapprehension that those of us who adopt a healthy diet are vegetarian and do not approve of eating meat, either because of moral or health reasons or both. Well, my experience is that many healthy eaters gradually begin to enjoy a varied diet, consequently eat less meat, experiment with alternative forms of protein and feel better for it.

The recipes in this book do not follow any strict regime. Vegetarian, vegans and meat-eaters will find full instructions on how they can adapt them to their own needs. To help you do this, all the nutritional information and special cookery instructions for unfamiliar ingredients are set out at the beginning of each lesson.

Whether you eat meat or not, the addition of wholefoods and the elimination of refined and overprocessed foods can only benefit your health. But no matter how healthy the food is, I think it should taste really good and not just be good for you; it should be reasonably simple for every day with added exotic flair for special occasions. This I have tried to fulfil in my course, which if followed, lesson by lesson will I hope open the doors to the joy of real food and healthier living.

DIET AND HEALTH

Basically we all have similar nutritional requirements whether we eat meat or not. It is, of course, a question of balance. The right amount of protein, unprocessed carbohydrates, fats and an adequate supply of vitamins and minerals are essential for a fit and healthy body. We require a high intake of fibre and a low consumption of fats, sugar and salt. But research has revealed that our modern Western diet is too low in fibre (roughage) and overloaded with saturated fats, sugar and salt. Added to which, most of our refined foods contain harmful additives. There is now strong evidence to suggest that these factors have all become an increasing threat to our health.

If you wish to change your diet to a healthier one it is important to educate the system slowly. Drastically reducing or cutting out foods without knowing which alternatives to introduce can endanger your health. Through experience I have found that it is not a good idea to eat too many pulses (dried peas, beans, lentils) without the previous introduction of more easily digested wholefoods such as whole grains. For this reason I have structured the course in such a way that grains, particularly wholewheat (wholemeal) in the first three lessons and a large variety of grains in the fourth lesson, are gradually introduced into the diet, in recipes which will not only be easy on the digestion but reasonably simple to prepare, even for the novice wholefood cook. The course is also designed to build-up a wholefood store cupboard gradually with ingredients you will use throughout the book.

WHAT ARE WHOLEFOODS?

There is nothing new or magical about wholefoods, they are simply unfragmented (unprocessed) foods as close to nature as possible with nothing added to them and nothing taken away. These foods include 100 per cent wholewheat (wholemeal) flour, unpolished brown rice and other whole grains, fresh fruit and vegetables, pulses (dried peas, beans and lentils), dried fruit, nuts and seeds, meat, fish and dairy produce. Unfortunately it is only the minority who can buy or grow pure organic plant food and even fewer who can obtain meat and dairy produce from naturally reared animals who have not been injected with hormones and antibiotics. But the demand for pure natural food is growing, so keep on hammering the producers and manufacturers and they will give you what you want. Remember, they have to please you or they won't make a profit.

A BALANCED DIET

Food gives the body energy but it should also supply it with essential nutrients for the maintenance, growth and repair of cells. The body is a complex machine with every part interdependent. It needs a balanced diet, which contains an adequate supply of protein, carbohydrates, fats, vitamins and minerals, to maintain its delicate chemical balance. This doesn't mean just feeding the stomach to fill it up. The brain and every cell in the body need certain nutrients to keep them not just alive but fit and well. This sounds quite simple but just as the body is complex so are the foods we eat. The more we understand how the body reacts to what we feed it with, the more likely we are to choose those foods which will keep it in good working order.

PROTEIN

The body does not store protein but it needs a constant supply, as protein is the builder of all body tissues including muscles, blood, skin, hair, nails and the internal organs such as the heart, brain, liver and kidneys. It also forms hormones, enzymes and antibodies. If the body does not get enough protein it will not sustain proper growth, and if protein intake is not complemented by enough energy-giving carbohydrates and fats, then the protein in muscle tissue can be converted into carbohydrates which, in turn, can lead to protein deficiency.

Not only does the body need protein, but it must be what is termed a 'complete' protein with all the amino acids in balance. Human protein is made up of twenty-two amino acids. The body produces fourteen, while the other eight, which are known as essential amino acids, must be obtained from your diet. Meat, fish, dairy produce and the soya bean have these essential amino acids in the necessary proportions, whereas grains, legumes (dried peas, beans and lentils), nuts and seeds are deficient in some of the essential amino acids. For this reason grains, legumes, nuts and seeds were once labelled as sources of second-class protein, but now research has shown that when these foods are complemented in various ways a proper amino acid balance can be achieved. To obtain enough usable protein you must combine the foods in one of the following ways:

● Grains with legumes (dried peas, beans or lentils).
● Grains with nuts and seeds.
● Grains with dairy produce.
● Legumes with nuts or seeds.

You can, of course, mix these combinations. For example a risotto could have grains, beans and a little cheese sprinkled on top.

Proportion-wise, you can't go wrong if the main meal consists of at least 50 per cent grains (cooked weight – remember most grains treble in size when cooked), 25 per cent of either legumes, nuts and seeds or dairy produce or a combination of all three, and the other 25 per cent land or sea vegetables either lightly steamed or in a salad.

I have devised the recipes in the book so that you do get a complete protein intake in all lunch and supper dishes. With practice, and a conscious awareness of the food you eat, you will be able to create many variations which will provide all the protein your body needs.

CARBOHYDRATES

Carbohydrates are our main source of calories (energy) and they consist of two main components – sugars (which includes starches) and fibre (roughage).

SUGARS
There are several types of sugars:

● *Monosaccharides* (or single sugars) such as glucose and fructose. Glucose is found in fruit juice and milk. Fructose is found in fruit and honey.
● *Disaccharides* (or double sugars). These are sucrose, lactose and maltose. Sucrose (common table sugar) is a combination of fructose and glucose and is produced from sugar cane and sugar beet. Sucrose is also found in most vegetables and fruit. Lactose is found in milk. Maltose is found in barley and other grains.
● *Polysaccharides* (or multiple sugars). These are what we call *starches*. They are found in root vegetables, pulses, grains and seeds.

The body needs sugar to give it energy but it can only use single sugars (monosaccharides) – our digestive system can extract these single sugars from the more complex sugars. However, ordinary common sugar (sucrose) and other sugar concentrates can also be harmful, especially as large amounts can be eaten far too easily. An excess of sugar is the main cause of tooth decay. It is also considered by experts in the field of nutritional research to be a major factor in the development of heart disease, obesity, diabetes and certain digestive disorders.

FIBRE

Carbohydrates also include substances such as cellulose, pectin and gums. These form the walls of plant cells and are collectively known as fibre (roughage). Dietary fibre was originally thought to be insoluble (not able to be absorbed by the body) thus the term 'unavailable carbohydrates', but recent research has revealed that there is soluble and insoluble fibre. Both have differing but beneficial effects on our digestive system. Soluble fibre breaks down more quickly and is said to assist in the lowering of blood cholesterol. Foods which contain soluble fibre include apples, other fruit and vegetables and oats. Insoluble fibre, particularly found in wheat, remains undigested. This fibre has been shown to have a greater effect on bowel functioning.

The main role of fibre in the body is that it absorbs water. It becomes sponge-like and grips onto the walls of the colon. The colon muscle can then work efficiently to expel waste products from the body. A lack of fibre in the diet causes constipation. If prolonged this condition leads to ruptures in the wall of the gut. The lining of the colon swells through these holes and causes little pouches (diverticulae) which often become inflamed and are extremely painful. This disease, which is called diverticulitis, can lead to abscesses and make elimination impossible and surgery inevitable. There is a strong connection between a low fibre intake and cancer of the colon. Findings also suggest that if we consume just over 28g/1oz, almost an average teacup full, of dietary fibre daily, we lessen the risk of coronary heart disease. Tests have also shown that fibre can alter bacteria in the bowel making it less prone to disease.

As you can see from the above, dietary fibre is vitally necessary if the body is to function properly. But findings have shown that eating too much fibre (particularly bran from wheat)

can be harmful. Fibre contains phytic acid which inhibits (blocks) the absorption of iron, calcium and zinc in the body. Yeasted bakes and certain heat processes apparently lessen the level of this acid, but as with most nutrients there is an optimum intake, which, if exceeded, causes vital foods to become harmful. It is not advisable to add neat bran by the spoonful to a diet containing a large proportion of refined foods as this will only serve to stop the body absorbing any remaining nutrients.

It would seem sensible then to obtain fibre from unrefined wholefoods which contain other nutrients vital for health. This means eating plenty of raw or lightly cooked vegetables, fresh fruit, whole grains, pulses (dried peas, beans and lentils), nuts and seeds.

Note: There is no fibre in meat, fish or dairy produce, so it is important to accompany these foods with those rich in fibre. So the next time you are serving, say a meat-based curry or goulash, then turn to page 79 and find out how to cook brown rice to perfection. Throw in one of the delicious salads in Lesson 8 and you will have a truly nutritious and fibre-full meal.

FATS

Fats are essential foods which are necessary to maintain health. They act as insulators of heat in the body as well as store energy for emergencies. They also form the major structural part of every cell wall in the body. But their most vital function is that they produce active biological substances necessary for the normal functioning of the body.

All fats, both animal and vegetable, are made up of triglycerides, each of which is a combination of fatty acids. The difference between fats is a result of the different fatty acids in them. Fats, however, break down into two main groups – those containing *saturated fatty acids* and those containing *polyunsaturated fatty acids*. These two groups have a considerable effect on our health:

● *Saturated Fats* include animal fats, lard, butter, cream, coconut oil, palm oil and some margarines (unless otherwise stated). Unfortunately most margarines, even some of those labelled 'high in polyunsaturates' are not a lot healthier than butter. Most are hydrogenated (chemically hardened) which is the process used to create a texture for spreading. This process changes polyunsaturated fat into saturated fat. Fats chemically altered in this way can make essential fatty acids unavailable to the body. There are a few margarines on the market which do not go through this process and are made largely with cold pressed oils. Findings have shown that if we eat large amounts of saturated fats we will produce too high a level of cholesterol in the blood and thus become more vulnerable to heart attacks, thrombosis and gallstones. Cholesterol is made by the body and is essential for certain functions; it is only when there is too much that problems arise.

● *Polyunsaturated Fats* include safflower seed oil (highest in linoleic acid which seems to play an important part in controlling cholesterol levels in the body), sunflower oil, corn oil, soya oil, sesame oil, grape seed oil, rape seed oil, wheatgerm oil and some vegetable margarines which are not chemically hardened (see *saturated fats* above). These polyunsaturated fats are high in linoleic acid which, as previously mentioned, helps lower the level of cholesterol in the blood. But it must also be mentioned that vitamins B and E are needed to maintain a low level of cholesterol.

Unsaturated fats also include *mono-unsaturated fats* (mono means one). Olive oil contains mono-unsaturated fatty acids which do not seem to contribute to heart disease. Although it is low in linoleic acid it has been found to increase the absorption of vitamins A, D, E and K and is easily digested. Groundnut/peanut oil is also largely mono-unsaturated.

What is of vital importance to the quality and nutritional value of these oils is the method used to extract them from their seeds. There are refined and cold pressed (virgin) oils. The most widely consumed are refined oils which are usually subjected to high temperatures to extract the oil quickly and cheaply. This process often destroys most of the nutrients. In many cases chemicals are then added. The better quality refined oils are less intensely treated and do retain some of their vitamins and minerals.

Cold pressed (or virgin) oil is whole and complete. This method of extraction is mechanical, the oil is simply pressed slowly from the seed, it retains all its nutrients and has a delicate flavour and fresh smell. These oils are best for salads and stir-fry vegetables.

Sesame oil does not turn rancid which is why it is most popular in tropical countries. It contains an ingredient called sesamol which analysis has shown is the natural stabilizing ingredient and prevents the oil from going off.

It would seem sensible then to replace saturated fats with unsaturated fats wherever possible and watch for hidden saturated fats in bought cakes and biscuits and other chemically prepared foods.

VITAMINS AND MINERALS

These are organic substances which are needed by the body, in small amounts daily, to assist growth and maintain health. Different vitamins and minerals behave differently in the body and adequate amounts can be got from eating a balanced diet. So unless there is a build up or a deficiency, due to inadequate diet or illness, we should not need to take extra vitamin or mineral supplements.

An important point for those on a vegan diet is that vitamin B_{12}, which is essential for the functioning of all body cells and is only rarely found in the plant world, must be included in the diet. Sources of B_{12} (other than meat, fish, dairy produce and eggs) include sprouted soya beans (see page 140) and other sprouted seeds, tempeh (a fermented soya bean food – see page 121), seaweed and comfrey if grown on soil rich in this vitamin. A deficiency of B_{12} can cause anaemia and may contribute to disorders in the central nervous system.

Particular care must be taken where babies (unless fed on mother's milk) and growing children are concerned to ensure that they eat foods which supply this vitamin. A vegetarian diet which includes dairy produce will supply adequate vitamin B_{12}.

LESSON 1

BREADS AND YEASTED PASTRIES

This lesson shows you how to make a variety of breads using different flours, including Indian unyeasted breads such as chapatis and puris, and delicious rich yeasted dough recipes for savarins, brioche and croissants. The variations on many of these recipes are endless so I have chosen tried and tested favourites. Follow the recipes carefully and you will succeed in making the most superb home bakes.

SHOPPING LIST

Here is a list of basic ingredients which will enable you to make many of the recipes in this lesson, as well as gradually build-up a larder of natural foods. These ingredients will all be of use in other lessons in the book.

Luxury recipe ingredients and fresh vegetables and fruit are not listed as these can be purchased when needed. Some of the ingredients below are not complete wholefoods but are used with discretion in the recipes. Replenish any item when used up, then you will always have a well-stocked larder.

100 per cent wholemeal or wholewheat stoneground flour, plain
81 per cent brown wheatmeal flour, plain
unbleached white flour, plain
rye flour
soya flour
soya oil (for any deep-frying)
raisins
sultanas
apricots
figs
dates
vegetable bouillon powder (or vegetable stock cubes)
black peppercorns
wholemeal chapati flour
sesame seeds
pumpkin seeds
jar of clear honey
fruit sugar (optional) see page 58
Barbados sugar
jar of malt extract
jar of molasses
large tin dried yeast
sunflower or corn oil
virgin olive oil
dried skimmed milk powder
dried basil
dried oregano
dried marjoram
dried tarragon
dried bay leaves
dry mustard powder
caraway seeds
mixed spice
nutmegs
ground cinnamon
natural vanilla essence

TYPES OF FLOUR

100 PER CENT WHOLEMEAL OR WHOLEWHEAT FLOUR contains all the bran (fibre) and wheatgerm and is 13 per cent protein. It is a good source of the B vitamins, vitamin E and various minerals. It is also higher in nutritional value than any product processed from the whole grain. *Stoneground* flour and *steel-milled* flour do differ. You can buy much cheaper steel-milled versions of 100 per cent wholemeal/wholewheat flour, because steel-milling is a much quicker and economical method of grinding, but often produces an inferior flour. This is because the steel plates reach such a high speed that the intensive heat generated can destroy the wheatgerm oil, causing it to become rancid and rendering it nutritionally useless. Stoneground flour is usually superior because the stone burrs, which grind the wheat, distribute the embryo (wheatgerm oil) at a

slow speed and do not reach a destructively high level of heat.

STRONG FLOUR, made from hard wheat, which has a higher protein (gluten) content than flour made from soft wheat, is best for yeasted dough mixtures (for more information on gluten see *Hints for perfect yeasted dough* on page 17).

85 PER CENT AND 81 PER CENT WHEATMEAL FLOUR has 15 to 19 per cent of the ground grain removed. This includes most of the bran and wheatgerm. It is lighter than 100 per cent wholemeal flour. Use it in moderation, although a good tip if you want to use lighter flour, say for a savoury or fruit pie, is to sieve 100 per cent wholemeal flour and add the bran left in the sieve to the pie fillings. This way you are still eating the wholegrain.

UNBLEACHED WHITE FLOUR has about 35 per cent of the grain, which includes all the bran and wheatgerm, removed. I use this occasionally in sauces and when making light bread. It is best to use it only in moderation as half and half unbleached white flour and 100 per cent wholemeal flour. Avoid ordinary white flour, which is chemically treated and bleached with chlorine dioxide (also used for cleaning drains).

GRANARY FLOUR is usually made from a mixture of flours and contains malt with added wholewheat berries which gives a crunchy texture. You can now buy a type of granary flour which is made with all wholewheat or wholemeal flour and toasted malted whole barley grains. This flour is called malthouse flour and makes the most delicious bread.

KIBBLED OR CRACKED WHEAT is wholewheat split by pressure machinery but still retaining its high nutritional value. It is really good sprinkled on top of bread or rolls before baking. Try the recipe for *Kibbled wheat bread* on page 21.

RYE FLOUR has a distinctive and I think delicious flavour. It is much lower in gluten

(protein) than wheat flour and, on its own, does not rise well enough to make a light loaf. I have found great success combining rye with wholewheat flour and using a batter or sponge method for preparing (see page 24 for *Dark rye, wholemeal and caraway seed bread*). There are two types of rye flour – dark and light. The darker variety has a higher fibre content and contains the valuable germ, so try to obtain this for your bread making.

OATMEAL (from oats) is a wholegrain that has been either ground or flaked by a simple rolling process. As no refining or processing takes place it retains its full nutritional value.

Oatmeal or porridge oats marked 'quick cooking' or 'instant' have been pre-heated before the rolling process and are nutritionally inferior. Oatmeal (including unrefined oat flakes called Jumbo Oats) is a highly nutritious high fibre grain containing 17 per cent protein. It is rich in minerals, especially iron and has more B vitamins than any other grain. Tests have shown that regular consumption of oats helps lower blood sugar level. Oatmeal comes in three grades – fine, medium and coarse (pin head). Fine oatmeal is good in bread making using approximately 85g/3oz oatmeal to 450g/1 lb flour. Medium oatmeal makes lovely crunchy savoury and sweet biscuits and coarse (pin head) oatmeal is delicious soaked in water and a little malt extract, then made into porridge for breakfast.

BARLEY FLOUR, if it is wholegrain, contains all the fibre and germ. It is great combined with strong wholemeal flour in bread making, but only use 55g/2oz barley flour to 450g/1lb flour. It adds a slightly sweet nutty malt taste to the finished loaf.

Malt extract is produced from barley and is made from the sprouted grain that has been dried at a low temperature. You can buy it in the form of a thick syrup as well as powdered. Malt is helpful in bread making because it is a food for yeast to feed on and helps convert starch into another form that ferments readily. It also softens gluten (see notes on gluten on page 96) and adds a nutty flavour. Be careful how you use malt because too much makes the bread sticky. Use just over 28g/1oz in syrup form or one heaped teaspoon of the powdered form to 1 Kg 375g/3 lb flour.

SOYA FLOUR is not from a grain but from the soya bean. I use it a great deal in bread making, as it adds lots of first class protein (see page 116 for nutritional information on soya flour). It will not make the bread heavy if you include it in the proportion of 55g/2oz to each 450g/1 lb of strong flour. Also, using a batter or sponge method lightens the dough considerably (see page 25 for *Wholemeal and soya bread* [batter method]).

WHOLEMEAL CHAPATI FLOUR (ATA) is obtainable from Indian grocers' shops. This flour is a very fine wholegrain flour which takes on a slightly sticky consistency when made into dough. It is ideal for Indian-type unyeasted chapatis, puris and samosas.

WHOLEGRAIN BAKING

It is of course better for your health to eat bread and other bakes made with wholegrain flours which contain the germ and fibre necessary for the body to function efficiently. But if your diet usually includes wholegrains, pulses, nuts and seeds and plenty of fresh fruit and vegetables then a little deviation from using the complete wholegrain flour in your baking should not cause problems to your health. In some of the following recipes I have used 81 per cent, 85 per cent and unbleached white flour combined with more wholesome ingredients to add a variety of taste and texture.

Baking bread and other yeasted dough using wholegrain flour is really quite a simple process. All you need is a bit of practice and patience and your recipes will turn out perfect every time. The following tips will save you time and hopefully help you avoid disappointments.

HINTS FOR PERFECT YEASTED DOUGH

- Kneading dough well releases the gluten (protein) in the flour. Gluten has a stretchy, rubbery quality and forms tiny bubbles which are filled with carbon dioxide. The carbon dioxide is made when yeast feeding on natural sugars in the dough multiplies. A draught can flatten these bubbles and make the resulting bread too heavy and crumbly. Your dough is well kneaded if it does not retain the impression of a finger.

- Too much heat kills the yeast but it needs warmth to live. A temperature of around 26°C/80°F is about right. For perfect yeasted doughs a warm kitchen, warm bowl and warm baking tins are essential.

- Do not leave your dough to rise too long as this will weaken it and dry it out. The resulting bread will have a flat, cracked surface, a coarse texture and holes in it.

- Although frozen dough will not result in the perfect loaf, sometimes it is necessary to freeze some for an emergency. It will taste better than most bought bread. The best time to freeze dough is when it has risen once, been knocked back and shaped and is in the tin ready to rise for the second time. Just place each tin in a good sized, oiled polythene bag, squeeze out the air, tie the opening 2.5cm/1 inch from the end and put it into the freezer. To defrost place the frozen tin still in its oiled polythene bag in a warm – not hot – place and leave to rise to double its size. It will then be ready for the oven.

- You can store yeasted doughs in a refrigerator for up to 48 hours after the first kneading. Make sure the dough is placed in a good sized, oiled polythene bag from which the air has been squeezed out. Tie 2.5cm/1 inch from the opening and place in the fridge. When ready to bake just knock back the dough, shape into loaves, place in tins and leave to rise in a warm place until double in size. Then bake as instructed in the recipe.

● One more very important tip is that 450g/ 1 lb and 900g/2 lb loaf tins vary enormously in size, so weigh your dough and make sure that the dough when placed in the tin reaches just over halfway up the tin, so that when the dough rises it will form a slight hump over the surface of the tin.

These tips are only guidelines. Remember, flours vary in texture depending on how finely the grains have been ground. The amount of liquid needed will vary according to the type of flour used, the fineness of the grain and the addition of any ingredient such as ground sesame seeds, soya flour or oatmeal that you might incorporate into the ingredients.

BREADS

WHOLEMEAL SESAME DOUGH
This is a favourite mixture which makes not only delicious bread but also superb pitta bread and pizza bases.

Makes 2½Kg/5½ lb dough.
This is sufficient for 2 x 675g/1½ lb loaves, 8 pitta breads and 1 large pizza base *or*
for bread only it will make 2 x 900g/2 lb loaves and 1 x 675g/1½ lb loaf *or*
for pitta bread only (which freezes well) it will make approximately 30 x 85g/3 oz *or*
for pizza bases only it will make 5 x 450g/1 lb and 1 x 225g/8 oz.

1 Kg 375g/3 lb wholemeal stoneground strong
*   flour*
1 level tablespoon sea salt (optional)
110g/4 oz sesame seeds
850ml/1½ pt warm water
28g/1 oz dried yeast or 55g/2 oz fresh yeast
1 level teaspoon either Barbados sugar or
*   molasses*
1 slightly rounded tablespoon malt extract –
*   just over 28g/1 oz*
2 tablespoons sunflower oil

1. Mix the flour, salt and sesame seeds in a large warm mixing bowl.
2. Put 285ml/½ pt of the required warm water in a small mixing bowl. Add sugar *or* molasses. Sprinkle on the dried yeast and stir well. If using fresh yeast then cream it with the sugar and a little of the 285ml/½ pt warm water until smooth, then gradually stir in the rest of the 285ml/½ pt warm water.
3. Cover and leave to froth in a warm place for about 7 minutes.
4. To the remaining 570ml/1 pt of warm water add the malt extract and oil. Stir well.
5. When yeast liquid is frothy make a well in the centre of the flour mixture and pour in the yeast and the malted liquids. Gradually work the flour into the liquid to form a soft dough. (Only after you have worked the dough well in the bowl can you be sure that you have added enough liquid. If too dry then add warm water a teaspoon at a time only.)
6. Knead the dough for 7 to 10 minutes. Flour your hands, not the surface, if the dough is a little sticky.
7. Place the dough in a large strong greased polythene bag, leaving enough room for it to rise to double its size. Press air out of the bag and secure 2.5 cm/1 inch from the top. Wrap loosely in a large thick warm towel and leave to rise for 45 minutes to 1 hour.
8. Knock back and knead for 1 minute more.

Your dough is now ready to make any or all of the three recipes that follow.

WHOLEMEAL SESAME BREAD
Makes 2 x 675g/1½ lb loaves.

You will need 2 x 675g/1½ lb loaf tins, greased and floured.

1 Kg 375g/3 lb Wholemeal sesame dough (see page 18).
little egg or milk to brush tops
few sesame seeds to sprinkle on top

1. Preheat the oven to 425°F/220°C/Gas Mark 7.
2. Divide the dough into 2 x 675g/1½ lb pieces.
3. Roll each to an oval shape, the length of the loaf tins, and roll up as you would a Swiss roll.
4. Press each piece gently into the prepared tins making sure that the dough touches all sides and corners. It should reach just over half-way up the tins.
5. Slide these into the greased polythene bags which should be big enough to let the bread rise to a slight hump just above the surface of the tin. Leave to rise for approximately 35 to 40 minutes in a warm place.
6. Brush tops with egg or milk and sprinkle on some sesame seeds.
7. Bake in the centre of a pre-heated oven for 10 minutes. Turn down heat to 375°F/190°C/Gas Mark 5, and continue to bake for 30 minutes more.

Note: If you want to use all the wholemeal sesame bread dough to make bread *only* then you will need the following:
2 x 900g/2 lb loaf tins and 1 x 675g/1½ lb loaf tin, greased and floured.

Break the dough into 2 x 900g/2 lb pieces and 1 x 675g/1½ lb piece.

Follow directions 3, 4, 5 and 6 but remember that the two larger loaves might take a little longer to rise. Put all three loaves in the centre of the pre-heated oven making sure to place the smaller loaf in front. Bake for 10 minutes. Turn down heat to 375°F/190°C/Gas Mark 5 and continue to bake the 675g/1½ lb loaf for 30 minutes more and the 2 x 900g/2 lb loaves for 50 minutes more.

WHOLEMEAL SESAME PITTA BREAD
Makes 8 pittas.
You will need 2 to 3 (depending on their size) baking trays, greased and lightly sprinkled with bran.

675g/1½ lb Wholemeal sesame dough (see page 18)
bran for rolling out

1. Preheat the oven to 450°F/230°C/Gas Mark 8.
2. Break dough into 8 x 85g/3 oz pieces. As you roll out each piece keep the others in the polythene bag. Roll each piece in a little bran into a 20 cm/8 inch long x 10 cm/4 inch wide, oval shape. I like to roll out pitta bread in a little bran as this does not dry the dough as much as flour.
3. Place each shape on the prepared trays and leave to rise in a warm place for 15 to 20 minutes (they will only rise a little).
4. Bake each tray separately on the top shelf of the hot oven for 5 minutes only. They will puff up completely or in places. Cool on a wire rack.

Note: If you want to use all the wholemeal sesame bread dough to make *only* pittas then the dough will make approximately 30 x 85g/3 oz pittas.

Follow the directions above and if you wish to freeze any for later use, allow to get completely cold on the rack before pressing each gently and freezing in polythene bags. They will not stick together. To defrost simply put in a warm oven for 2 to 3 minutes.
Serving Suggestions: Anyone can make a meal in a minute with a pitta. Simply cut in half widthwise. Open each piece to form a pocket. Stuff with either *Nutty pâté* (see page 94) or *Chick pea and sunflower seed dip* (see page 105), or grated cheese and salad vegetables, such as beansprouts, sliced cucumber, tomato or red pepper, spring onions and cress.

WHOLEMEAL SESAME PIZZA
Makes 1 x 30 cm/12 inch pizza.
You will need 1 x 30 cm/12 inch pizza tray, well oiled with virgin olive oil and a greased polythene sheet.

450g/1 lb Wholemeal sesame dough (see page 18)
1 tablespoon warm virgin olive oil (optional)

1. Put the dough into a mixing bowl and knead in the tablespoon of oil until the dough is smooth and silky. You can leave out this extra oil but it does add a delicious flavour and crispens the edges beautifully.
2. Roll out the dough to a circle to fit the pizza tray.
3. Fit the dough onto the tray, cover loosely with the greased polythene sheet and leave to rise in a warm place for about 30 minutes. While rising preheat the oven to 450°F/230°C/Gas Mark 8 and prepare the sauce and topping.

Pizza sauce and topping
Fills 1 x 30 cm/12 inch pizza base. You can use either black or green olives to top the pizza which is traditional, but children often find these too salty so try sprinkling on a few pumpkin seeds instead.

110g/4 oz onion, weight when peeled and
    chopped
1 large clove of garlic, peeled and chopped
2 sticks celery, chopped
1 tablespoon either virgin olive oil or sunflower
    oil
1/2 small red pepper
1/2 small green pepper
or 1 small green pepper, de-seeded and
    chopped
55g/2 oz firm button mushrooms, wiped and
    chopped
1 level teaspoon basil or 1 level tablespoon
    fresh, chopped
1 large bay leaf
1 level teaspoon vegetable bouillon powder
little freshly ground black pepper
1 x 397g/14 oz can tomatoes (less 2 tablespoons
    of the juice)
1 rounded tablespoon tomato purée
225g/8 oz either Farmhouse Cheddar or
    Mozzarella cheese, grated
10 black or green olives, stoned and halved or
    2 tablespoons pumpkin seeds
1 level teaspoon dried oregano or marjoram

1. Sauté onion, garlic and celery in the oil for 10 minutes with the lid on.
2. Add the peppers, mushrooms, basil, bay leaf and vegetable bouillon powder and cook for 3 minutes more.
3. Add black pepper, tomatoes (less 2 tablespoons of juice) and tomato purée.
4. Cook briskly, stirring for 1 minute.
5. Turn down heat and simmer for 15 minutes with the lid off. This evaporates the liquid and concentrates the sauce and makes it rich and thick.
6. To fill the risen pizza base sprinkle on 3 tablespoons of the cheese. Spoon on the hot sauce then sprinkle on the rest of the cheese.
7. Either dot with olives or pumpkin seeds and sprinkle on the oregano or marjoram.
8. Bake in the preheated oven for 10 minutes, then turn down heat to 375°F/190°C/Gas Mark 5 and continue to bake for 25 minutes more or until the top is golden brown.

Note: If you want to use all the wholemeal sesame dough for pizzas *only*, either for freezing or a buffet party, then the dough will make 5 x 450g/1 lb and 1 x 225g/8 oz pizza bases.

Follow the directions above (5 times the sauce will be enough as you can take a few spoonfuls out of this amount to fill the small pizza base). If you wish to freeze, allow to get completely cold and freeze in polythene bags. When needed defrost for about 2 hours then heat in a moderate oven 375°F/190°C/Gas Mark 5 for 15 minutes only.

Vegan pizza: All you need to alter in the previous recipe is the cheese topping. Lay thin slices of tofu (see page 119) over the pizza sauce instead of the cheese. Roughly chop the pumpkin seeds, mix these with a vegetable bouillon powder and oregano and sprinkle this on top of the tofu. This gives a savoury taste to the bland tofu.

SPROUTED GRAIN BREAD
All sprouted seeds, which include sprouted grains, dried peas, beans, whole lentils, alfalfa seeds and sunflower seeds are highly nutritious (see Lesson 7). They are also delicious in bread and many other bakes.

To make *Sprouted grain bread*, simply omit the sesame seeds from the *Wholemeal sesame* dough recipe (see page 18) and add 110g/4 oz sprouted wheat or barley grains (see page 142) instead.

This recipe will produce enough dough for 2 x 900g/2 lb loaves and 1 x 675g/1½ lb loaf. Prepare it for baking as described in the *Wholemeal sesame bread* recipe (see page 18) but remember that the two larger loaves might take a little longer to rise and that after the oven has been turned down to 375°F/190°C/Gas Mark 5, the two larger loaves need to bake for 50 minutes more while the smaller loaf needs 30 minutes more.

KIBBLED WHEAT BREAD
Kibbled or cracked wheat adds a lovely crunchy texture to bread but you have to soak the kibbled wheat before using.

To make, omit the sesame seeds from the *Wholemeal sesame dough* recipe (see page 18) and add 170g/6 oz kibbled wheat instead. Soak the kibbled wheat in the malt, oil and 570 ml/1 pt of the warm water for 1 hour before mixing in. Remember this water is part of the required water needed for the recipe, i.e. 850ml/1½ pt in all.

Follow the directions for making the dough and preparing it for baking. There should be enough dough for 2 x 900g/2 lb loaves and 1 x 675g/1½ lb loaf. Egg wash the tops when ready to bake and sprinkle on a little cracked wheat.

The oven temperature is the same as for *Wholemeal sesame bread* (see page 18), but remember that the two larger loaves need to bake for 50 minutes and the smaller loaf for 30 minutes, after the oven has been turned down to 375°F/190°C/Gas Mark 5.

GRANARY BREAD
No sweetener is needed for these loaves as the malt in the flour is quite sweet enough.
Makes 5 x 450g/1 lb loaves.

You will need 5 x 450g/1 lb loaf tins (you can use round cake tins) greased and floured.

850ml/1½ pt warm water
1 Kg 375g/3 lb granary flour (wholewheat granary)
28g/1 oz dried yeast or 55g/2 oz fresh yeast, crumbled

1 level tablespoon sea salt
2 tablespoons sunflower or corn oil

1. Put the warm water in a mixing bowl.
2. Stir in 110g/4 oz of the flour and the yeast. Mix well and let it stand for 15 minutes until frothy.
3. Add all the other ingredients and form into a soft dough. It might be a bit sticky but do not add any more flour until you have mixed the ingredients well.
4. Knead for 7 minutes, flouring your hands as you do so if the dough is still sticky.
5. Put into a large greased polythene bag and leave in a warm place for about 5 minutes or until double in size.
6. Knock back and knead for 2 minutes. Break dough into 5 equal parts, shape these to the size of your tins.
7. Press gently into tins making sure the dough touches all sides and corners of the tins.
8. Slide these into large greased polythene bags leaving enough room for them to rise.
9. Allow to rise for 25 minutes in a warm place.
10. Set the oven to 450°F/230°C/Gas Mark 8.
11. Brush the tops with warm water and bake in the preheated oven for 10 minutes then turn down the heat to 400°F/200°C/Gas Mark 6 and continue to bake for a further 20 to 25 minutes.

GRANARY GARLIC FRENCH LOAVES
For this recipe I have used a combination of wholewheat granary flour and unbleached white flour with the result that the bread is very light. Sprinkling the water on as directed in the recipe helps crispen the loaves. You can omit the garlic and add some to polyunsaturated margarine or butter just before serving.

Makes 5 x 450g/1 lb loaves.
You will need 2 large baking sheets, greased.

55g/2 oz fresh yeast or 28g/1 oz dried yeast
1 generous teaspoon honey or Barbados sugar
850ml/1½ pt warm water
900g/2 lb wholewheat granary flour

450g/1 lb unbleached strong white flour
1 level tablespoon sea salt (optional)
1 large free range egg (optional)
2 tablespoons sunflower or corn oil
6 large juicy cloves garlic, peeled and crushed
lukewarm water to brush tops
kibbled wheat to top

1. If using fresh yeast, cream with the sugar in a small mixing bowl and add 285ml/½ pt of the warm water. Stir well, cover and leave to froth in a warm place for 5 to 10 minutes.
2. If using dried yeast then pour 285ml/½ pt of the warm water into the bowl. Stir in the honey or sugar and sprinkle on the dried yeast. Stir well and leave to froth as above.
3. Mix flours and salt together in a large mixing bowl.
4. Whisk egg with oil and crushed garlic. When yeast liquid is frothy make a well in the centre of the flour and pour in the yeast liquid, egg mixture and the remaining 570ml/1 pt of warm water.
5. Form into a soft dough. If too sticky after mixing well then add a little more flour.
6. Knead for 7 minutes then place in a greased polythene bag, press out air and secure with a wire tie 2.5cm/1 inch from the top. Wrap in a warm towel and leave to rise in a warm place for about 40 minutes until double in size.
7. Knock back and divide dough into 5 equal parts. Roll out each piece to an oval shape about 25.5cm/10 inch long and 18cm/7 inch wide. Roll up as you would a Swiss roll pressing the dough gently together. Form into a French loaf shape 30cm/12 inch long.
8. Place three loaves onto one baking sheet and the two loaves on the other sheet, leaving enough space for rising.
9. Slide into large greased polythene bags and leave to rise until double in size (about 30 minutes).
10. Set oven to 425°F/220°C/Gas Mark 7.
11. When the loaves have risen make 5 slanting indents in each with the back of a knife (do not cut the dough). Brush with lukewarm water and sprinkle on a little kibbled (or cracked) wheat.
12. For best results bake in two batches in the preheated oven on the shelf just above centre for 10 minutes. Then sprinkle on a little lukewarm water and continue to cook for 6 minutes more (this helps to crispen the crust). Turn loaves upside down and cook for 2 minutes more. Cool on a wire rack.

EASY WHEATMEAL BURGER BAPS

These are quick to prepare and need only one proving. The use of ascorbic acid (vitamin C) quickens the whole process and results in light, easy to fill, baps. I use a mixture of wholemeal and unbleached white flour which also helps to lighten the dough, but you can use all wholemeal flour which will give you a heavier but still delicious roll.

Makes approximately 30.
You will need 3 large baking sheets, greased and lined.

675g/1½ lb strong wholemeal flour
675g/1½ lb unbleached white flour
1 level tablespoon sea salt
570ml/1 pt warm water
1 level teaspoon clear honey
28g/1 oz dried yeast
4 x 25mg ascorbic acid tablets, crushed
330ml/12 fl oz warm milk
2 tablespoons sunflower oil
1 level tablespoon clear honey
milk for brushing
few sesame seeds to top

1. Put both flours and sea salt in a large warm mixing bowl and mix well together.
2. Stir the 1 teaspoon of clear honey into the warm water and sprinkle on the yeast and ascorbic acid. Cover and leave to froth for 5 to 7 minutes.
3. Stir the tablespoon of honey into the warm milk. Make a well in the centre of the flours and pour in the frothy yeast liquid, the milk and honey mixture and the oil.
4. Form the lot into a soft dough and knead for 10 minutes.

5. When well kneaded place in a large greased polythene bag and leave to rest for 3 minutes only.

6. Pull out 70g/2½ oz pieces, one at a times and roll each with your hands into a ball. Arrange them on the prepared baking sheets, leaving enough space for them to double in size.

7. Brush tops with milk and sprinkle on some sesame seeds. Slide the baking sheets into large polythene bags and leave in a warm place for about 40 minutes until the baps are double in size.

8. Preheat the oven 20 minutes before needed to 425°F/220°C/Gas Mark 7.

9. Bake two trays at a time, one just above centre and one just below centre for 10 minutes. Change the trays around and continue to bake for 10 minutes more. To bake one tray alone then do so in the centre of the oven for 15 minutes only.

10. Cool on a wire rack.

CRUNCHY WHEATGERM BREAD STICKS
These are easy to make and good to eat on their own and especially delicious accompanied with a savoury dip or soup.

Makes 25.
You will need several baking sheets lightly oiled with virgin olive oil.

280g/10 oz wholemeal flour
55g/2 oz raw or toasted wheatgerm
2 level teaspoons dried yeast
1 level teaspoon brown sugar
1 tablespoon virgin olive oil
140ml/¼ pt warm water
140ml/¼ pt warm milk
2 tablespoons vegetable bouillon powder or 1 teaspoon sea salt
milk for brushing
poppy seeds for coating

1. Blend the flour with the wheatgerm in a mixing bowl.

2. Stir the sugar into the warm water and sprinkle on the yeast. Cover and leave to froth for 7 minutes.

3. Stir vegetable bouillon powder or salt and oil into the warm milk.

4. Make a well in the flour and pour in the frothy yeast liquid and the milk liquid.

5. Form into a soft dough.

6. Knead, flouring your hands if necessary, for 4 minutes only.

7. Put into a greased polythene bag and leave in a warm place for 30 minutes or until double in size.

8. Divide the dough into 25 pieces. Shape into balls and roll into sticks (pencil thin). Lay onto the warm oiled tins, brush with milk and sprinkle on some poppy seeds.

9. Slide into large greased polythene bags and leave to rise until double in thickness (about 25 to 30 minutes).

10. Preheat the oven 15 minutes before needed to 375°F/190°C/Gas Mark 5. Bake two trays at a time for 20 minutes, changing the trays around after 10 minutes and also turning the sticks over to bake more evenly and crisply.

Note: If they do not snap easily when nearly cool then return to the turned-off warm oven on the cooling tray and let them dry off.

CRUNCHY WHEATGERM AND GARLIC STICKS
Simply add 3 large juicy crushed cloves of garlic to the milk liquid in the previous recipe.

CRUNCHY SESAME SEED STICKS
Simply add 4 tablespoons of lightly toasted and ground sesame seeds to the flour instead of the wheatgerm in the *Crunchy wheatgerm bread sticks* recipe, and sprinkle on sesame seeds instead of poppy seeds before baking.

BREAD MAKING – BATTER OR SPONGE METHOD
Some mixtures for bread making improve in texture enormously by preparing a batter with

half the flour, the yeast and all the liquid, letting this stand for at least 1 hour then incorporating the rest of the dry ingredients. This is particularly helpful when including low gluten flours such as rye and oatmeal or no gluten flour such as soya flour (see notes on gluten on page 96).

For best results it is advisable to make the batter, let it stand as directed, then after incorporating the rest of the flour or flours, knead for 7 minutes. Then let the dough rise until double in size before forming your loaves, which will have to rise again in the tins before baking.

Except when using rye flour, you can by-pass the first rising by simply following the batter and kneading stages and immediately forming the dough into loaf shapes and letting them rise once only in the tins before baking. The results will still be good but not as light and perfect as following the double-rising method.

DARK RYE, WHOLEMEAL AND CARAWAY SEED BREAD

This is absolutely delicious and ideal sliced thinly for open or ordinary sandwiches.

Before I was a yoghurt fan I used sour cream which is traditionally an ingredient in this recipe. Both give very good results. Use Greek yoghurt as ordinary yoghurt tends to be a bit too sharp. The inclusion of yoghurt and eggs helps lighten the bread considerably. For an even lighter loaf use less rye flour, say 450g/1 lb instead of the 675g/1½ lb in the recipe and add 275g/½ lb unbleached white flour instead.

Makes 3 or 4 loaves.
You will need 3 x 675g/1½ lb loaf tins or 4 x 450g/1 lb tins, greased and floured.

600ml/just under 1¼ pt warm water
1 generous tablespoon molasses
28g/1 oz dried yeast
2 large eggs
1 x 225g/8 oz carton Greek yoghurt
2 rounded tablespoons caraway seeds
3 tablespoons sunflower oil
675g/1½ lb strong wholemeal flour
675g/1½ lb whole grain rye flour
1 level tablespoon sea salt (optional)

milk or egg to glaze
few caraway seeds to top

1. Pour 285ml/½ pt of the required warm water into a large mixing bowl. Stir in 1 level teaspoon of the required molasses and sprinkle on the yeast. Stir well, cover and leave to froth for 7 to 10 minutes.
2. Whisk eggs until frothy and blend in the yoghurt.
3. Stir in the rest of the molasses with the remaining warm water.
4. When yeast water is frothy then stir in the yoghurt mixture and the molasses water.
5. Add the wholemeal flour and the caraway seeds and using a wooden spoon in an upward motion beat gently, incorporating as much air as possible into the batter for 1 minute (about 100 strokes).
6. Cover with a greased polythene sheet and a warm towel.
7. Leave to rise in a warm place until double in volume (about 1 hour).
8. Stir in the oil. Blend the rye flour with the sea salt (if using) and add this to the risen batter mixture a cupful at a time. Form into a dough and knead, using a little more wholemeal flour if the dough gets too sticky, for 7 minutes.
9. Place in a large greased polythene bag and wrap loosely in a warm towel and leave to rise in a warm place until double in size (this could take 1 to 2 hours).
10. Knock back and knead the dough for 2 minutes. Break into 3 or 4 equal pieces depending on the size of your tins.
11. Roll each into a loaf shape and press gently into the tins, making sure the dough is touching all sides and corners of the tin and reaches just above halfway.
12. Slide into large greased polythene bags and leave to rise in a warm place until the dough is slightly humped above the level of the tin (this could take 1 to 1½ hours).
13. Preheat the oven about 20 minutes before needed to 400°F/200°C/Gas Mark 6.

14. When risen, brush tops with either beaten egg or milk and sprinkle on a few caraway seeds.

15. Bake in the centre of the preheated oven for 10 minutes, turn down heat to 350°F/180°C/Gas Mark 4, and continue to bake the 675g/1½ lb size loaves for 45 minutes more and the 450g/1 lb size loaf for 35 minutes more.

WHOLEMEAL AND SOYA BREAD

The addition of soya flour (see nutritional notes on soya flour on page 116) will give you a high protein loaf. The bread will not be heavy if you do not add too much soya flour. I find the best results are achieved using 55g/2 oz soya to 450g/1 lb flour in any bread recipe.

Makes 4 loaves.
You will need 4 x 450g/1 lb tins, greased and floured.

850ml/1½ pt warm water
1 level teaspoon clear honey
28g/1 oz dried yeast
1 level tablespoon more clear honey (optional)
675g/1½ lb strong wholemeal flour
175g/6 oz full fat soya flour
500g/1 lb 2 oz more strong wholemeal flour
1 level tablespoon sea salt
milk to brush tops
few sesame seeds or rolled oats to top

1. Pour 285ml/½ pt of the warm water into a large mixing bowl. Stir in the teaspoon of honey and sprinkle on the yeast. Mix well then cover and leave to froth in a warm place for 7 to 10 minutes.

2. Stir the tablespoon of honey (if using) into the remaining warm water and add this to the yeast water when frothy.

3. Stir in the 675g/1½ lb wholemeal flour and beat using an upward motion incorporating as much air as possible into the batter. Do this for 1 minute.

4. Cover with a greased polythene sheet and a warm towel and leave to rise for 40 minutes.

5. Sieve the rest of the wholemeal flour, soya flour and salt (if using) together and gradually add this to the batter mixture.

6. Form into a dough and knead lightly,

flouring your hands as you do so, for 7 minutes.

7. Put into a large greased polythene bag, cover with a warm towel and leave to rise in a warm place until double in size (about 40 minutes).

8. Knock back and knead for 2 minutes more. Break into four equal pieces. Roll each piece into a thick oval shape then roll up like a Swiss roll. Press each into the prepared tins, making sure the dough touches all sides and corners of the tin and reaches a level just above halfway.

9. Slide tins into large polythene bags and leave to rise until the dough is a slight hump above the level of the tin (about 30 to 40 minutes). Preheat the oven at this stage to 450°F/230°C/Gas Mark 8.

10. When risen, brush tops with milk and sprinkle on sesame seeds or rolled oats.

11. Bake for 10 minutes in the centre of the preheated oven then turn down heat to 375°F/190°C/Gas Mark 5 and continue to bake for 25 minutes more.

12. Cool in the tins for a few minutes then turn out and cool on a wire rack.

BAGUETTES (FRENCH LOAVES)

I rarely make bread with as much unbleached white flour as in these loaves, but the inclusion of some wholemeal flour makes them a slightly healthier alternative to the traditional all white French loaves. I also use a little more yeast in this recipe than when making other breads. They freeze well when cooled. When required simply defrost for 30 minutes, sprinkle with a little warm water and rebake at 375°F/190°C/Gas Mark 5, for about 7 minutes or until the crust is crisp.

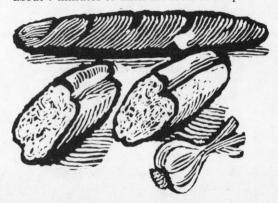

Makes 6 loaves.
You will need 2 large baking sheets, greased and floured.

850ml/1½ pt warm water
1 level teaspoon fruit sugar
28g/1 oz plus 1 teaspoon dried yeast
1 level tablespoon more fruit sugar
450g/1 lb strong wholemeal flour
2 tablespoons virgin olive oil
900g/2 lb strong unbleached white flour
1 level tablespoon sea salt
warm water to sprinkle on top
a few sesame seeds to top

1. Pour 285ml/½ pt of the warm water into a large mixing bowl. Stir in the teaspoon of fruit sugar and the yeast. Cover and leave to froth for 7 minutes.
2. Stir the tablespoon of fruit sugar into the remaining water and pour this into the yeast water when frothy.
3. Stir the wholemeal flour into the liquids using an upward motion, incorporating as much air into the mixture as possible and beat for 1 minute.
4. Cover with a greased polythene sheet and a warm towel and leave to rise in a warm place for 30 minutes only.
5. Stir in the oil. Mix the salt with the unbleached flour and gradually add this to the batter, forming it into a soft dough.
6. Knead with lightly floured hands for 7 minutes.
7. Put into a large greased polythene bag and leave to rise for 40 minutes or until double in size.
8. Knock back and knead for 2 minutes more. Break the dough into 6 equal pieces, roll out each to an oval shape approximately 20 cm x 10 cm/8 inch x 4 inch, then roll each up as you would a Swiss roll and press gently into a French loaf shape about 30 cm/12 inch long.
9. Place these on the prepared baking sheets, 3 to each tray, making sure they have space to rise.
10. Slide the trays into large greased polythene bags and leave to rise until double in size (about 30 minutes).
11. Preheat oven at this stage to 425°F/ 220°C/Gas Mark 7.
12. Pour 2.5cm/1 inch of boiling water into a roasting tin and place on the floor of the oven.
13. When the loaves have risen, cut 4 diagonal shallow slits (using the back of a knife) on top of each loaf, brush with warm water and sprinkle on a few sesame seeds.
14. Bake on two shelves, one just above centre and one just below centre for 8 minutes.
15. Change the trays around and continue to bake for a further 8 minutes.

MUSHROOM, CHEESE AND HERB PLAIT

You will need 450g/1 lb of the baguette dough to make this tasty and simple recipe so when making *Baguettes* (see page 25) make 5 instead of 6. This should leave you with just under 450g/1 lb of dough to spare.

The plait is delicious served with a side salad for lunch or if preceded by a warming nutritious soup such as *Lentil and miso soup* (see page 111) it will make a tasty and satisfying evening meal for 4.

I have chosen to use this light baguette dough, but you can use the *Easy wheatmeal burger bap* dough (see page 22) or the *Wholemeal sesame dough* (see page 18), but avoid heavier doughs which include rye flour.

Makes 1 loaf.
You will need a large baking tray, lined with kitchen parchment and oiled.

450g/1 lb Baguette dough, risen (see page 00)
2 tablespoons virgin olive oil
170g/6 oz button mushrooms
1 large juicy clove garlic, crushed
½ teaspoon dried tarragon
½ teaspoon dried oregano or basil, or 1 rounded tablespoon fresh, chopped
freshly ground black pepper
1 level tablespoon Greek yoghurt
110g/4 oz crumbled mature Lancashire cheese, or Farmhouse Cheddar, grated
28g/4 oz Farmhouse Cheddar cheese to top, or simply egg glaze

1. Heat the oil in a pan and sauté the mushrooms and garlic for 3 minutes on

high heat stirring constantly.

2. Take out with a slotted spoon and let them get cool.
3. Stir in the herbs and yoghurt and freshly ground black pepper to your taste and leave to absorb the flavours.
4. Knock back the dough and knead for 2 minutes. Roll out onto a floured surface to a rectangle about 30cm/12 inch x 12cm/6 inch.
5. Place this on the lined and oiled tray.
6. Spoon 55g/2 oz of the cheese in the centre of the dough allowing a border of approximately 5cm/6 inch dough. Spoon on the cold mushroom mixture with a slotted spoon so that it is not too wet.
7. Top with another 55g/2 oz cheese. Make even diagonal cuts every 2cm/¾ inch along both sides of the rectangle. Fold the ends of the dough onto the filling, then plait the diagonally cut pieces over the top of the filling. Cover loosely with a greased polythene sheet and leave to rise in a warm place for 20 minutes only.
8. Preheat the oven at this stage to 400°F/200°C/Gas Mark 6. When ready for the oven brush the top with beaten egg *or* sprinkle on the 28g/1 oz Cheddar cheese. Bake in the centre of the oven for 20 minutes.
9. Serve immediately.

SOURDOUGH BREADS
These breads are quite simple to make and require a sourdough starter in which micro-organisms grow and cause the bread to rise. The starter stays in the fridge and should be used and replenished as directed below once a week.

Starter
There are two ways to make your starter. One uses dried yeast as the main fermenting ingredient (method described below) and the other more ancient method uses any sour food such as two-day old cooked cereals, milk, fruit or vegetables. The yeast or the sour food ingredient is mixed with water and a little wholemeal flour to a spongy consistency and left to ferment over a few days, stirring daily until a strong sour smell arises.

1 level tablespoon dried yeast
585ml/1 pt warm water
2 level teaspoons honey or dark sugar
280g/10 oz strong wholemeal flour

1. Combine the ingredients to form a spongy, muddy texture.
2. Put in a container with a lid which is double in volume to the mixture, because it rises a little during storage in the fridge.
3. Allow this to stand overnight to sour. Refrigerate and stir once daily for 3 days.
4. Your starter is now ready to use in the following recipes.

Note: Make sure you replenish your starter from each batch of bread you make as directed in the recipes. It will last indefinitely with a little fresh starter mixture. Always stir the starter before taking any out.

SOURDOUGH WHOLEMEAL BREAD
This bread is made in two stages. Start making it the day before you wish to bake it or in the morning if baking in the evening.

Makes 2 x 900g/2 lb loaves.
You will need 2 x 900g/2 lb loaf tins, greased and lightly floured.

560g/1¼ lb strong wholemeal flour
225g/8 oz starter (see above – stir before taking out)
850ml/1½ pt warm water
3 tablespoons sunflower oil
1 rounded dessertspoon sea salt
785g/1¾ lb more strong wholemeal flour

1. Place the 560g/1¼ lb flour in a large mixing bowl.
2. Make a well in the centre, add the starter and beat well using a wooden spoon while adding the warm water a cupful at a time until you have the consistency of a thick muddy batter.
3. Continue to beat with an upward motion, getting as much air in as possible for half a minute.
4. Cover with a greased polythene sheet and a warm towel and leave to stand in a warm place overnight or for at least 8 hours.

5. Take 225g/8 oz of the batter mixture and stir into the starter in the refrigerator to replenish it.
6. Fold the oil into the remaining batter.
7. Mix the salt with the 785g/1¾ lb flour.
8. Gradually beat the flour mixture into the batter, first with a wooden spoon then with your hands to form a dough. This dough will be softer and a little stickier than a full yeasted dough.
9. Flour a work surface and knead for 5 minutes only.
10. Divide into two equal pieces and mould each to fit snugly into the prepared tins.
11. Slide each into large greased polythene bags and leave to rise in a warm place for 2 hours.
12. Preheat the oven 20 minutes before needed, 425°F/220°C/Gas Mark 7.
13. Brush tops with a little warm water and bake in the centre of the oven for 20 minutes then lower the heat to 375°F/190°C/Gas Mark 5 and continue to bake for 1 hour more.

SOURDOUGH RYE AND WHOLEMEAL BREAD

Follow the previous recipe for *Sourdough wholemeal bread,* but instead of using the 785g/1¾ lb strong wholemeal use 340g/¾ lb strong wholemeal and 450g/1 lb rye flour (you can use more rye flour but the bread will be heavier). Proceed and bake in the same way as the previous recipe.

These loaves may also be shaped into ovals or rounds and baked on oiled trays. You can also add 55g/2 oz caraway seeds to the dough.

INDIAN BREADS

The following three recipes help complete a true Indian meal.

BASIC CHAPATI AND PURI DOUGH
Makes 12 chapatis or 24 puris.

340g/12 oz wholemeal chapati flour (ata – see page 17)
½ level teaspoon sea salt

2 tablespoons sunflower or corn oil (slightly warmed)
225ml/8 fl oz water

1. Sift the flour and salt and rub in the oil.
2. Gradually add the water to make a smooth dough then knead for 10 minutes.
3. Cover with a damp cloth or place in a greased polythene bag and leave to rest for 1 hour at least. Your dough is now ready.

CHAPATIS
These are flat breads which need no baking in the oven. They are simply dry cooked in a heavy pan or griddle.

Makes 12.

1 recipe quantity Basic chapati and puri dough

1. Divide the dough into 12 balls.
2. Take one ball between the palms of your hands, flatten it and flip it from palm to palm a few times, then roll it out on a floured surface to approximately 18cm/7 inch round.
3. Heat the pan or griddle to very hot. Pop on the chapati and press it gently with the back of a large spoon to encourage it to bubble in places.
4. When the bottom of the chapati is turning brown, flip it over and cook the other side. They cook very quickly. Keep warm in a very low heated oven.

PURIS
These are little puffed breads which are deep fried. They swell up and are cooked in seconds so very little fat is absorbed. They look like little flying saucers and are very tasty and light in texture.

Makes 24.

1 recipe quantity Basic chapati and puri dough
soya oil for deep frying

1. Pinch off walnut sized pieces of the dough. Form into balls and flatten each with an oiled rolling pin.

2. Roll out on a slightly oiled surface to rounds 7.5cm/3 inch in diameter.
3. Heat the oil as for deep frying chips and when hot drop the puris in one at a time.
4. As the puri pops up to the surface, press it gently with the back of a spoon (this happens very quickly). It will puff up like a balloon.
5. When golden, flip over and cook the other side for a few seconds only.

SAMOSAS (curried pasties)

You can use the *Basic chapati and puri dough* (see page 28) for these, as I did for many years until I experimented with yoghurt in the dough. The results were much lighter but both doughs make lovely samosas. Deep fry in soya oil. These are great as an appetizer.

Makes 16.

225g/8 oz chapati flour
½ level teaspoon sea salt
4 tablespoons sunflower or corn oil
2 tablespoons water
2 tablespoons natural yoghurt
675g/1½ lb potatoes
1 tablespoon sunflower or corn oil
1 medium onion finely chopped
1 large clove of garlic, crushed
2.5cm/1 inch knob ginger grated
1 rounded teaspoon garam masala
1 just above level teaspoon cayenne pepper
1 rounded teaspoon methi (fenugreek leaf)
2 tablespoons fresh parsley or coriander leaves, chopped
2 tablespoons lemon juice
170g/6 oz frozen peas (defrosted only)

1. To make the dough, put the flour and salt into a bowl and rub in the oil with your finger tips until the mixture resembles fine breadcrumbs.
2. Mix the water with the yoghurt and gradually add this to the flour mixture and form into a firm dough.
3. Knead the dough for 10 minutes until very smooth (this is important).
4. Form into a ball and rub with a little oil, put into a polythene bag and leave to rest for 1 hour at least (2 hours would be best). During this time prepare the filling.
5. If large then cut the potatoes in four and steam until cooked but not mushy. Cut into small cubes.
6. Sauté the onion and garlic and brown slightly (do not burn). Add the ginger, garam masala, cayenne and methi and fry for 1 minute. Stir in the lemon juice.
7. Combine all the ingredients in a bowl taking care not to mush the potatoes. Coat the vegetables well with the onion and spices. Allow this filling mixture to cool completely.
8. When the dough is rested, knead for 2 minutes and then divide into 16 pieces.
9. Keep the pieces in the polythene bag as you make the samosas one by one. Roll each ball out on a slightly oiled surface with an oiled rolling pin into a 7.5cm/ 3 inch circle.
10. Spoon about 2 teaspoons of the filling mixture onto one half of each circle, dampen the complete edge, fold over the other half and press edges gently together. Flute the seam with fingers or press together with the prongs of a fork.
11. Heat enough soya oil for deep frying and when the oil is medium hot, fry four or five samosas at a time, keeping the temperature moderately hot. Turn frequently until they are golden brown and crisp.
12. Drain on absorbent kitchen paper.

RICH YEASTED DOUGHS

Once you have mastered the basic technique of making bread, you can quite easily prepare the following yeasted bakes which are enriched with ingredients such as eggs, milk, sugar or honey, fats, dried fruit, nuts, seeds and spices. These bakes are for special treats rather than everyday and are far healthier than any shop-bought teatime treats.

BASIC RICH YEASTED DOUGH
Makes about 900g/2 lb dough.

560g/1 lb 4 oz either all strong wholemeal flour
  or half and half wholemeal and unbleached
  white
1 level teaspoon sea salt
2 level tablespoons either fruit sugar or clear
  honey
1 large egg
28g/1 oz fresh yeast
2 x 25mg ascorbic acid (vitamin C tablets)
  crushed
285ml/½ pt warm water
2 rounded tablespoons dried skimmed milk
  powder
55g/2 oz melted butter or polyunsaturated
  margarine

1. Mix flour with salt in a mixing bowl.
2. Whisk sugar or honey and egg together
   until frothy.
3. Cream yeast with a little of the warm
   water and the ascorbic acid tablets.
4. Stir the milk powder into the remaining
   warm water.
5. Make a well in the flour and pour in the
   egg mixture, the yeast mixture, the milk
   and water liquid and the melted butter or
   margarine. Form quickly into a soft
   dough. It will be a little sticky but just
   flour your hands and knead the dough on
   a lightly floured surface for 10 minutes
   until it is smooth.
6. Place in an oiled polythene bag, press out
   the air and secure the top with a wire tie.
   Cover with a towel and leave to rise for
   about 30 minutes in a warm place (or
   until double in size). Your dough is now
   ready to use in the following recipes:

YEASTED MUFFINS
Makes 12.
You will need an oiled baking sheet and if
cooking on top of the stove instead of oven
baking you will need a heavy based non-stick
pan or griddle.

1 recipe quantity Basic rich yeasted dough,
  risen (see page 29)
little whole cornmeal for dusting

1. Punch down the dough and let it rest in
   the bag for 10 minutes.
2. Roll out to 1cm/½ inch thickness. Cut into
   7.5cm/2 inch rounds or triangles and place
   on the oiled baking sheet.
3. Dust with cornmeal, slide baking sheet
   into an oiled polythene bag and leave to
   rise until doubled in size.
4. If cooking on a griddle, or in a pan, then
   heat the pan or griddle to hot. Then
   reduce heat to medium and carefully take
   each muffin off the tray with a fish slice
   and cook on the griddle or pan until
   lightly browned (about 5 minutes on each
   side).
5. If baking, then preheat the oven while the
   muffins are rising to 450°F/230°C/Gas
   Mark 8 and bake for 10 minutes, turning
   the muffins after 5 minutes' cooking time.
6. To serve, break open muffin and butter
   while warm.
7. To reheat muffins bake in a moderate
   oven for 5 minutes or split open and toast.

HOT CROSS BUNS
Makes 15
You will need two oiled baking sheets.

1 recipe quantity Basic rich yeasted dough (see
  page 29, but add the currants, rind and
  spices listed below to the flour and salt
  mixture)
140g/5 oz currants
coarsely grated rind of 1 orange
coarsely grated rind of 1 lemon
½ teaspoon mixed spice
½ level teaspoon cinnamon
½ level teaspoon nutmeg, freshly ground
little honey water (mix 1 teaspoon honey with 1
  teaspoon warm water) to glaze

1. After the dough has risen, punch down and knead for 2 minutes.
2. Divide the dough into 15 pieces.
3. Roll each into a ball then into a bun shape.
4. Arrange well apart on the baking sheets. Slide sheets into large polythene bags and leave to rise for about 30 minutes until double in size.
5. Preheat oven to 375°F/190°C/Gas Mark 5.
6. Make a cross on the top by using the back of a knife to indent.
7. Bake for 20 minutes one tray just above centre and one below, changing the trays around after 10 minutes.
8. While still warm, brush tops with a little honey water to glaze.

EASTER LOAF
Makes 2 x 450g/1 lb loaves.
You will need 2 x 450g/1 lb loaf tins, greased and lightly floured.

Use ingredients as for Hot Cross Buns (see page 30) and when the dough has risen proceed as follows:

1. Punch down and knead the dough for 2 minutes.
2. Break in two equal pieces and form into loaf shapes.
3. Press gently into the tins making sure the dough reaches all sides and corners of the tins.
4. Slide into greased polythene bags and allow to rise in a warm place until double in size (about 30 minutes).
5. Preheat the oven to 400°F/200°C/Gas Mark 6.
6. Brush tops with honey water and bake in the centre of the oven for 15 minutes. Turn down heat and continue to bake for 15 minutes more. Allow to cool slightly in tins for 5 minutes, then cool on a wire rack.

APRICOT AND PECAN NUT TEA RING
You will need 1 baking sheet, greased and lightly floured.

½ recipe quantity Basic rich yeasted dough (see page 29)

110g/4 oz dried apricots, soaked overnight in apple juice
3 cardamon seeds (pod them and grind the seeds with a pestle and mortar)
2 teaspoons clear honey
50g/2 oz pecan nuts, chopped
few pecan nut halves to decorate
a little clear honey to glaze

1. Cook the soaked apricots, ground cardamon seeds and honey with the soaking water for 5 minutes. Liquidize with some of the juice until smooth but not runny.
2. After rising take the dough and knock it back, then roll out into a rectangle, 35cm x 25cm/14 inch x 10 inch.
3. Spread the apricot mixture onto the rolled out dough leaving 2.5cm/1 inch of dough free of filling along one long side.
4. Sprinkle on the chopped pecans.
5. Start rolling from the long side which has filling to the edge on it (as you would a Swiss roll). Dampen the clear end and seal.
6. Place on the baking sheet and curl the roll around into a ring. Dampen the ends and seal together. Cut slits in the top half-way through the dough at 3cm/1½ inch intervals.
7. Slide into an oiled polythene bag and leave to rise in a warm place until double in size, about 30 to 40 minutes.
8. Preheat the oven 400°F/200°C/Gas Mark 6.
9. Bake in the centre of the oven for 15 minutes. Turn down heat to 375°F/190°C/Gas Mark 5 and continue to cook for 20 minutes more.
10. While still hot brush with honey and stick on a few pecan nut halves to decorate.

FIG AND ANISEED TEA RING
You will need 1 baking sheet, greased and lightly floured.

½ recipe quantity Basic rich yeasted dough (see page 29)
170g/6 oz dried figs, chopped and soaked overnight in apple juice and 1 teaspoon aniseed

2 tablespoons pine nuts
little beaten egg white and honey to glaze
2 fresh figs to decorate, thinly sliced (optional)

1. Cook the soaked figs in their juice until pulp-like. Mash with a potato masher until smooth and jam-like (not runny).
2. Spread this over the dough rolled out as for *Apricot and pecan nut tea ring* (see page 31).
3. Sprinkle on the pine nuts and roll up as directed.
4. Follow rest of the method for the *Apricot and pecan nut tea ring*.
5. When baked brush with the glaze while still warm and decorate the top with fresh fig slices, if using.

BRIOCHE

I have experimented using all wholemeal flour and with a mixture of wholemeal and unbleached white. Both gave good results but obviously the mixture of flours tended to lighten the dough considerably. The addition of ascorbic acid (vitamin C) is not essential but it does quicken the proving (rising) process.

Makes 12.
You will need 12 individual 6cm/2½ inch fluted patty tins, well oiled and standing on a baking sheet or in deep bun tins.

14g/½ oz fresh yeast
1 x 25 mg tablet ascorbic acid (vitamin C) crushed
3 tablespoons warm water
110g/4 oz strong wholemeal flour and 110g/ 4 oz strong unbleached white flour or all wholemeal flour
good pinch sea salt
1 level tablespoon fruit sugar or demerara sugar
55g/2 oz melted butter or polyunsaturated margarine
2 eggs well beaten until frothy
little beaten egg to glaze

1. Cream the yeast, ascorbic acid and warm water together.
2. Put flour, sugar and salt in a mixing bowl and blend well.

3. Pour in the yeast mixture, the melted butter and the well beaten eggs. Form into a dough. It will be a little sticky but just knead on a lightly floured surface flouring your hands as you do so for 6 minutes.
4. Place dough in a large oiled polythene bag, press out the air and secure top with a wire tie. Cover with a towel and leave to rise in a warm place for 30 to 40 minutes (or until double in size).
5. Knock back and knead for 2 minutes. Put back in the polythene bag.
6. Take out a 40g/1½ oz piece of dough, pull off a quarter of this and roll the rest into a ball. Press gently into a patty tin. Roll the small piece left into a knob shape which tapers to a point. Using a floured finger press a hole in the dough in the patty tin and insert the pointed end of the knob into this. The result will look like a small cottage loaf. Use the remaining dough to make 12 of these altogether.
7. Egg brush the tops.
8. Slide into a large oiled polythene bag and leave to rise in a warm place until the bottom piece of dough reaches a fraction below the rim of the tins (takes 20 minutes).
9. Preheat the oven 20 minutes before needed to 450°F/230°C/Gas Mark 8.
10. Bake in the centre of the oven for 5 minutes. Turn heat down to 400°F/200°C/ Gas Mark 6 and continue to bake for 7 to 8 minutes more.

SAVARIN

This is a very simple dessert to prepare as there is no kneading to do, but it is extremely rich so reserve this recipe for a special occasion. Traditionally savarins are drowned in a very sweet mixture of honey and water with a touch of rum. I drown mine with a syrup made from fruit juice concentrates, water and a touch of whatever liqueur I feel like flavouring it with. The alcohol is optional. I also prefer to fill the savarin with a fresh fruit salad just to balance the richness.

Serves 6 to 8.

You will need 1 x 23 cm/9 inch savarin mould, well greased.

225g/8 oz either strong wholemeal or half and
half strong wholemeal and unbleached
white flour
¼ teaspoon sea salt
28g/1 oz either fruit or soft brown sugar
28g/1 oz fresh yeast
1 x 25 mg ascorbic acid tablet (vitamin C)
140ml/¼ pt warm milk
4 eggs, well beaten
4 drops of natural vanilla essence
110g/4 oz butter or polyunsaturated margarine,
melted

1. Put flour in a mixing bowl with the salt and the sugar.
2. Cream the yeast with the crushed ascorbic acid tablet and the warm milk until smooth.
3. Pour this with the beaten eggs, vanilla and the melted butter or margarine into the flour and beat thoroughly for about 3 minutes (this is important as it lightens the mixture considerably).
4. Pour this into the savarin mould.
5. Slide into a large greased polythene bag and leave to rise in a warm place until it reaches almost to the top of the mould (this should take about 30 to 40 minutes).
6. Preheat the oven 15 minutes before needed to 400°F/200°C/Gas Mark 6.
7. Bake in the centre of the oven for about 35 to 40 minutes.

Fruit syrup for savarins
You can buy a variety of fruit juice concentrates such as apple, raspberry, cherry, strawberry, blackcurrant and exotic fruit (see page 184 for more information). These are naturally sweet but if not sweet enough for your taste then simply add a little honey. I use the exotic fruit juice concentrate for this recipe.

8 tablespoons exotic fruit juice concentrate
8 tablespoons water
2 to 3 tablespoons of either rum, brandy or
liqueur of your choice

1. Heat all ingredients but do not boil.
2. Pour over the still warm savarin and cool before serving.

Fruit filling for savarins
When the syrup-soaked savarin is cool and ready to serve, fill it with a fresh fruit salad. Try a mixture of peaches, apricots, pineapple, papaya, kiwi fruit, banana and strawberries (when available).

Serve the savarin with Greek yoghurt or a mixture of Greek yoghurt and cream whipped together in equal amounts.

YEASTED PASTRIES

BASIC YEAST PASTRY

This pastry is much lower in fat than any other pastry and is simple to work with because the dough is pliable, which makes it easier to roll out and mould. For this reason it is particularly ideal as a covering for savoury and sweet filled parcels and pastries.

You can use all strong wholemeal flour or half and half wholemeal and unbleached white. Obviously the mixture of flours achieves a lighter dough but both give very good results.

100 ml/3½ fl oz warm milk
1 heaped teaspoon dried yeast
1 teaspoon clear honey or brown sugar
225g/8 oz strong wholemeal flour or half and
half wholemeal and unbleached white
¼ teaspoon sea salt
1 egg, beaten

Note for vegans: Omit the ordinary milk and the egg and use 140 ml/¼ pt soya milk instead. Leave to rise for 30 minutes instead of 15, as directed below in stage 6. Also, brush edges and tops of parcels with soya milk instead of beaten egg.

1. Measure out the warm milk, stir in the honey and sprinkle on the yeast. Stir well. Cover and leave to froth for 7 minutes.
2. Put flour and salt into a mixing bowl and make a well in the centre.

3. When yeast liquid is ready pour this with the beaten egg into the flour.
4. Form into a soft dough.
5. Knead for 3 minutes only on a lightly floured surface.
6. Put into a greased polythene bag and leave in a warm place for 15 minutes only.

APRICOT AND ALMOND PARCELS
Makes 8.
You will need a large baking sheet, oiled.

1 recipe quantity Basic yeast pastry (see page 33)
560g/1½ lb fresh, ripe apricots or 200g/7 oz dried (soaked overnight in apple juice then drained)
1 egg white
1 teaspoon lemon juice
2 drops natural almond essence
2 tablespoons clear honey
110g/4 oz almonds, finely ground
little beaten egg to seal edges and glaze top

1. Cut fresh apricots in half, stone and chop. If using dried then drain well after soaking and chop roughly.
2. Whisk egg white, lemon juice, essence and honey together until well blended and gradually add the ground almonds to form a paste.
3. Roll the pastry out on a lightly floured surface until slightly thinner than ordinary pastry.
4. Cut it into 8 x 10 cm/4 inch squares.
5. Spoon equal amounts of the apricots onto one half of each pastry square, then top the apricot with equal amounts of the almond paste.
6. Brush the edges of each pastry square with a little beaten egg, fold the other half of the pastry over the filling and press the edges together with a fork or flute with your fingers. Brush the tops with beaten egg to glaze and prick lightly with a fork.
7. Place each parcel on the prepared baking sheet and bake in a preheated oven, 400°F/200°C/Gas Mark 6, for 25 minutes.

Note for vegans: In the filling use honey instead of fruit sugar, omit the egg white and blend the honey, lemon juice, essence and almonds well together. It will form a gooey paste but it tastes great.

APPLE, RAISIN AND NUT PARCELS

Makes 8.
Follow the recipe for *Apricot and almond parcels* (see above), but make the filling by mixing together 450g/1 lb cored and thinly sliced cooking apples, 85g/3 oz raisins, 55g/2 oz roughly chopped nuts (either walnuts or hazelnuts), 1 tablespoon clear honey, ½ teaspoon cinnamon, ½ teaspoon freshly ground nutmeg, ½ teaspoon clove powder and 55g/2 oz wholemeal breadcrumbs.

Other fruit fillings could include stoned and chopped plums, blackberries with apple, or date and apple, with or without the spices.

MUSHROOM, POTATO AND CHEESE PARCELS
Makes 8.
You will need a large baking sheet, oiled.

1 recipe quantity of Basic yeast pastry (see page 33), cut into 8 x 10 cm/4 inch squares
225g/8 oz new potatoes, scrubbed and chopped in small cubes
2 tablespoons virgin olive oil
170g/6 oz mushrooms, wiped and sliced
6 good size spring onions, chopped (use green stems as well)
1 heaped teaspoon vegetable bouillon powder
1 tablespoon parsley, finely chopped
1 teaspoon dried marjoram or 1 tablespoon fresh leaves, chopped
1 egg yolk
1 tablespoon Greek yoghurt
freshly ground black pepper to taste

*140g/5 oz either Gruyère or Farmhouse
  Cheddar cheese, grated*

1. Steam the cubed potatoes for 5 minutes.
2. Heat oil in a pan and sauté the
   mushrooms for 2 minutes on high heat
   stirring constantly.
3. Stir in the potatoes and cook for 1 minute
   only.
4. Take off heat, stir in the spring onions,
   vegetable bouillon powder, parsley and
   marjoram, then take out with a slotted
   spoon and put into a mixing bowl to cool
   slightly.
5. Whisk egg yolk with the yoghurt and stir
   this with 85g/3 oz of the cheese into the
   mushroom mixture. Season with black
   pepper to your taste.
6. Sprinkle 28g/1 oz cheese onto one half of
   each pastry square.
7. Spoon the mushroom mixture in equal
   amounts onto the cheese and top this with
   the remaining 28g/1 oz of cheese. Then
   fold, seal, glaze and bake the parcels as
   directed in stages 6 and 7 of the *Apricot
   and almond parcels* recipe (see page 34).

Note for vegans: Simply omit the dairy
produce and stir in about 170g/6 oz firm tofu
chopped in small pieces, correcting the
seasoning as the tofu is rather bland.

CURRIED VEGETABLE PARCELS
Makes 8.

Follow the recipe for *Mushroom, potato and
cheese parcels* (see page 33), but use the filling
for *Samosas* (see page 29).

CROISSANTS
These I have never succeeded in making with
all wholemeal flour or using polyunsaturated
margarine instead of butter, so don't waste
your time and effort by trying – the results
are far too heavy. Both croissants and the
following recipe for *Danish pastries,* which use
the same dough, are high in saturated fat but
the use of half wholemeal flour makes them a
slightly healthier alternative to the shop-
bought variety.
   The method used is time consuming so

make double if you're in the mood and freeze
half.

Makes 12.
You will need 2 large baking sheets, greased.

225g/8 oz strong wholemeal flour
225g/8 oz strong unbleached white flour
1 rounded teaspoon sea salt
28g/1 oz polyunsaturated margarine
28g/1 oz fresh yeast
*2 x 25 mg tablets ascorbic acid (vitamin C),
  crumbled*
225ml/8 fl oz warm water
1 egg, well beaten
170g/6 oz butter, cold
*1 small egg, beaten, 2 teaspoons water, and ½
  teaspoon sugar, mixed together for the glaze*

1. Sift flours and sea salt together in a
   mixing bowl.
2. Rub in the margarine.
3. Blend the yeast with the warm water
   and ascorbic acid tablet. Pour this with
   the egg into the flour mixture and mix to
   a soft dough.
4. Turn onto a floured surface and knead
   for 5 minutes.
5. Cover with the upturned mixing bowl
   and leave to rest for 5 minutes.
6. On a floured surface roll out the dough to
   a rectangle 50 cm x 20 cm/20 inch x 8
   inch and mark into thirds.
7. Dot half the butter over ⅔ of the dough
   leaving a small border clear.
8. Fold the dough in three, folding in the
   unbuttered third first so that it is
   sandwiched between the buttered areas.
9. Seal the edges well with the rolling pin.
   Wrap in an oiled polythene bag and chill
   for 30 minutes, then roll out and repeat
   the whole procedure with the remaining
   half of the butter.
10. After folding the dough over and sealing
    the edges, if still cold, then roll and fold
    three more times, without adding any
    more butter. If the dough is not cold then
    chill for 10 minutes before the final three
    rollings.
11. Wrap in an oiled polythene bag and chill
    for at least 1 hour or overnight in the fridge.

12. Remove from the fridge and fold in three once more, then roll out to a strip 50 cm x 10 cm/20 inch x 4 inch long. Turn so that you have a perfect rectangle shape 45 cm/18 inch long. Cut into equal triangles 7.5 cm/3 inch at the base.

13. Brush them with the glaze and roll up each triangle from the long base and shape to form a crescent.

14. Place 6 on each warmed and oiled tray. Slide trays into large polythene bags and leave in a warm place to rise for 30 minutes until puffed up.

15. Preheat the oven 15 minutes before baking to 425°F/220°C/Gas Mark 7.

16. Brush the tops gently with a little more glaze and bake one tray at a time in the centre of the oven for 20 minutes. Cool on a wire rack.

DANISH PASTRIES

Traditionally these pastries contain much more fat than is used in this recipe but I make them with the same dough as for *Croissants* (see page 35) with very good results.

Also, most Danish pastries are dribbled with icing but I have devised one using honey, egg white and vanilla (see below), which is also good for topping cup cakes.

Makes 16.
You will need 3 large baking sheets, greased.

1 recipe quantity Croissant dough (see page 35), ready to roll and cut in squares (i.e. up to stage 12 of the Croissant recipe).
fillings, and honey icing as suggested below
55g/2 oz flaked almonds, lightly toasted in an oven until golden

1. After chilling for the last time roll and fold the dough once more then roll out into a rectangle 50 cm/20 inch long and 13 cm/5 inch wide.

2. Cut into 16 squares, 6 cm/2½ inch x 6 cm/2½ inch.

3. Place a heaped teaspoon of one of the fillings below into the centre of each square.

4. To make star shapes simply make diagonal cuts from the corners of each square to within 1 cm/½ inch of the centre. Fold one corner of each cut section into the centre and press the points firmly into the filling. Brush with beaten egg.

5. To make envelope or cushion shapes simply fold all the corners of each square into the centre on top of the filling and brush with beaten egg.

6. Place whichever filled shapes you have onto the oiled baking sheets and slide these into greased polythene bags. Leave to rise in a warm place for about 30 minutes.

7. Preheat the oven to 425°F/220°C/Gas Mark 7.

8. When puffed up bake the pastries 2 trays at a time, one just above centre and one just below for 20 minutes, turning the trays around after 10 minutes. If baking one tray then do so in the centre of the oven for 15 minutes only.

9. Cool on a wire rack.

10. When cold spread with a little honey icing (see below) and sprinkle on a few toasted flaked almonds.

Apricot and almond paste filling

110g/4 oz dried apricots, soaked in apple juice overnight
1 small egg white
2 tablespoons fruit sugar
few drops almond essence
85g/3 oz almonds, finely ground

1. Purée the soaked apricots with a little of the soaking water to achieve a purée consistency.

2. Whisk egg white with sugar and almond essence until frothy, then gradually blend enough of this with the ground almonds until you have a thick paste.

3. Allow 1 teaspoon of the apricot purée and 1 level teaspoon of the almond paste for each pastry and shape, glaze and bake as directed above.

Cinnamon, apple and sultana filling

1 large cooking apple
little honey to sweeten to your taste

1 level teaspoon ground cinnamon
2 rounded tablespoons sultanas

1. Thinly peel, core and chop apple into small chunks.
2. Steam in a colander in which you have put a piece of muslin (not to come over the edge, just to contain the apple) for 5 minutes until soft.
3. Scrape apple off the muslin and mash in honey to your taste, cinnamon and the sultanas.
4. Allow 1 heaped teaspoon of this mixture for each pastry shape, glaze and bake as directed above.

Honey icing

6 tablespoons honey
1 egg white
1 teaspoon vanilla essence
2 teaspoons lemon juice

1. Bring honey to boil in a small heavy based saucepan and let it boil for 5 minutes until putty-like then remove from heat.
2. Beat the egg white with an electric hand whisk and gradually add the warm honey. Continue to beat for 3 minutes or until the mixture is of a spreading consistency.
3. Finally beat in the vanilla and lemon juice.
4. Spread a thin layer on top of the cooled pastries then sprinkle on a few toasted almonds.

Note: Keep uneaten iced pastries in the refrigerator. Unlike sugar icing, honey icing does not harden.

Honey icing is also great for topping buns or cup cakes (see page 63). If you want to colour it pink then you can buy a completely natural red colouring which is an extract from beetroot, so now you can have a reasonably harmless pink icing.

LESSON 2
PASTRY

This lesson covers a wide range of delicious pastry using 100 per cent wholemeal flour or a mixture of flours rather than all white flour. In my baking I have for very good reasons tried to used wholemeal wherever possible, but there are some pastry recipes such as *Rich sweet pastry* (Pâte sucrée – see page 48) and *Choux pastry* (see page 54), which do not produce the best results using wholegrain flour. For these I have successfully used 81 per cent brown wheatmeal flour.

I have not included flaky or puff pastry, as they are so time consuming to prepare and only successful if made with large quantities of saturated fat. If you want to have a go then rest assured that using 81 per cent brown wheatmeal flour instead of white flour in any recipe you have for flaky or puff pastry will be successful and a little bit healthier, but using polyunsaturated margarine instead of butter does not work very well.

You will also find recipes for savoury and sweet crumble mixtures, which can be frozen and sprinkled on fillings while still frozen.

Most pastry freezes well so it is a good idea to double or treble the recipes and freeze what you do not immediately need. This cuts the preparation time by half in many of the recipes that follow.

SHOPPING LIST

Where a page number is given next to any item then look it up if you are not familiar with that particular ingredient. In this lesson, you will find a few recipes using pulses, such as aduki beans and lentils, which are discussed fully and more extensively used in Lesson 5. Both these pulses are quick cooking and easy to digest, but as previously mentioned in the Introduction (see page 00) it is best to let the body adjust to eating wholegrains before adding too many pulses.

100 per cent wholewheat flour, plain	strawberry, raspberry, cherry and exotic fruit
81 per cent brown wheatmeal flour, plain	dried mushrooms (see page 148)
aduki beans (see page 99)	arrowroot
red split lentils (see page 101)	agar agar (see page 184)
shoyu (naturally fermented soya sauce – see page 116)	ground almonds spices listed in Lesson 1
pure maple syrup	ground coriander
pure fruit juice concentrates (see page 184) – these include apple,	cinnamon sticks ground cumin clove powder fennel seeds ground mace cardamons

SAVOURY PIES AND CRUMBLES

BASIC WHOLEMEAL SHORTCRUST PASTRY
You will notice that I use a slightly different method for making shortcrust pastry than is traditionally used. I find the creaming and light kneading method described below releases the gluten (see page 96) in the flour and helps make the dough more manageable and easy to roll out, especially when using wholemeal or wheatmeal flours. It also lightens the end result considerably.

110g/4 oz polyunsaturated margarine
3 tablespoons cold water

pinch sea salt (optional)
225g/8 oz wholemeal flour

1. Put the margarine, water and salt, plus 2 tablespoons of the flour into a mixing bowl. Cream together with a wooden spoon for 1 minute.
2. Gradually add the rest of the flour and mould with your hands as the mixture gets too stiff to use the spoon.
3. Form into a dough and knead for 1 minute with lightly floured hands. You can use this immediately, but it is easier to roll out if placed in a polythene bag and chilled for 20 minutes.

WHOLEMEAL CHEESE SHORTCRUST PASTRY
Simply add 55g/2 oz either Farmhouse Cheddar, Pecorino, Parmesan, or Gruyère cheese, finely grated, to the previous recipe.
   Incorporate the cheese into the creamed mixture just before adding the flour.

SAVOURY WHOLEMEAL CHEESY CRUMBLE MIX

225g/8 oz wholemeal flour
good pinch sea salt
110g/4 oz cold polyunsaturated margarine
55g/2 oz either Farmhouse Cheddar or Gruyère cheese, finely grated

1. Mix flour and salt together in a mixing bowl and rub in the margarine with cool fingertips until the mixture resembles fine breadcrumbs.
2. Toss in the grated cheese with a fork.

Note: Make sure the cheese is cold when you grate it or you will get lumps of it in the mixture.

SAVOURY WHOLEMEAL SESAME SEED CRUMBLE MIX
Omit the cheese from the previous recipe and fork in 3 tablespoons of sesame seeds instead.

Note: If you toast the seeds in a dry pan stirring constantly on a moderate heat for 5 minutes the crumble will be even tastier.

Allow the seeds to cool before adding to the mixture.

LEEK AND POTATO PIE
This is a real hearty pie and great for a cold winter evening.

Serves 6.
You will need a deep pie dish 30 cm x 20 cm/ 12 inch x 8 inch.

1½ times the recipe quantity for Basic wholemeal shortcrust pastry (see page 38), chilled
3 good size potatoes, scrubbed and chopped into 1 cm/½ inch cubes (leave the skins on)
1 rounded teaspoon vegetable bouillon powder
4 good size leeks, trimmed and cut into 2.5 cm/ 1 inch pieces
3 sticks celery, chopped
700 ml/1¼ pt mixed milk and stock from cooking the vegetables
2 rounded tablespoons 81 per cent wheatmeal flour, plain
1 level tablespoon soya flour
½ level teaspoon dry mustard powder
140g/5 oz Farmhouse Cheddar cheese, grated
2 tablespoons freshly chopped parsley
little freshly ground black pepper
little beaten egg to glaze

1. Bring 425ml/¾ pt of water to boil, add the potato cubes and the vegetable bouillon powder. Cook for 3 minutes then add the leeks and celery and continue to cook for a further 3 minutes. The vegetables should still be firm.
2. Drain, saving the cooking liquid, and place the parboiled vegetables in the pie dish.
3. Add enough hot milk to the cooking liquid to make 570ml/1 pt.
4. Blend another 140ml/¼ pt of cold milk with the flours and the mustard powder until smooth, then gradually add a little of the hot liquid.
5. Bring the hot liquid to boiling point then quickly stir in the flour mixture. Stir constantly until well blended. Bring back to boil, still stirring, and cook for a further 1 minute. Remove from heat.

6. Add parsley, cheese and black pepper. Taste and add a little salt if needed.
7. Preheat the oven to 375°F/190°C/Gas Mark 5.
8. Pour the sauce over the vegetables and let the mixture cool before topping with the pastry.
9. Roll out the pastry to fit the top of your dish and place over the vegetables and sauce. Trim and crimp the edges. With the trimmings cut out four leaf shapes. Brush the top of the pastry with beaten egg, stick on the leaf shapes and then brush the tops of these.
10. Bake in the preheated oven for 35 minutes until golden brown.
11. Serve with a little made mustard and a fresh green salad.

Note for vegans: In the recipe above use soya milk instead of ordinary milk. Omit the cheese and add 225g/8 oz of firm tofu. Blend the tofu into the cooked sauce. This is best done in a liquidizer or food processor. Taste and add more vegetable bouillon powder if needed.

ADUKI BEAN PIE
This pie is delicious hot or cold.

Serves 6 to 8.
You will need a 25 cm/10 inch round flan dish, greased.

1½ times recipe quantity of Wholemeal cheese shortcrust pastry (see page 39) or Basic wholemeal shortcrust pastry (see page 38), chilled
225g/8 oz aduki beans (dry weight), soaked and cooked (see page 99)

4 tablespoons sunflower oil
225g/8 oz onion (weight when peeled and chopped)
1 large clove garlic, crushed
2 sticks celery, chopped
110g/4 oz mushrooms, sliced (optional)
2 rounded tablespoons parsley, chopped
396g/14 oz can tomatoes, chopped
¼ teaspoon freshly ground black pepper
1 teaspoon dried basil or 1 tablespoon fresh, chopped
1 tablespoon shoyu (naturally fermented soya sauce)
little beaten egg to glaze

1. Set the oven to 400°F/200°C/Gas Mark 6.
2. Roll out and line the flan dish with half the pastry. Prick the base and bake blind in the centre of the oven for 10 minutes. Allow to cool. Keep the other half of the pastry in the fridge while you prepare the filling.
3. Most of the cooking water will have been absorbed when cooking the beans (if not then drain them).
4. Sauté the onion, garlic, and celery for 6 minutes in a covered pan.
5. Add the mushrooms and continue to fry for 3 minutes more. Stir in the parsley and the tomatoes and cook for 3 minutes with the lid off.
6. Stir in the drained beans, black pepper, basil and shoyu. Take off the heat and leave to cool.
7. Spoon the cold bean mixture into the baked pastry case.
8. Roll out the other half of the pastry to fit on top of the filling. Place over the filling, crimp the edges, prick the top and brush with a little beaten egg.
9. Turn down the heat to 375°F/190°C/Gas Mark 5 and bake for 40 minutes.
10. Serve with lightly steamed green vegetables or a fresh green salad.

ADUKI BEAN CRUMBLE
Serves 6.

Spoon the filling in the previous recipe into a deep 20 cm/8 inch round pie dish and sprinkle on either the *Savoury wholemeal cheesy crumble mix* (see page 39) or the *Savoury wholemeal sesame seed crumble mix* (see page 39). Bake as in the previous recipe.

LENTIL AND MUSHROOM PIE
Serves 6.
You will need a 25 cm/10 inch round pie or flan dish, greased.

1½ times recipe quantity of Wholemeal cheese shortcrust pastry (see page 39) or Basic wholemeal shortcrust pastry (see page 38), chilled
225g/8 oz red split lentils or whole brown or green lentils
425 ml/¾ pt water
1 tablespoon vegetable bouillon powder or vegetable stock cube
1 cinnamon stick
1 bay leaf
2 tablespoons sunflower oil
1 large onion, peeled and chopped
170g/6 oz mushrooms, sliced
1 rounded teaspoon ground coriander
4 medium size tomatoes, skinned and chopped
2 tablespoons lemon juice
½ level teaspoon freshly ground black pepper
1 tablespoon tomato purée
2 tablespoons finely chopped parsley
1 egg beaten
little beaten egg to glaze

1. Set the oven to 400°F/200°C/Gas Mark 6.
2. Roll out and line the pie dish with half the pastry. Prick the base and bake blind in the centre of the oven for 10 minutes. Allow to cool. Keep the rest of the pastry in the fridge while you prepare the filling.
3. Wash the lentils by placing in a sieve and letting cold water run over them. Pick over for little stones.
4. Bring them to boil with the water, vegetable bouillon powder, cinnamon stick and bay leaf, then allow to simmer with the lid on for 15 to 20 minutes (or for 30 minutes if using the brown or green lentils) by which time all the water should have been absorbed (if not drain it off).
5. Remove the cinnamon stick and bay leaf and leave to cool.
6. Sauté the onion in the oil on a moderate heat with the lid off until golden brown. Add the mushrooms and coriander and cook for 2 minutes stirring with a wooden spoon.
7. Add the tomatoes, lemon juice, black pepper and tomato purée.
8. Cook for 2 minutes more then stir in the parsley and the cooked lentils. Let the lot get cold before stirring in the beaten egg.
9. Fill the baked pastry case with the lentil mixture.
10. Roll out the other half of the pastry to fit on top of the filling. Place over the filling, crimp the edges, prick the top all over with a fork and brush with the beaten egg. Bake 375°F/190°C/Gas Mark 5 for 40 minutes.

Note for vegans: The egg in the lentil mixture is not essential, it simply firms the filling a little.

LENTIL AND MUSHROOM CRUMBLE
Serves 6.

Spoon the filling in the previous recipe into a deep 20 cm/8 inch round pie dish and sprinkle on either the *Savoury wholemeal cheesy crumble mix* (see page 39) or the *Savoury wholemeal sesame seed crumble mix* (see page 39) and bake as in the previous recipe.

LENTIL AND BROCCOLI LAYER PIE
This is a wonderful pie to serve hot with the *Vegetable gravy* (see page 170), creamed potatoes and steamed carrots, or cold with a fresh salad. It is deliciously satisfying and goes a long way, so any left over can be eaten cold for a packed lunch or a quick, healthy lunch the next day.

Serves 6.
You will need a 23 cm/9 inch round x 5 cm/2 inch deep pie dish (a loose-bottomed, non-stick tin is ideal).

1½ times recipe quantity of Wholemeal cheese shortcrust pastry (see page 39) or Basic

*wholemeal shortcrust pastry (see page 38),
chilled*
225g/8 oz red split lentils
400 ml/¾ pt hot water
1 level tablespoon vegetable bouillon powder
curl of lemon peel
1 bay leaf
*175g/6 oz onion (weight when peeled and
    chopped)*
1 clove garlic
*2 tablespoons cold pressed sunflower or corn
    oil*
1 rounded teaspoon ground coriander
1 level teaspoon ground fennel seeds
*110g/4 oz mushrooms, wiped and finely
    chopped*
1 level teaspoon ground cumin
1 tablespoon lemon juice
1 level tablespoon tomato purée
freshly ground black pepper
350g/12 oz broccoli florets, green or purple
1 level teaspoon dried tarragon
1 tablespoon Greek yoghurt
sprinkling of vegetable bouillon powder

1. Pick over the lentils for small stones,
   wash and drain.
2. Bring the water to boil, add the lentils,
   vegetable bouillon powde, lemon peel and
   bay leaf. Boil without the lid for 1
   minute, turn down to simmer and cook
   for 15 minutes with the lid on. The water
   will all be absorbed. Allow to cool.
   Remove the lemon peel and bay leaf.
3. Sauté the onion and garlic in the oil for
   10 minutes with the lid on.
4. Add the chopped mushrooms and the
   ground spices, and cook for 3 minutes on
   a moderate to high heat stirring
   constantly, then stir in the lemon juice
   and the tomato purée.
5. Blend all together and stir this into the
   cooled lentils. You should have a thick
   mixture.
6. Add freshly ground black pepper and
   leave to cool while you prepare the
   broccoli.
7. Wash and steam the broccoli until just
   tender.
8. Roughly chop the florets, then purée in a
   blender with the tarragon, Greek yoghurt

and a sprinkling of vegetable bouillon
powder.
9. Set the oven to 400°F/200°C/Gas Mark 6.
10. Roll out half the pastry on a lightly
    floured surface and line the greased pie
    dish.
11. Spoon in half the lentil mixture then
    spread all of the puréed broccoli over
    this.
12. Top with the remaining lentil mixture.
13. Roll out the remaining pastry, ease it
    onto the rolling pin and cover the pie.
14. Trim and flute the edges, and decorate
    the top with pastry leaves if you wish.
15. Brush the top with egg or milk.
16. Bake in the centre of the oven for 15
    minutes, then turn down heat to 375°F/
    190°C/Gas Mark 5 and continue to bake
    for another 10 minutes until the top is
    golden brown. Allow to stand for 10
    minutes before slicing.

Note for vegans Simply omit the Greek
yoghurt from the broccoli layer and blend with
a little tofu and 1 teaspoon of lemon juice.

RICH SAVOURY BROWN WHEATMEAL PASTRY

I use this pastry for savoury tartlets and
miniature pastries or turnovers. Filled with a
variety of tasty mixtures, they are great for
buffet parties or as appetizers. You can use
fluted brioche or boat-shaped barquette
moulds, but these are fiddly so I use bun tins
and a fluted biscuit cutter slightly larger than
the rim of the bun tin moulds instead.
   You can use all wholemeal flour for this

recipe, but for these small delicate pastries I think the 81 per cent brown wheatmeal flour will make the dough more manageable and give you light, melt-in-the-mouth results.

225g/8 oz 81 per cent brown wheatmeal flour
pinch sea salt
110g/4 oz cold butter or polyunsaturated
    margarine
3 rounded tablespoons Pecorino or Parmesan
    cheese, finely grated
1 egg yolk (save the white for brushing pastry)
1 tablespoon ice-cold water
1 tablespoon ice-cold lemon juice

1. Mix flour and salt together. If using butter, grate this into the flour then rub in until the mixture resembles fine breadcrumbs. If using margarine, simply rub this in until you achieve the same texture.
2. Stir in the cheese with a fork.
3. Whisk the egg yolk, water and lemon juice together until frothy.
4. Sprinkle this into the flour mixture and blend together using the fork. Then with cupped hands, lightly mould together to form a dough.
5. Place in a polythene bag and chill for at least 1 hour before using.

Note for vegans: Omit the cheese and the egg yolk and use 2 tablespoons of sesame seeds and an extra tablespoon of cold water. Proceed with the method as above.

BROCCOLI AND TARRAGON TARTLETS
Makes 24.
You will need 2 x 12 mould bun trays, oiled.

1 recipe quantity Rich savoury brown
    wheatmeal pastry (see page 42)
170g/6 oz fresh or frozen broccoli florets
3 standard eggs
170g/6 oz cottage cheese
3 rounded tablespoons Gruyère cheese, finely
    grated
110g/4 oz Greek yoghurt
1 level teaspoon vegetable bouillon powder
1 level teaspoon dried tarragon
1/3 level teaspoon ground mace

1 clove garlic, crushed
freshly ground black pepper to taste

1. Roll out the pastry as thinly as possible, using a lightly floured surface. Cut out rounds with a fluted biscuit cutter slightly bigger than the rim of the bun moulds.
2. Ease each round into the oiled bun tin moulds and brush the surface of the pastry with well beaten egg white. Slide into polythene bags and chill while you prepare the filling.
3. Preheat the oven to 375°F/190°C/Gas Mark 5.
4. Steam the broccoli for 10 minutes only. Leave to cool, then chop into small bits.
5. Whisk the eggs until frothy.
6. Using a fork, stir in the broccoli, 1½ tablespoons of the Gruyère cheese and the rest of the ingredients. Blend well without mashing the broccoli.
7. Sprinkle a little of the remaining Gruyère cheese onto the base of each pastry case.
8. Spoon on the broccoli mixture until it reaches to the top of each pastry case.
9. Bake the bun tin trays on two shelves – one just above centre and one just below centre – for 12 minutes. Change the trays around and continue to bake for another 12 minutes or until the filling has risen and become light golden brown on top.

MUSHROOM, ROASTED AUBERGINE AND PEPPER 'CAVIAR' TARTLETS
Makes 24.
You will need 2 x 12 mould bun tins, oiled.

1 recipe quantity Rich savoury brown
    wheatmeal pastry (see page 42)
10 small dried mushrooms
2 x 280g/10 oz aubergines
1 medium size green pepper
1 medium size red pepper
2 tablespoons virgin olive oil or sunflower oil
170g/6 oz onion, peeled and finely chopped
1 large clove garlic, crushed
1/4 teaspoon cayenne pepper (more if you like)
2 rounded tablespoons parsley, finely chopped
2 tablespoons lemon juice
1 tablespoon tomato purée
thin strips of red and green pepper
25 black olives, stoned (optional)

1. Preheat the oven to 400°F/200°C/Gas Mark 6.
2. Roll out the pastry and line bun tin moulds as for *Broccoli and tarragon tartlets* (see page 43).
3. Bake blind in the centre of the preheated oven for 5 minutes. Turn down heat to 375°F/190°C/Gas Mark 5 and continue baking for 10 minutes more. Leave to cool.
4. Soak the mushrooms in hot water for 15 minutes.
5. Wash and wipe the aubergines and the peppers. Make 3 slits in the aubergines. Leave peppers whole.
6. Heat the grill to maximum for 3 minutes, then turn down heat to moderate and grill the aubergines and peppers, turning them continuously until the skins are blistered and charred all over and the flesh soft.
7. Pop the aubergines and peppers into a colander and rinse in cold water, then gently rub the skins off. Pat dry, roughly chop the aubergines, cut peppers in half, remove pith and seeds, and chop roughly.
8. Sauté the onion and garlic in the oil for 5 minutes.
9. Drain the mushrooms, cut off woody stems and discard. Chop the mushroom caps into tiny pieces and sauté with the onions for 7 minutes.
10. Stir in cayenne, parsley, lemon juice and tomato purée.
11. Put aubergines, peppers and onion mixture into a blender and process until smooth. Cover and chill until ready to fill the pastry cases. (Do this just before serving.)
12. When ready to serve, spoon the filling into the baked tartlet cases, garnish with criss-cross thin strips of red and green pepper and place one olive in the centre of each.

Note for vegans: Use the vegan version of the *Rich savoury brown wheatmeal pastry* recipe (see page 42). The filling remains the same.

FRENCH-STYLE MUSHROOM TARTLETS

Traditional French mushroom tartlets contain lots of cream. These French-style tartlets, using thick Greek yoghurt, are just as tasty but much lower in fat. Do not add the yoghurt to the mushroom mixture before you have gently cooked it with the egg and the arrowroot first, otherwise the mixture will curdle. Flour and eggs stabilize the yoghurt. The Madeira is optional but delicious.

Makes 24.
You will need 2 x 12 mould bun tins, oiled.

1 recipe quantity Rich savoury brown wheatmeal pastry (see page 42)
1 medium onion, peeled and very finely chopped
3 tablespoons sunflower or virgin olive oil
450g/1 lb button mushrooms (as small as possible, slice if necessary)
2 tablespoons Madeira
1 rounded teaspoon arrowroot
1 egg yolk
225g/8 oz carton Greek yoghurt
sea salt and freshly ground black pepper to taste
good pinch cayenne pepper (optional)
fresh parsley, very finely chopped, to garnish

1. Prepare the baked pastry cases as in stages 1, 2 and 3 of the previous recipe.
2. Sauté the onion in 2 tablespoons of oil for about 10 minutes until soft.
3. Add another tablespoon of oil and sauté the mushrooms briskly for 3 minutes only, turning them to achieve even cooking.
4. Add the Madeira and stir well. Remove from heat.
5. Blend the arrowroot with a very little cold water to achieve a smooth, runny paste.
6. Warm the yoghurt in a small, thick saucepan on a very low heat. As it is warming, whisk in the beaten egg yolk with a balloon whisk, then beat in the arrowroot mixture. Keep whisking until the mixture thickens.
7. Take the egg, yoghurt and arrowroot mixture off the heat and stir into the mushroom and onion mixture. Heat gently to boiling point, stirring all the time, and

cook gently for 2 minutes. Add the cayenne if using.

8. When ready to serve, spoon the hot mixture into the baked tartlet cases and place under the grill for one minute. Sprinkle on a little fresh parsley and serve hot.

Note: You can use this filling for 1 x 25 cm/10 inch baked pastry case instead of the tartlet cases.

MINIATURE DRIED MUSHROOM STUFFED PASTIES

These are delicious hot or cold. You can make them well in advance and freeze before cooking. To bake after freezing leave to defrost almost completely for 1 hour, then bake in the preheated oven as directed in the method below.

Makes 25.

1 recipe quantity of Rich savoury wheatmeal pastry (see page 42)
little beaten egg to seal pasties
110g/4 oz dried mushrooms
170g/6 oz onion, finely chopped
2 tablespoons sunflower oil or butter
2 slices rye bread (wholemeal will do)
1 rounded teaspoon dried dill weed or
½ teaspoon fennel seeds, finely ground
little sea salt and freshly ground black pepper
2 tablespoons Greek yoghurt
2 hard-boiled eggs

1. Soak the mushrooms in hot water for 15 minutes, then cook them in the soaking water for 20 minutes until soft.
2. Drain, reserving the water, cut off and discard woody stems, then chop the caps roughly.
3. Put into a food processor and chop very finely.
4. Sauté the onion with the finely chopped mushrooms for 10 minutes.
5. Meanwhile, strain the mushroom soaking liquid (to get rid of grit) and soak the bread in it.
6. Using a potato masher, mash the soaked bread into the mushroom and onion mixture.

7. Sieve in the hard-boiled eggs, and stir in the yoghurt and the dill or ground fennel seed.
8. Season with a little sea salt and freshly ground black pepper, tasting as you do so.
9. Cook on very low heat for 10 minutes more, stirring occasionally. Leave to cool.
10. Preheat the oven to 375°F/190°C/Gas Mark 5.
11. Roll out the chilled pastry on a lightly floured surface. Cut out circles 7.5 cm/ 3 inch in diameter with a plain round cutter.
12. Place one generous teaspoon of the filling in the centre of each round, brush all round the edge of the pastry and bring together in a semi-circle on top of the filling.
13. Seal the edges together, pressing gently and fluting as you do so.
14. Place on lightly greased baking sheets and brush the tops with beaten egg.
15. Bake in the preheated oven one tray just above centre, the other tray just below centre, for 20 minutes. Change the trays around after 10 minutes.

Note for vegans: Use the vegan version of the *Rich savoury brown wheatmeal pastry* recipe, (see page 43). Then in the filling, use 110g/ 4 oz smoked or firm tofu and mash it in instead of the hard boiled eggs and yoghurt at stage 7 in the method above. Follow all other directions.

QUICHES

The following fillings for quiches will give you deliciously flavoured and firm texture results instead of the wobbly, omelette type of quiche I have sampled through the years.

The true French quiche filling contains cream to achieve the perfect texture, but I use a mixture of milk, thick Greek yoghurt and eggs – or you can use a mixture of milk, ordinary yoghurt, milk powder and eggs, as well as a variety of herbs, spices and vegetables. The basic liquids for my 25 cm/ 10 inch quiche contain four standard eggs plus either 140 ml/¼ pt milk and 140 ml/¼ pt Greek yoghurt *or* 140 ml/¼ pt milk, 2 rounded tablespoons of dried milk powder and 3 tablespoons of ordinary yoghurt. So the liquid, including the eggs, will reach a level of 500 ml/ just under 1 pt in your measuring jug.

For a 20 cm/8 inch quiche, cut all the ingredients in the recipe by a quarter.

Note for vegans: The next five recipes are traditional quiches, packed with dairy produce, but I have devised delicious alternative tofu and vegetable quiche fillings in Lesson 6 on the soya bean. They are worth trying, even if you aren't a vegan.

LEEK AND TOMATO QUICHE
Serves 6.
You will need a 25 cm/10 inch quiche dish, greased.

¾ recipe quantity of Basic wholemeal
*   shortcrust pastry (see page 38), chilled*
225g/8 oz leeks, chopped in thin rings
2 tablespoons sunflower or virgin olive oil
140 ml/¼ pt milk
140g/5 oz Greek yoghurt
4 standard eggs
1 level teaspoon dried tarragon
½ teaspoon ground mace
¼ teaspoon dried mustard powder
¼ teaspoon black pepper, freshly ground
¼ teaspoon sea salt
140g/5 oz Cheddar cheese, grated
3 medium size tomatoes, sliced
little extra dried tarragon to top

1. Preheat the oven to 375°F/190°C/Gas Mark 5.
2. Roll out the pastry to fit the quiche dish and line the dish. Trim edges, prick the base and bake blind for 12 minutes until lightly golden brown. Leave to cool.
3. Heat the oil in a pan and sauté the leeks on low heat until just soft (about 7 minutes), stirring occasionally. Leave to cool.
4. Either in a blender or using a egg whisk, mix milk, Greek yoghurt, tarragon, mace, mustard powder, pepper, salt and eggs together until frothy.
5. When pastry and leeks are cool, sprinkle 55g/2 oz of the cheese on the pastry. Spoon the leeks over this and top with another 55g/2 oz of the cheese.
6. Pour on the milk and egg liquid. Arrange the tomatoes on top, pressing them in gently.
7. Sprinkle on the remaining 28g/1 oz of cheese and a little dried tarragon.
8. Bake in the centre of the oven for 40 to 45 minutes until the filling rises a little and is golden brown on top. Leave to cool for 5 minutes before cutting.

ONION AND TOMATO QUICHE
Serves 6.

Substitute one large onion, peeled and cut in thin rings, for the leeks in the previous recipe, and use basil or oregano instead of the tarragon. Sauté the onion for 4 minutes only and leave to drain in a colander. Proceed as in the previous recipe.

GREEN AND RED PEPPER QUICHE
Serves 6.
You will need a 25 cm/10 inch quiche dish, greased.

¾ recipe quantity of Basic wholemeal
*   shortcrust pastry (see page 38), chilled*
4 standard eggs
140 ml/¼ pt milk
140g/5 oz Greek yoghurt
½ teaspoon ground mace
¼ teaspoon dried mustard powder
¼ teaspoon black pepper, freshly ground

¼ *teaspoon sea salt*
1 teaspoon oregano
140g/5 oz Cheddar cheese, grated
1 small onion, peeled and finely chopped
½ *medium size red pepper, deseeded and cut*
in thin rings
½ *medium size green pepper, deseeded and cut*
in thin rings
little oregano to top

1. Preheat the oven to 375°F/190°C/Gas Mark 5.
2. Roll out the pastry to fit the quiche dish, line the dish and prick the base. Bake blind in the centre of the oven for 12 minutes until tinged with gold. Leave to cool.
3. Whisk eggs, milk, Greek yoghurt, mace, mustard, black pepper, salt and oregano together until frothy.
4. Sprinkle 55g/2 oz of the cheese onto the cooled pastry case. Spoon the finely chopped onion evenly over this, then top with another 55g/2 oz of the cheese.
5. Pour the egg and milk mixture evenly over the onion and cheese.
6. Arrange the red and green pepper slices on top in two overlapping circles.
7. Sprinkle on the remaining 28g/1 oz of cheese and a little oregano.
8. Bake in the centre of the oven for 40 to 45 minutes until slightly risen and golden brown. Leave to stand for 5 minutes before cutting.

SPINACH AND GOAT'S CURD (OR COTTAGE CHEESE) QUICHE

Fresh spinach, lightly steamed, is best for this quiche. If using fresh, you will need 450g/1 lb raw spinach. Steam for 7 minutes, press out all the liquid and chop very finely.

If using frozen, you will need a 225g/8 oz packet. Cook on very low heat until melted, then drain in a sieve, pressing to extract as much liquid as possible.

Serves 6.
You will need a 25 cm/10 inch quiche dish, greased.

¾ *recipe Basic wholemeal shortcrust pastry*
(see page 38), chilled

4 standard eggs
225g/8 oz goat's curd or cottage cheese
225g/8 oz spinach (cooked weight), cooled
55g/2 oz Pecorino, Parmesan or Cheddar
cheese, finely grated
140g/5 oz Greek yoghurt
⅓ *teaspoon ground mace or nutmeg*
1 large clove garlic, crushed
freshly ground black pepper to taste
little sea salt to taste, if needed

1. Preheat the oven to 375°F/190°C/Gas Mark 5.
2. Roll out the pastry to fit the quiche dish, line the dish and prick the base. Bake blind in the centre of the oven for 12 minutes until tinged with gold. Leave to cool.
3. Whisk the eggs until frothy.
4. If using goat's curd cheese, blend this with the eggs in a food processor. If using cottage cheese, stir this into the beaten eggs.
5. Add all the other ingredients, tasting before you add the salt (you might not need it). Stir with a fork and pour into the cool pastry case.
6. Bake in the centre of the oven for 40 minutes. Leave to stand for 5 minutes before cutting.

SWEET PIES AND CRUMBLES

I am going to give you four versions of sweet pastry; the third is the nearest to the traditional French recipe for pâte sucrée, so take your pick, according to how healthy you want your pastry to be. Obviously the third version – which uses 81 per cent brown wheatmeal flour, fruit sugar, egg yolks and butter – is not a good choice if you are on a special diet, but for the occasional very special dessert it is absolutely delicious. Versions 1 and 2 can be used for most of the recipes in this section, but versions 3 and 4 should only be used where stated.

WHOLEMEAL SWEET PASTRY

This is the healthiest version. I use apple juice concentrate to sweeten this pastry. The result is a very slightly sweet taste, so it is great if you haven't a sweet tooth but like just a hint of sweetness.

110g/4 oz polyunsaturated margarine
1 tablespoon apple juice concentrate
2 tablespoons cold water
225g/8 oz wholemeal flour
pinch sea salt (optional)

1. Cream the margarine, apple juice concentrate, water and two tablespoons of the flour in a mixing bowl until smooth.
2. Gradually add the rest of the flour (to which you have added the salt, if you are using it) beat it in with a wooden spoon, then mould with your hands to form a soft dough.
3. Knead the dough on a lightly floured surface for 1 minute.
4. Place in a polythene bag and chill for 30 minutes, when your dough will be ready to use.

WHEATMEAL SWEET PASTRY

If you do not wish to use the egg yolk, then add one more tablespoon of cold water to the recipe below.

110g/4 oz polyunsaturated margarine
1 rounded tablespoon fruit sugar
2 tablespoons cold water, less 1 teaspoon
1 teaspoon lemon juice
1 egg yolk
225g/8 oz 81 per cent brown wheatmeal flour
pinch sea salt (optional)

1. Cream the margarine and fruit sugar for half a minute.
2. Whisk the water, lemon juice and egg yolk together until frothy, then add this with 2 tablespoons of the flour to the margarine and sugar.
3. Beat well together until smooth. Now follow the directions for *Wholemeal sweet pastry* (see above), from stage 2.

RICH SWEET PASTRY (PATE SUCREE)

You can use polyunsaturated margarine in this recipe with good results, but using butter gives a melt-in-the-mouth texture. It is best to use the rubbing-in method for this recipe.

225g/8 oz 81 per cent brown wheatmeal flour
pinch sea salt
2 level tablespoons fruit sugar
110g/4 oz cold butter, grated, or cold
    polyunsaturated margarine
3 large egg yolks, beaten, or 2 egg yolks plus 1
    tablespoon cold water

1. Mix flour, salt and sugar together in a mixing bowl.
2. Rub in the grated butter or margarine with cool fingertips, as quickly as possible, until the mixture resembles fine breadcrumbs.
3. Make a well in the centre and pour in the 3 egg yolks (or 2 egg yolks plus 1 tablespoon of water) and fold the flour mixture over this, forming it, with light fingertips, into a dough.
4. Knead for a few seconds and place in a polythene bag, flatten slightly and chill for 1 hour. Your pastry is now ready to use.

CAKE-LIKE SWEET WHOLEMEAL PASTRY

This is great for fruit slices, where you want a softer, spongy type of pastry. It is the only pastry I use baking powder in. If you like, you can omit the egg yolk and add 1 extra tablespoon of water and ½ teaspoon more of baking powder to keep the spongy texture.

150g/5 oz polyunsaturated margarine
1 rounded tablespoon clear honey

1 egg yolk
1 tablespoon cold water
4 drops natural vanilla essence
225g/8 oz strong wholemeal flour, plain
1 rounded teaspoon baking powder

1. Cream the margarine and honey for half a minute.
2. Whisk the egg yolk with the water and vanilla essence and beat this with 2 tablespoons of the flour into the margarine and honey.
3. Mix the baking powder with the rest of the flour and gradually fold this into the creamed mixture. (Never beat mixtures with baking powder in them; always fold, or the dough will become heavy.)
4. Form into a dough, kneading together for a few seconds only.
5. Place into a polythene bag and chill for 1 hour. (If you want to use immediately, you will have to press the dough into the baking tins; it will only roll out easily when well chilled.) After chilling, your dough is ready to use.

SWEET CRUMBLE MIX
This is great for quick puddings. Make plenty and freeze what you do not need. You can use the frozen mixture without defrosting, as long as you don't press it together before freezing.

225g/8 oz wholemeal flour
110g/4 oz cold polyunsaturated margarine
good pinch sea salt
1 to 2 tablespoons demerara sugar (according to taste)
2 tablespoons of either sesame seeds, ground sunflower seeds or ground hazel nuts

1. Rub the margarine into the flour with cool fingertips until the mixture resembles fine breadcrumbs.
2. Stir in the sugar, salt, and seeds or ground nuts.
3. If freezing, lay on a tray and freeze before putting into a freezer bag. Do not press together.

Note: Try this crumble mix over any of the fillings suggested in the next three recipes.

They are all ideal for crumbles, which will take you half the time it takes to prepare double-crusted pies.

SPICED APPLE PIE
The filling for this delicious fruit-filled pie uses honey and a little natural maple syrup instead of sugar to sweeten. It tastes wonderful hot or cold, and is delicious served with Greek yoghurt.

Serves 6.
You will need a 23 cm/9 inch pie dish, greased.

1½ times recipe quantity of Wholemeal sweet pastry (see page 48) or Wheatmeal sweet pastry (see page 48), chilled
little beaten egg or milk to brush top of pastry
900g/2 lb cooking apples, cored and thinly sliced (but not peeled)
1 tablespoon lemon juice
1 level tablespoon arrowroot
2 level tablespoons runny honey
2 tablespoons natural maple syrup
½ level teaspoon nutmeg, freshly ground
½ level teaspoon ground cinnamon
pinch clove powder
55g/2 oz sultanas (optional)

1. Preheat the oven to 425°F/220°C/Gas Mark 7.
2. Roll out just over half the pastry to a circle big enough to line the pie dish and overhang the sides a little.
3. Roll out the rest of the pastry to a circle which will just fit on top of the filling.
4. Cut out a small, 2.5 cm/1 inch hole with a tiny cutter in the centre of the pastry topping.
5. Put the sliced apples in a mixing bowl and toss with the lemon juice.
6. Blend the arrowroot with the honey, maple syrup and spices until smooth.
7. Stir this into the apple mixture using a fork, then sprinkle on the sultanas (if using) and distribute these into the mixture.
8. Fill the pastry-lined pie dish with the fruit and spice mixture just before baking.

9. Top with the pastry lid and seal the edges with a little beaten egg or milk, then either flute with fingertips or press all round the edge with the back of a fork.
10. Brush the top with egg or milk and bake in the centre of the preheated oven for 15 minutes. Turn down heat to 350°F/180°C/ Gas Mark 4, and continue to bake for about 30 minutes longer or until the crust is golden brown on top and the apples feel tender when poked with a skewer or steel knitting needle.

FRESH APRICOT PIE
Serves 6.
You will need a 23 cm/9 inch pie dish, greased.

Follow the recipe for *Spiced apple pie* (see above), but substitute 900g/2 lb fresh, stoned and sliced apricots for the apples and lemon juice. Omit the sultanas and use the finely ground seeds from 2 cardamon pods instead of the clove powder.

CRANBERRY AND APPLE PIE
Serves 6.
You will need a 23 cm/9 inch pie dish, greased.

This is great during the Christmas season when cranberries are easily available. Follow the recipe for *Spiced apple pie* (see above), but substitute 560g/1¼ lb apples (cored and thinly sliced) and 340g/12 oz cranberries for the apples alone and omit the clove powder and sultanas.

Note: There are many more variations on the fruit-filled pie theme using seasonal fruits – for example, *Apple and blackberry pie* (675g/ 1 lb apples to 225g/8 oz blackberries), *Cherry pie* (900g/2 lb cherries, stoned) and, of course, *Plum pie* (900g/2 lb plums). All are delicious sweetened with honey and maple syrup. Experiment with different spices and you will never be lost for a healthy, satisfying and tasty dessert.

MEXICAN FRUIT CRUMBLE
For this recipe I imagined I was a native of Mexico and having read an English recipe for apple crumble, I decided to create my own. I must admit it is very different from our traditional pudding but I'm sure you will love it.

Start the night before because the fruit is best if left to marinate in the delicious juices and spices. You can vary the fruit according to the seasons. If using part-dried fruit then weigh after soaking.

Serves 6.
You will need a 30 cm/12 inch square ovenproof dish.

675g/1½ lb fresh apricots
450g/1 lb crisp, ripe eating apples
3 large bananas
juice of 2 large oranges
juice of 1 good size lemon
4 tablespoons either apple juice concentrate, maple syrup or raw cane syrup
2 tablespoons brandy or 1 each of rum and brandy
1 rounded teaspoon freshly grated ginger
½ level teaspoon ground cinnamon
½ teaspoon aniseed
110g/4 oz yellow cornmeal
110g/4 oz medium fine oatmeal
110g/4 oz wholemeal flour, plain
55g/2 oz sesame seeds
85g/3 oz either freshly grated coconut or desiccated coconut
good pinch sea salt (optional)
170g/6 oz polyunsaturated margarine
½ level teaspoon ground allspice
1 rounded tablespoon clear honey
grated peel of 2 oranges and 1 lemon

1. Blanch the apricots in boiling water for 30 seconds, peel, cut in half and remove the stones. Slice each half into 3 segments.
2. Wash the apples, cut in quarters and core (leave the skins on), then cut quarters into very thin slices.
3. Peel and slice bananas into 0.5 cm/ ¼ inch rounds.

4. Put the fruit into a bowl, pour on orange juice, lemon juice, whichever syrup you choose and the brandy. Stir into the fruit, add the spices and again stir well in.

5. Cover and leave to marinate overnight or for at least 2 hours.

6. Put the cornmeal, oatmeal, flour, sesame seeds, coconut and salt into a mixing bowl.

7. Melt the margarine in a saucepan over a pan of hot water. Stir in the allspice, honey and grated rind of the oranges and lemon, blend well.

8. Pour into the dry ingredients and rub all together with your fingertips. The mixture will be like sticky breadcrumbs.

9. Put the marinated fruit into a lightly greased ovenproof dish with all of the juices. Spread the crumble mixture over the top in an even layer and bake at 375°F/190°C/Gas 7 for 35 minutes until the top is golden brown.

10. Serve hot or cold with Greek yoghurt.

DRIED APRICOT, APPLE AND ALMOND FLAN

Serves 6.
You will need a 25 cm/10 inch round, loose-bottomed, flan tin, well greased.

1 recipe quantity of either Wholemeal or
*   Wheatmeal sweet pastry (see page 48)*
170g/6 oz dried apricots, soaked in 425 ml/
*   ¾ pt apple juice overnight*
1 large cooking apple, peeled, cored and
*   chopped*
85g/3 oz ground almonds
1 level teaspoon ground cinnamon
2 tablespoons clear honey
1 tablespoon maple syrup
1 large cooking apple (leave whole until
*   wanted)*
1 tablespoon lemon juice
1 glacé cherry to decorate (optional)

1. Preheat the oven to 400°F/200°C/Gas Mark 6.
2. Roll out the pastry of your choice and line the flan dish. Trim and prick the base and bake blind in the centre of the oven for 12

minutes. Leave to cool.

3. Liquidize the soaked apricots with the chopped apples and the fruit juice until smooth.

4. Scoop out into a bowl and stir in the ground almonds, cinnamon and 1 tablespoon of the honey.

5. Spread this mixture onto the base of the cooked and cold pastry case.

6. Core and thinly slice the other apple (leave skin on) into very thin wedges. Sprinkle with the lemon juice and arrange the slices overlapping each other in two circles over the almond filling.

7. Melt the remaining 1 tablespoon of honey with the maple syrup and trickle this over the apples.

8. Turn the oven down to 375°F/190°C/Gas Mark 5 and bake in the centre of the oven for 25 minutes until the apples are soft.

9. Serve hot or cold with Greek yoghurt or a mixture of Greek yoghurt and cream.

MINCE PIES

Makes 12.
You will need 1 bun mould tray (moulds 6.5 cm/2½ inch in diameter) greased.

1 recipe quantity either Wholemeal or
*   Wheatmeal sweet pastry (see page 48)*
450g/1 lb mincemeat (or follow the method for
*   the mincemeat filling in the Mincemeat*
*   stuffed apples recipe on page 00, using four*
*   times the quantity of ingredients)*
little sugar for dusting (optional)

1. Preheat the oven to 400°F/200°C/Gas Mark 6.
2. Roll out the pastry as thinly as possible on a lightly floured surface.
3. Cut out 12 rounds with a 7.5 cm/3 inch fluted cutter and 12 smaller rounds using a 5.5 cm/2¼ inch fluted cutter. Line the bun tray moulds with the larger rounds.
4. Spoon on a generous teaspoon of mincemeat into the centre of each pastry round.
5. Dampen the edges of the small pastry rounds and place on top. Make a small slit on top of each one.

6. Bake in the centre of the oven for 20 minutes.
7. Dust tops with sugar while still hot (optional).

MINCE SLICE

I always make Mince slice instead of pies for a Christmas buffet party as it is simpler to prepare.

Makes 24.
You will need a 20 x 15 cm/8 inch x 6 inch rectangle baking tin.

1 recipe quantity of either Wholemeal or Wheatmeal sweet pastry (see page 48), chilled
450g/1 lb mincemeat (or follow the method for the mincemeat filling in the Mincemeat stuffed apples recipe on page 190, using four times the quantity of ingredients)
little beaten egg to glaze
little sugar for sprinkling (optional)

1. Preheat the oven 350°F/180°C/Gas Mark 4.
2. Roll out half the pastry as thinly as possible between two sheets of polythene to a rectangle to fit the base of the baking tin.
3. Spoon on the mincemeat and spread evenly.
4. Roll out the other half of the pastry to fit the top of the tin. Trim edges and pattern with a fork. Prick the top evenly all over.
5. Brush with beaten egg and bake in the centre of the oven for 35 to 40 minutes.
6. While still hot sprinkle with a little sugar (optional).

MIXED BERRY TARTLETS OR FLAN

Makes 12 tartlets or 1 x 23 cm/9 inch flan.
You will need 12 individual fluted tartlet moulds (7.5 cm/3 inch diameter brioche moulds are perfect) or a 23 cm/9 inch loose-bottomed flan tin brushed with oil.

1 recipe quantity of Rich sweet pastry (pâte sucrée) (see page 48), well chilled
450g/1 lb mixed strawberries, raspberries, blackcurrants and redcurrants
1 tablespoon clear honey

2 tablespoons pure raspberry juice concentrate
250 ml/9 fl oz water
1 rounded teaspoon of agar agar granules or 1 tablespoon agar agar flakes
1 tablespoon lemon juice

1. Preheat the oven to 400°F/200°C/Gas Mark 6.
2. If making the tartlets, roll out the pastry into a sausage shape and cut into 12 equal pieces. If making the flan, ignore stages 2, 3, 4 and 5 and follow stages 6, 7 and 8 instead.
3. Roll each piece into a ball then roll out on a lightly floured surface to a circle slightly larger than the tops of the tartlet moulds.
4. Ease these gently into the moulds, lightly pressing the pastry against the sides.
5. Trim excess pastry with a sharp knife, prick the base all over with a fork and bake blind in the centre of the oven for 12 minutes until light golden brown. Leave to cool completely before filling.
6. Alternatively, for the flan roll pastry into a ball and flatten it between two sheets of polythene then roll it out to a circle slightly larger than the top of the flan tin.
7. Ease the pastry onto the rolling pin, still between the sheets, gradually taking the bottom sheet off as you lay the pastry into the tin.
8. Press the pastry gently against the sides, trim the edges with a sharp knife, prick the base and bake blind in the preheated oven for 15 minutes or until light, golden brown. Leave to cool completely before filling.

9. If strawberries are big then slice in half and put all the fruit into a mixing bowl.

10. Heat the honey, raspberry juice concentrate and water to warm. Sprinkle on the agar agar granules or flakes and stir continuously as you bring the mixture to boil. Continue to boil until the agar agar has completely dissolved.

11. Take off heat and stir in the lemon juice.

12. Pour this liquid over the fruit stirring gently with a fork to coat the fruit well.

13. Leave to cool to room temperature then chill for 1 hour until it begins to set.

14. Spoon into the tartlet cases or flan case and chill until set.

15. Just before serving top with scoops of ice cream (see page 184 for ice cream recipes) or *Vanilla yoghurt cream* (see page 191), and garnish with sprigs of mint or lemon balm or seasoned edible flowers (for example, primroses or violets in spring).

Note: This recipe can be made using only one type of berry and its pure fruit juice concentrate in the filling.

YELLOW FRUIT TARTLETS OR FLAN

The choice of soft yellow fruits can include fresh pineapple, apricots, peaches, mangos, papayas, oranges, banana and kiwi. (I know it's green but just one small kiwi is delicious with any of the other fruits mentioned. Do not use too much because it is quite sharp.) The weight of the fruit in the ingredient list is its chopped weight after peeling, stoning or de-seeding etc.

Makes 12 tartlets or 1 x 23 cm/9 inch flan. You will need 12 individual fluted tartlet moulds (7.5 cm/3 inch diameter brioche moulds are perfect) or a 23 cm/9 inch loose-bottomed flan tin brushed with oil.

1 recipe quantity Rich sweet pastry (pâte sucrée) (see page 48), well chilled
450g/1 lb mixed yellow fruit (see above)
1 tablespoon clear honey
140 ml/¼ pt pure pineapple juice
140 ml/¼ pt pure orange juice
1 rounded teaspoon of agar agar granules or 1 tablespoon agar agar flakes
1 tablespoon lemon juice

1. Preheat the oven to 400°F/200°C/Gas Mark 6.

2. Prepare and bake the tartlet cases or flan case as in previous recipe.

3. Put prepared and chopped fruit into a bowl.

4. Heat the honey and fruit juice to warm, sprinkle on the agar-agar stirring as you bring the liquid to boil. Allow to boil until the agar-agar has completely dissolved.

5. Take off heat, stir in the lemon juice and pour over the fruit. Stir well to coat all the fruit and leave to cool at room temperature then chill for 1 hour until beginning to set.

6. Spoon into the tartlet pastry cases or flan case and chill until set.

7. Just before serving top as suggested for *Mixed berry tartlets* or *flan* (see page 52).

FIG AND ANISEED SLICE
Serves 6.
You will need a baking tin approximately 20 cm/8 inch x 30 cm/12 inch or a 25 cm/10 inch square tin about 4 cm/1½ inch deep, well greased.

2 x the recipe quantity of Cake-like sweet wholemeal pastry, chilled (see page 48)
450g/1 lb dried figs
285ml/½ pt water
3 teaspoons aniseed, ground
little beaten egg to glaze

1. Preheat the oven to 375°F/190°C/Gas Mark 5.

2. Cut the pastry in half and roll out one half between two sheets of polythene (otherwise it will break) to a rectangle or square the size of the base of the tin only.

3. Ease the pastry up, still with the sheets on and gently lay the pastry on the bottom of the tin, gradually peeling off the bottom sheet as you do this. Press gently into the tin, prick the base and bake blind in the centre of the oven for 12 minutes. Leave to cool.

4. Cut stalks off the figs, wash well and chop as small as possible.

5. Soak in the water for 1 hour then cook with the soaking water and the aniseed until soft and pulp-like.

6. Leave to cool then spread onto the cooked pastry base.
7. Top with the other half of the pastry, rolling it out and easing it on gently as described for the base. Trim and mark the edges with the back of the prongs of a fork.
8. Brush with egg or milk and bake in the preheated oven for 45 minutes to 1 hour.

DATE AND APPLE SLICE
Serves 6.
You will need a baking tin approximately 20 cm/8 inch x 30 cm/12 inch or a 25 cm/10 inch square tin about 4 cm/1½ inch deep, well greased.

Follow the instructions for preparing pastry and baking in the recipe for *Fig and aniseed slice* (see page 53) but do the following filling:

450g/1 lb cooking apples, thinly peeled, cored and chopped
½ teaspoon clove powder
1 teaspoon ground cinnamon
140ml/¼ pt water
450g/1 lb dates, chopped

1. Put the apples, spices and water into a heavy-based saucepan and bring to boil.
2. Turn down to simmer and add the dates. Leave to simmer with the lid on until the fruit is pulp-like.
3. Stir to mix well and leave to cool.

APRICOT, PRUNE AND APPLE SLICE
Serves 6.
You will need a baking tin approximately 20 cm/8 inch x 30 cm/12 inch or a 25 cm/ 10 inch square tin about 4 cm/1½ inch deep, well greased.

Follow the instructions for preparing the pastry and baking in the recipe for *Fig and aniseed slice* (see page 53) but do the following filling:

225g/8 oz dried apricots
225g/8 oz stoned dried prunes
140ml/¼ pt apple juice
1 large cooking apple, peeled, cored and chopped
1 rounded teaspoon ground cinnamon
½ teaspoon ground nutmeg
1 rounded teaspoon fresh ginger, grated (optional)
1 tablespoon honey

1. Steam the apricots and prunes until softish, about 20 minutes, then chop.
2. Put apple juice, chopped apple, spices and honey into a heavy-based saucepan and bring to boil.
3. Turn down to simmer and add the chopped apricots and prunes. Simmer on very low heat until the mixture is pulp-like. Leave to cool.

CHOUX PASTRY

This light, airy pastry is extremely versatile and can be used as the basis of a huge variety of savoury and sweet delicacies.

You can use wholemeal or 81 per cent brown wheatmeal flour and polyunsaturated margarine or butter. The lighter flour and butter combination puffs up slightly more but both combinations are quite successful.

All choux pastry-based dishes are best made and eaten on the same day. For hot fillings you can prepare and bake the pastry in the morning and re-heat in a moderate oven just before filling and serving.

BASIC PLAIN CHOUX PASTRY

55g/2 oz unsalted butter or polyunsaturated margarine
140ml/¼ pt water
½ level teaspoon sugar
good pinch sea salt
70g/2½ oz 81 per cent wheatmeal flour, sifted
2 standard eggs (not large), beaten

1. Heat the butter and water in a small heavy-based saucepan until the butter has melted then bring to boil.
2. Take off heat and immediately tip in all the flour and salt and beat with a wooden spoon until well blended and the dough leaves the sides of the pan. Do not beat too vigorously or the mixture will become too fatty.
3. Cool for 1½ minutes then beat the beaten eggs in, this time beating vigorously, in four goes, making sure each addition is completely absorbed before adding more egg. The dough should be shiny and not floppy but just soft enough to pipe. Your dough is now ready to use.

Note: If not using immediately you can leave to stand for a few hours but you must cover with a piece of greaseproof paper and then cover the saucepan with a tight lid to prevent the pastry drying out.

PLAIN CHOUX BUNS

These can be stuffed with a variety of savoury or sweet fillings.

If you want the buns to puff up enormously then you will have to cover the baking sheet with a lid – a large deep baking or roasting tin near to the size of your baking sheet will do – and bake the buns in their own steam. Don't lift the lid until the baking time is up. This is not essential but very effective. The buns will still swell up if baked uncovered in the usual way.

Makes 16.

2 x recipe quantity of Basic plain choux pastry (see page 54)

1. Preheat oven 400°F/200°C/Gas Mark 6.
2. Using a tablespoon, spoon level spoonfuls of the pastry mixture onto greased baking sheets, forming little moulds. Rough up the tops with a fork. Alternatively use a piping bag and pipe out plump-based rounds bringing them up to a slight point at the top.
3. Bake in the preheated oven for 40 minutes if covered and 45 minutes if uncovered.

They are cooked when crisp and golden.

4. Cool on a wire rack for 1 minute then slit horizontally to release the steam. If filling with a cold savoury or sweet mixture then leave on the rack to cool completely. If filling with a hot mixture then either fill immediately and serve or re-heat the buns later for 5 minutes in a moderate oven just before filling and serving.

MUSHROOM AND YOGHURT CREAM CHOUX BUNS

These are delicious as an appetiser or as a special lunch for 6 accompanied with a fresh salad and a choice of cheeses.

Makes 16.

16 Plain choux buns (see opposite)
450g/1 lb small mushrooms, sliced
3 tablespoons virgin olive or sunflower oil
1 large clove garlic, crushed
1 level teaspoon dried tarragon
2 level tablespoons parsley, finely chopped
1 level tablespoon arrowroot
3 tablespoons white wine or water (wine is lovely in this)
225g/8 oz Greek yoghurt
sea salt and freshly ground black pepper to taste

1. Have the warm buns ready to fill.
2. Sauté the mushrooms, garlic and tarragon in the oil until soft.
3. Stir in the parsley then remove from heat.
4. Blend the arrowroot with the wine or water until smooth then stir this into the yoghurt, mixing well.
5. Add the yoghurt mixture to the mushrooms and re-heat. Cook gently stirring constantly until the mixture thickens. Season with salt and black pepper.
6. Slit the warm buns and spoon in the filling just before serving. Eat immediately before the pastry gets soggy.

AVOCADO, RICOTTA AND VEGETABLE FILLING

The filling is cold for this recipe but the combination of the cold filling with the hot choux buns is a delight to the taste buds.

Makes 16.

16 Plain choux buns (see page 55).
2 ripe avocados, peeled, stoned and chopped
2 tablespoons lemon juice
225g/8 oz Ricotta or goat's curd cheese
½ teaspoon Dijon mustard
1 scant teaspoon clear honey
¼ teaspoon cayenne pepper
¼ teaspoon fennel seeds, crushed
1 clove garlic, crushed
1 rounded teaspoon sweet mixed herbs or 1
    tablespoon fresh, chopped herbs
1 tablespoon parsley, finely chopped
1 rounded teaspoon vegetable bouillon powder
    or ½ level teaspoon sea salt
1 small sweet red pepper, deseeded and very
    finely chopped
7.5 cm/3 inch cucumber, cut in tiny pieces
6 average size spring onions, finely chopped

1. Have the warm buns ready to fill.
2. Mix the avocado, ricotta, lemon juice,
   mustard, honey, cayenne, ground fennel
   seeds, garlic, herbs, parsley and bouillon
   powder or salt well together in a blender.
3. Scoop out and stir in the peppers,
   cucumber and spring onions. Chill the lot.
4. To stuff the buns slit while still warm and
   spoon in the filling just before serving.
   Serve immediately.

SWEET YOGHURT CREAM AND CAROB COATED CHOUX BUNS

I make these special buns for children's
parties or for a special tea-time treat.

Makes 30.

1 recipe quantity Basic plain choux pastry (see
    page 54)
1 recipe quantity Vanilla yoghurt cream (see
    page 191), chilled
225g/8 oz plain, unsweetened block of carob
    (see page 58)
3 tablespoons maple syrup

1. Follow the recipe for *Plain choux buns,*
   but put mounds of pastry mixture on the
   greased baking trays using either a
   teaspoon (instead of a tablespoon) or a

piping bag with a 1 cm/1½ inch nozzle to
form 30 walnut-sized mounds. Then bake
for only 15 minutes uncovered or 25
minutes covered in the preheated oven
until golden. Leave to cool.
2. Break up the carob bar into small pieces
   and melt in a bowl over simmering water.
3. Gently heat the maple syrup on low heat.
   Take off the heat and stir in the melted
   carob.
4. When buns are cold, slit and fill with the
   yoghurt cream.
5. Using a spoon trickle the warm carob
   topping over the filled buns. Chill until
   the topping sets and serve.

FRUITY 'CREAM' FILLED, CAROB COATED CHOUX BUNS

Makes 30.

Follow the previous recipe but add 170g/6 oz
of any finely chopped soft fruit to the 'cream'
filling. Fresh pineapple, fresh apricots,
peaches, stoned cherries, raspberries or
strawberries are ideal.

GRUYERE PUFF PIE

This is delicious and will make a light lunch
or supper dish if accompanied by a hearty
soup.

Serves 4.
You will need a 20 cm/8 inch round pie tin or
dish, lightly greased.

1 recipe quantity of Basic plain choux pastry
    (see page 54) – see note on making in
    method below
85g/3 oz Gruyère cheese, finely grated
¼ teaspoon cayenne pepper
¼ teaspoon dry mustard powder

1. Preheat the oven to 400°F/200°C/Gas Mark
   6.
2. Prepare the recipe for *Basic plain choux
   pastry,* but add the cayenne and mustard
   powder to the flour, and beat most of the
   cheese into the mixture after the egg (save
   1 rounded tablespoon for the topping).
3. Spread the dough over the prepared

baking dish, roughing the top a little.

4. Sprinkle on the remaining cheese.
5. Bake in the centre of the preheated oven uncovered for about 40 minutes until well risen and browned.
6. Serve hot immediately.

ASPARAGUS, MUSHROOM AND WHITE WINE SAUCE STUFFED CHOUX RING

This is a rich, tasty recipe and perfect for a special dinner party.

Serves 6.

You will need a round ovenproof dish, 23 cm/9 inch in diameter or you can use a pizza tray, lightly floured.

2 x recipe quantity of Gruyère puff pie pastry
*   mix (see page 57), ready to spread over the*
*   baking dish*
little milk for glazing
450g/1 lb asparagus, fresh or frozen
1 scant teaspoon lemon peel finely grated
2 rounded tablespoons Greek yoghurt
1 egg yolk (optional)
285ml/½ pt white wine
55g/2 oz unbleached white flour
2 tablespoons sunflower oil
170g/6 oz onion, peeled and finely chopped
225g/8 oz small mushrooms, sliced
285ml/½ pt hot water
1 level tablespoon vegetable bouillon powder
1 bay leaf
½ teaspoon ground mace or nutmeg
¼ teaspoon freshly ground black pepper to
*   taste*

1. Preheat the oven to 400°F/200°C/Gas Mark 6.
2. Draw a circle 7.5 cm/3 inch from the centre of the lightly floured baking dish or tin and pipe or spoon the dough around the outside of this circle. Brush the surface lightly with milk.
3. Bake in the centre of the preheated oven for 40 to 45 minutes until well risen and golden brown. While baking make the filling.
4. If using fresh asparagus then cut off woody ends and steam the asparagus for 20 minutes until tender. If using frozen then steam for 10 minutes maximum. (If you haven't a steamer then use a colander which fits snugly into the rim of a saucepan.)
5. When the asparagus is tender cut off 4 cm/1½ inch tips and put these aside. Chop the stems roughly.
6. Using a liquidizer or food processor, blend the chopped stems with the lemon peel, yoghurt, egg yolk, 140ml/¼ pt of the wine and the flour until smooth. Spoon into a jug.
7. Heat the oil in a large heavy-based saucepan and sauté the onion until tender. (Keep the lid on.)
8. Add the sliced mushrooms and continue to fry for 3 minutes more.
9. Pour in the hot water, vegetable bouillon powder, bay leaf, mace, black pepper and the remaining 140ml/¼ pt wine and bring to boil.
10. Pour a little of this hot broth to the blended yoghurt mixture and mix well together then pour the yoghurt mixture into the saucepan, whisking briskly as you do so with a balloon whisk. Keep whisking as you bring the sauce to boil on moderate heat then leave to simmer on a very low heat for 5 minutes, stirring occasionally.
11. Take off heat and stir in most of the asparagus tips, saving a few to garnish.
12. When choux ring is cooked remove from the oven and slice off the top half with a bread knife. Spoon on half the sauce, replace the top and spoon the rest of the sauce into the centre of the ring.
13. Garnish with the reserved tips and serve hot as soon as possible after assembling.

LESSON 3

CAKES, SCONES, BISCUITS AND PANCAKES

You should now have a reasonable stock of wholefoods which will include some of the dried fruit and spices needed in this lesson, but there are a few more ingredients to add to your store. Honey and lots of dried fruit are used in many recipes so stock up with those mentioned in Lessons 1 and 2 and add any extras listed below.

Nuts and seeds are also frequent ingredients in the following recipes (see Lesson 4 for further information on any of these).

SHOPPING LIST

100 per cent wholewheat or wholemeal flour, self-raising	natural almond essence
carob powder (see opposite)	natural food colourings, various (see page 59)
porridge oats	dried apple
jumbo oats	dried mango
fine oatmeal	dried fruit listed in Lessons 1 and 2
desiccated coconut	pecan nuts
baking powder	walnuts
bicarbonate of soda	hazelnuts
instant decaffinated coffee	whole almonds
raw cane sugar	flaked almonds
Barbados sugar	ground almonds
shredded vegetable suet	sunflower seeds
natural vanilla essence	pumpkin seeds
	peanut butter
	sunflower seed spread

SOME UNUSUAL INGREDIENTS

CAROB POWDER or flour is a product prepared from the locust bean which grows on the Mediterranean carob or locust tree. It is similar in flavour to chocolate but unlike cocoa powder it is naturally sweet. It is a much cheaper and healthier alternative to cocoa or chocolate, as cocoa beans are high in caffeine and contain oxalic acid which 'locks in' calcium in the diet and makes it unavailable to the body. Carob is also higher in fibre and iron and lower in crude fat and sodium than cocoa.

Carob comes in powdered form which can be used in any cake or biscuit recipe where cocoa is an ingredient. Carob bars are made in a variety of flavours, just like chocolate bars, and can be melted down to use in sweet sauces or in your baking.

FRUIT SUGAR is great to use in cheesecake recipes (see page 64) as it will not discolour the cheese mixture. It is also sweeter than ordinary castor sugar so you use less.

SHREDDED VEGETABLE SUET is available in health stores and many supermarkets and can be used in any recipe that requires animal suet. It gives results indistinguishable in appearance from animal suet dishes but tastes much better. It is made from vegetable oil and a little wheat flour.

DECAFFINATED COFFEE is just as good in flavour as ordinary coffee for using in cake making – see *Banana, hazelnut and coffee tea cake* (see page 62) which uses decaffinated instant coffee granules and tastes very good.

NATURAL FOOD ESSENCES are easily available from healthfood stores and some supermarkets. They are expensive but they are free from additives and a little goes a long way. Their flavour is superb.

NATURAL FOOD COLOURINGS are available from healthfood stores and come in three colours at present – pink, yellow and green. Beetroot is the colouring agent for the pink.

CAKES

You can make most of your favourite traditional cakes, and a lot more variations you haven't thought of yet, using whole, natural ingredients. I hope the following recipes will prove to you that cakes can be made light and delicious using wholemeal flour instead of white.

These recipes are designed to set you off in cake making using wholesome ingredients, but experiment for yourself and you will find that if you stick to the basic recipe you can substitute with great success. For example, you can use sunflower or corn oil instead of margarine in most cake recipes. You can use honey instead of sugar and you can even make cakes with tofu (soya bean curd – see page 119 for more information) and oil or margarine instead of eggs and butter. The results are just as pleasant in texture and perfect if you are on a low fat diet and crave a bit of cake.

A note here is necessary about the size of baking tins used. It is important to stick to the size given for individual recipes but, if for example, you use a 23 cm/9 inch cake tin instead of a 20 cm/8 inch tin required for the recipe then the cooking time will be approximately 10 to 15 minutes less as the cake will be thinner. To check if a cake is done, insert a skewer or tooth pick into the centre of it: if it comes out clean and dry then the cake is ready.

DEVONSHIRE APPLE AND SULTANA CAKE

This simple and delicious recipe will use up lots of apples when there is a glut in the autumn. It freezes well so make several cakes when cooking apples are cheap and plentiful. It is lovely served hot as a pudding with a custard sauce or cold, sliced. You can make one large round, or two small loaf shape cakes.

You will need a 25 cm/10 inch round cake tin or 2 x 450g/1 lb loaf tins greased and lined.

340g/12 oz wholemeal self-raising flour
¼ teaspoon clove powder
1 teaspoon ground cinnamon
225g/8 oz polyunsaturated margarine
225g/8 oz Barbados sugar
170g/6 oz sultanas
450g/1 lb cooking apples, cored and diced in
  smallish chunks
4 large eggs, separated

1. Preheat the oven to 350°F/180°C/Gas Mark 4.
2. Put flour and spices in a large mixing bowl and with cool fingertips rub in the margarine until the mixture resembles fine breadcrumbs.
3. Stir in the sugar, sultanas and diced apples.
4. Beat egg whites for 1 minute in a small bowl.
5. Beat egg yolks for 1 minute in another small bowl.
6. Stir both gently into the other ingredients

with a fork. Do not beat in. The mixture will not seem wet enough but it will become moist as the raw apples cook.

7. Spoon into the prepared large tin or the 2 small tins.

8. Bake in the centre of the preheated oven, 1¾ hours for the large cake and 1 hour for the two small cakes.

9. Leave to stand in the tin for 10 minutes only then cool on a wire rack.

APPLE AND DATE CAKE

Follow the previous recipe for *Devonshire apple and sultana cake*, but use 170g/6 oz Barbados sugar instead of 225g/8 oz and substitute 170g/6 oz of chopped dates for the 170g/6 oz of sultanas.

DRIED MANGO, APPLE AND GINGER CAKE

Dried mango tastes very like fresh mango after soaking overnight. For this recipe I only soak the mango in hot apple juice for 1 hour or it gets too soggy for this particular mixture. Try to use fresh, not dried, ginger, as the flavour is much better.

You will need a 25 cm/10 inch round cake tin, greased and lined or 2 x 450g/1 lb loaf tins, greased and lined.

110g/4 oz dried mango pieces
apple juice for soaking
340g/12 oz wholemeal self-raising flour
1 rounded teaspoon mixed spice
225g/8 oz polyunsaturated margarine
225g/8 oz Barbados sugar
225g/8 oz cooking apples, cored and chopped
  into smallish chunks
1 rounded tablespoon raw fresh ginger, finely
  grated
4 large eggs, separated

1. Preheat the oven to 350°F/180°C/Gas Mark 4.

2. Soak the dried mango in hot apple juice for 1 hour (make sure all of it is submerged while soaking). Drain (you will not need the liquid for this recipe) and chop each piece in half.

3. Put flour and spice in a large mixing bowl

and with cool fingertips rub in the margarine until the mixture resembles fine breadcrumbs.

4. Stir the freshly grated ginger into the chopped mango pieces then mix this with the apples.

5. Stir this fruit mixture gently into the flour mixture using a fork.

6. Whisk egg whites for 1 minute in a bowl.

7. Whisk egg yolks for 1 minute in another bowl, then stir these into the other ingredients. Do not beat but merge the ingredients gently together.

8. Spoon the mixture into the large tin or the 2 small tins and bake in the centre of the preheated oven for 1¾ hours for the larger cake and 1 hour for the smaller cakes.

GINGER AND HONEY CAKE

Moist and deliciously gingery, just as it should be!

You will need a 23 cm/9 inch round cake tin, greased and lined.

350g/12 oz wholemeal self-raising flour
1 heaped teaspoon mixed spice
85g/6 oz polyunsaturated margarine
280g/10 oz clear honey
85g/6 oz fresh ginger, peeled and finely grated
3 large eggs, well beaten until frothy
2 tablespoons milk

1. Preheat the oven to 325°F/160°C/Gas Mark 3.

2. Put the flour and spice into a mixing bowl.

3. Melt the margarine and honey on a very low heat, do not boil.

4. Stir in the freshly grated ginger.

5. Pour this into the flour and blend gently in until well mixed. Do not beat.

6. Gradually add the beaten egg (again do not beat).

7. Finally stir in the milk.

8. Spoon into the prepared tin and bake in the centre of the oven for 1½ hours.

SIMPLE CARROT CAKE SLICE

You can bake this in a flat 23 cm/9 inch x 32.5 cm/13 inch rectangular tin, the depth of a Victoria sponge tin, well oiled, or in a 23 cm/

9 inch x 13 cm/5 inch wide loaf tin. The loaf tin should be greased and lined.

110ml/4 fl oz sunflower or corn oil
170g/6 oz clear honey
6 drops vanilla essence
½ level teaspoon clove powder
½ teaspoon ground cinnamon
2 large eggs
225g/8 oz carrots finely grated (weight when grated)
225g/8 oz wholemeal self-raising flour
2 level tablespoons dry milk powder
good pinch sea salt

1. Preheat the oven to 375°F/190°C/Gas Mark 5.
2. Beat the oil and honey together until smooth and thick then add the vanilla essence and spices.
3. Beat in the eggs one at a time vigorously.
4. Stir in the finely grated carrots.
5. Mix flour, milk powder and sea salt together and gradually fold this into the wet ingredients until well blended.
6. Pour this into either the flat tin or the loaf tin and bake in the centre of the oven for 30 to 35 minutes for the flat tin and 1 hour for the loaf tin. (Test the centre of the loaf shape cake with a skewer or tooth pick after 1 hour, as it may need 10 minutes longer.)
7. Spread with *Vanilla yoghurt cream* (see page 191) before serving.

RICH CARROT AND PECAN NUT CAKE
Pecan Nuts are similar to walnuts but a little sweeter.

You will need a 25 cm/10 inch round or 2 x 700g/1½ lb loaf tins, greased and lined.

285ml/½ pt sunflower or corn oil
225g/8 oz Barbados sugar
1 level teaspoon clove powder
good pinch sea salt
4 large eggs, separated
340g/12 oz wholemeal self-raising flour
450g/1 lb carrots, finely grated
110g/4 oz pecan nuts, chopped

1. Preheat the oven to 325°F/160°C/Gas Mark 3.
2. Using a wooden spoon beat the oil with the sugar and the clove powder for 2 minutes. Add the salt.
3. Whisk the egg whites for 1 minute until frothy.
4. Whisk the egg yolks for 1 minute until frothy.
5. Add the whites and then the yolks to the oil and sugar and beat well in.
6. Gradually fold in the flour (do not beat) and mix together gently until well blended.
7. Finally stir in the carrots and the chopped nuts using a fork.
8. Spoon into the prepared tin or tins and bake in the centre of the oven for 2 hours for the large cake or 1½ hours for the smaller cakes.
9. Leave to stand in the tin for 10 minutes before cooling on a wire rack.

BANANA AND WALNUT CAKE
You will need a 25 cm/10 inch round cake tin, greased and lined, or 2 x 700g/1½ lb loaf tins, greased and lined.

225g/8 oz polyunsaturated margarine
225g/8 oz clear honey or Barbados sugar
pinch sea salt
4 large eggs, separated
450g/1 lb ripe bananas, mashed
110g/4 oz walnuts, chopped
340g/12 oz wholemeal self-raising flour

1. Preheat the oven to 325°F/160°C/Gas Mark 3.
2. Cream the margarine with the honey or sugar until smooth (1 minute if using honey, 3 minutes if using sugar). Add salt.
3. Beat the egg whites for 1 minute then the egg yolks for 1 minute.
4. Add the egg whites to the margarine mixture then the egg yolks, beating well in.
5. Stir in the mashed bananas and the walnuts and beat well.
6. Gradually fold in the flour, do not beat, until well mixed.

7. Spoon into the tin or tins and bake in the centre of the oven for 2 hours for the large cake and 1¼ hours for the smaller cakes. (Check if the cake or cakes are cooked by inserting a skewer or a toothpick in the centre. If it comes out clean then the cake or cakes are cooked.)

BANANA, HAZELNUT AND COFFEE TEA CAKE

You will need a 450g/1 lb loaf tin, greased.

225g/8 oz wholemeal self-raising flour
good pinch sea salt
170g/6 oz Barbados sugar
1 tablespoon instant decaffinated coffee
  granules
140ml/¼ pt milk or yoghurt
55g/2 oz polyunsaturated margarine
55g/2 oz hazelnuts, finely chopped (not
  powdery)
2 medium size bananas
1 large egg, beaten

1. Preheat the oven to 350°F/180°C/Gas Mark 4.
2. Mix flour, salt, sugar and coffee granules together.
3. Bring milk to boil or warm the yoghurt (do not let it boil), take off heat and stir in the margarine and the hazelnuts. Leave to stand for 5 minutes.
4. Mash bananas, stir into the milk or yoghurt mixture then add this with the beaten egg to the flour mixture.
5. Blend gently but thoroughly together.
6. Put mixture into the greased tin and bake in the centre of the oven for 1 hour. Leave to stand in the tin for 10 minutes after baking then cool on a wire rack.

RICH CAROB BIRTHDAY OR SWEETHEART CAKE

This cake is great for children's birthday parties or if made in a heart-shape for a Valentine celebration. Ideas for decorating are given after the recipe.

You will need a 23 cm/9 inch diameter heart-shaped or round cake tin, greased and lined. Line the heart-shaped tin with foil, by pressing it into the base and sides; the creases will not affect the cake. Lightly grease the foil.

225g/8 oz wholemeal self-raising flour
28g/1 oz carob powder
55g/2 oz ground almonds
225g/8 oz polyunsaturated margarine
225g/8 oz clear honey
6 drops vanilla essence
4 large eggs, separated

1. Preheat the oven to 350°F/180°C/Gas Mark 4.
2. Sieve the flour, carob powder and almonds into a bowl.
3. Cream the margarine and honey in another bowl for 1 minute then add the vanilla essence.
4. Put egg whites in one bowl and egg yolks in another.
5. Beat the egg yolks lightly with a fork and gradually beat into the margarine and honey.
6. Gradually fold in the flour mixture until well mixed but do not beat.
7. Whisk the egg whites until stiff and fold them into the creamed mixture, again do not beat.
8. Spoon into the prepared tin and bake in the centre of the oven for 1 hour. Leave to cool in the tin for 10 minutes then cool on a wire rack.

Suggestions for decorating: Prepare *Yoghurt, carob or chocolate and hazelnut 'icing'* (see below) and spread over the cake as directed in the recipe.

If the cake is for a children's birthday party, make *Gingerbread people* (see page 72) and stand them up around the cake. Secure with a ribbon.

YOGHURT, CAROB OR CHOCOLATE AND HAZELNUT 'ICING'

110g/4 oz either plain sweetened carob or
*   chocolate bar*
1 tablespoon Greek yoghurt
1 tablespoon double cream
1 teaspoon finely grated orange peel
45g/1½ oz toasted chopped hazelnuts (optional)

1. Melt the carob or chocolate bar by placing on a heatproof plate or dish over a pan of hot water.
2. Whisk the cream in a small bowl.
3. Stir in the yoghurt, grated peel and the melted carob or chocolate bar.
4. Spread over the top of the cake when completely cold.
5. If using hazelnuts then toast these in the oven, 325°F/160°C/Gas Mark 3, for 15 minutes (or 15 minutes before the end of cooking time of cake on a shelf just below it). Place the toasted nuts between 2 sheets of polythene or a teatowel and crush them by rolling over the top with a rolling pin.
6. Sprinkle the crushed toasted hazelnuts over the top of the 'icing' as soon as you have spread it on.
7. Keep the cake in a cool place for the 'icing' to set.

Note: Double the 'icing' recipe if you want to spread it on the sides as well as the top of the cake.

BASIC WHOLEMEAL VICTORIA SPONGE

If you think you can't make a light sponge using all wholemeal flour then try this recipe and I think you will find that it is not only just as light as when using white flour but is much more flavoursome.

I find using a mixer is labour saving and gives much lighter results when making sponges, especially when creaming the margarine and sugar until light and fluffy, but a mixer is not essential.

You will need 2 x 20 cm/8 inch sponge tins. Try to get the non-stick or use those with a little handle which eases the sponge away from the tins. If using ordinary sponge tins then grease as well as line the bottom of the tins.

170g/6 oz polyunsaturated margarine
170g/6 oz soft brown sugar or honey
3 large eggs, separated
1 tablespoon cold water
few drops natural vanilla essence
170g/6 oz wholemeal self-raising flour
pinch sea salt (optional)

1. Preheat the oven to 350°F/180°C/Gas Mark 4.
2. Cream together the margarine and the sugar until light and fluffy. If using honey then cream for 3 minutes.
3. Whisk the egg yolks with the cold water and the vanilla essence as you count to 20. Gradually beat these into the creamed mixture.
4. Sieve the flour and salt and gradually fold this thoroughly but gently into the mixture.
5. Whisk the egg whites until a thick foam but not stiff then fold them, again gently and thoroughly, into the mixture.
6. Divide the mixture equally between the two tins (it's a good idea to weigh these so that they are exact).
7. Bake in the centre of the preheated oven for 25 minutes.
8. Leave to stand in the tin for 2 minutes, then cool on a wire rack.
9. When cold sandwich between a layer of no-sugar jam.

CAROB WHOLEMEAL SPONGE

Follow the recipe for *Basic wholemeal Victoria sponge* (see opposite) but take one rounded tablespoon of wholemeal flour out and add 1 rounded tablespoon of carob powder. Sieve the carob with the flour and salt and then proceed as in the basic recipe.

PINK WHOLEMEAL SPONGE

Follow the recipe for *Basic wholemeal Victoria sponge* (see opposite) and add a few drops of beetroot natural red colouring (see notes on natural food colourings – page 59) to the mixture just before folding in the flour.

THREE-TIERED BIRTHDAY SPONGE CAKE
You will need 3 x 23 cm/10 inch sponge tins.

For the top and bottom layer make *Carob wholemeal sponge* mixture (see above) using 225g/8 oz margarine, 225g/8 oz sugar or honey, 4 large eggs and 225g/8 oz wholemeal self-raising flour (less 1 rounded tablespoon) and 1 rounded tablespoon carob flour. Divide this mixture equally between 2 tins.

For the centre layer make the *Pink wholemeal sponge* mixture (see page 63) using 110g/4 oz margarine, 110g/4 oz sugar or honey, 2 large eggs, 110g/4 oz wholemeal self-raising flour and the beetroot natural red colouring as directed.

Bake all three layers for 30 minutes.

When cold top with the *Yoghurt, carob or chocolate and hazelnut 'icing'* (see page 63). Keep the cake in a cool place after icing.

CUP CAKES
Makes 18.

The mixtures for the *Basic wholemeal Victoria sponge* (see page 63) and the two variations, *Carob wholemeal sponge* (see page 63) and *Pink wholemeal sponge* (see page 63) will each make 18 cup cakes. Simply divide whichever mixture you choose equally between 18 paper bun cases (stand paper cases in bun tray moulds) and bake in a preheated oven, 375°F/190°C/Gas Mark 5, for 15 to 20 minutes. If using two trays, place one tray just above centre and one tray just below centre and change the trays around after 10 minutes.

The following are more varieties of cup cakes for you to try:

CHOCOLATE AND ORANGE CUP CAKES
Makes 22.

Adding coconut to the mixture will mean you can make 4 more cup cakes than the *Basic wholemeal Victoria sponge* mixture (see page 63) will give you.

Simply fold in 110g/4 oz desiccated coconut and the juice and rind of 1 small orange gently after the flour. Do not beat in. Spoon the mixture into the paper cases and bake as directed for *Cup cakes* above.

ALMOND CUP CAKES
Makes 18.

Simply take out 55g/2 oz of wholemeal flour from the *Basic wholemeal Victoria sponge* recipe (see page 63) and add 55g/2 oz ground almonds instead. Use a few drops of natural almond essence instead of vanilla. Spoon into the paper cases and bake as directed for *Cup cakes* above.

CAROB AND ORANGE CUP CAKES
Makes 18.

Simply add the grated rind of 1 small orange to the *Carob wholemeal sponge* mixture (see page 63). Spoon into the paper cases and bake as directed for *Cup cakes* above.

YOGHURT AND CAROB DEVIL'S CAKE
You will need a 23 cm/9 inch x 13 cm/5 inch loaf tin, oiled and floured.

2 level tablespoons carob flour
225g/8 oz wholemeal flour, plain
1 level teaspoon baking powder
1 level teaspoon bicarbonate of soda
1 level teaspoon ground cinnamon
110g/4 oz polyunsaturated margarine
225g/8 oz clear honey
3 large eggs
1 level teaspoon natural vanilla essence
225ml/8 fl oz natural yoghurt

1. Preheat the oven, 350°F/180°C/Gas Mark 4.
2. Sieve dry ingredients into a bowl.
3. Cream the margarine and honey until smooth.
4. Beat in the eggs one at a time making sure each one is well blended before adding the next.
5. Beat in the vanilla essence.
6. Gradually add the flour mixture alternately with the yoghurt, folding it in gently but thoroughly (do not beat).
7. Spoon into the prepared loaf tin and bake in the centre of the oven for 1 hour. Leave to cool in the tin for 10 minutes then cool on a wire rack.

SWISS COOKED YOGHURT CHEESECAKE

This cake is deliciously light in texture, but rich and expensive to make. It will give you 12 portions, so save it for a special occasion.

You will need a 23 cm/9 inch spring-form cake tin, greased.

170g/6 oz wholewheat digestive biscuits
55g/2 oz sesame seeds
½ level teaspoon ground cinnamon
85g/3 oz polyunsaturated margarine, melted
85g/3 oz either dried mango or apricot pieces
apple juice to soak dried fruit
225g/8 oz yoghurt cheese (see page 181)
110g/4 oz cream cheese
170g/6 oz Ricotta or goat's curd cheese
85g/3 oz fruit sugar or clear honey
4 eggs, separated
1 teaspoon natural vanilla essence
1 tablespoon lemon juice
1 teaspoon finely grated lemon rind
2 tablespoons toasted and roughly ground
    mixed almonds and pumpkin seeds, to
    decorate

1. Preheat oven 300°F/150°C/Gas Mark 2.
2. Use either a blender or potato masher to break up the biscuits. Then stir in the sesame seeds, cinnamon and melted margarine.
3. Press this biscuit mixture into the base of the cake tin and bake in the preheated oven for 5 minutes only. Leave to get completely cold before filling.
4. Soak the mango or apricot pieces in hot apple juice for a few hours then puree with a little of the soaking juice until you have a smooth jam consistency (not runny). Leave to one side.
5. Preheat the oven, 325°F/170°C/Gas Mark 3.
6. Cream the yoghurt cheese, cream cheese, Ricotta or goat's curd cheese and fruit sugar or honey until smooth. Take out 2 rounded tablespoons of this mixture and place in a covered dish in the fridge for topping.
7. Beat in the egg yolks one at a time until well mixed.
8. Stir in the vanilla, lemon juice and rind.
9. Beat the egg whites until stiff. Fold this gently into the cheese mixture.
10. Spread the fruit puree onto the cold biscuit base. Pour in the cheese filling and bake in the centre of the preheated oven for 1 hour 10 minutes. Cover with a sheet of greaseproof paper if browning too much after 45 minutes.
11. Turn off oven, open the door and let the cake stand in the warm atmosphere for 20 minutes. This stops the mixture dipping in the centre.
12. Leave to get cold before spreading the reserved 2 tablespoons of cheese mixture in a thin layer on top of the cake. To finish sprinkle on the roughly ground nut and seed mixture. Chill well before slicing. This cake freezes extremely well.

SPICY MIXED FRUIT CAKE

You will need a 23 cm/9 inch round or 20 cm/8 inch square, deep cake tin, greased and lined.

225g/8 oz polyunsaturated margarine
170g/6 oz Barbados sugar or clear honey
grated rind of 1 lemon and ½ an orange
4 eggs, beaten
1 teaspoon natural vanilla essence
1 level teaspoon nutmeg, freshly grated
½ level teaspoon allspice
¼ level teaspoon ground clove powder
280g/10 oz wholemeal flour, plain
55g/2 oz ground almonds
85g/3 oz each sultanas, raisins and currants
55g/2 oz dried apricots, chopped
55g/2 oz dried apple, finely chopped
55g/2 oz glace cherries (ones without
    colouring), cut in half
1 tablespoon sherry or milk
110g/4 oz whole blanched almonds

1. Preheat oven, 325°F/160°C/Gas Mark 3.
2. Cream the margarine, sugar and lemon and orange rind together until light and fluffy (about 5 minutes).
3. Gradually beat in the eggs and the vanilla essence.
4. Mix the spices, flour, ground almonds and fruit together and gently stir this into the creamed mixture.

5. Finally stir in the sherry or milk (do not beat).
6. Spoon mixture into the prepared tin and make a hollow in the centre by pushing the mixture towards the sides, to prevent a bump forming in the middle.
7. Arrange the blanched almonds on top and bake in the centre of the oven for 2½ to 3 hours.
8. Check after 2 hours – if nice and brown, then turn down heat to 300°F/150°C/Gas Mark 2, and bake for a further 30 minutes. Then test with a skewer – let cook the full 3 hours if the skewer does not come out clean.

CHRISTMAS OR CELEBRATION CAKE
This rich fruit mixture makes a wonderful Christmas, wedding or special occasion cake.

You will need a 28 cm/11 inch round or 25 cm/10 inch square cake tin. If making for a wedding, then bake in a heart-shaped tin 25 cm/10 inch wide at the widest point.

3 tablespoons brandy
juice and rind of 1 orange
juice and rind of 1 lemon
560g/1¼ lb wholemeal flour, plain
1 rounded teaspoon freshly ground nutmeg
1 level teaspoon freshly ground allspice
1 level teaspoon ground cinnamon
½ level teaspoon clove powder
450g/1 lb polyunsaturated margarine
225g/8 oz Barbados sugar

8 large eggs, beaten
340g/12 oz currants
340g/12 oz raisins
340g/12 oz sultanas
170g/6 oz dried apricots, finely chopped
170g/6 oz dried pineapple (unsweetened), finely chopped
170g/6 oz dried papaya (unsweetened), finely chopped
170g/6 oz glace cherries, washed, dried and cut in quarters
110g/4 oz dried apple flakes or rings, if rings, cut in small pieces
170g/6 oz pecan nuts, chopped (almonds will do)
little brandy to soak cake after cooking

To decorate the top if not icing
110g/4 oz pecan nut halves
55g/2 oz blanched almonds
55g/2 oz glace cherries

1. The day before, mix orange rind and juice, lemon rind and juice and brandy together. Store in a screw-top jar.
2. Mix fruit with the nuts.
3. Sieve flour and spices together.
4. Cream the margarine and sugar until light and fluffy.
5. Gradually beat in the eggs adding a little flour if the mixture curdles.
6. Gradually fold in the flour alternatively with the fruit and nut mixture (do not beat).
7. Stir in the brandy, orange and lemon mixture.
8. Spoon into the prepared cake tin, level gently using the back of the spoon and then hollow the middle a little or the cake will rise in the centre too much.
9. If not icing later, then decorate the top before baking with alternate circles of pecans, glace cherries (cut in half) and blanched almonds. Press them in gently.
10. Preheat oven 300°F/150°C/Gas Mark 2, and when correct temperature is reached place cake on the bottom shelf of the oven and bake for 5 hours. Turn down heat to 250°F/130°C/Gas Mark ½ and continue to cook for about 2 hours more. The cake will be cooked when a skewer inserted in the centre comes out clean. If

the cake is browning too quickly on top place a sheet of greaseproof paper over it. Let it cool in the tin for 1 hour then turn out onto a wire rack.

11. If you like, prick the top in several places with a skewer and trickle on a little brandy. Let it cool completely then wrap in greaseproof paper and store upside down in an airtight tin for 2 months.

Decorating ideas For Christmas, simply decorate the top with nuts and cherries, as described in the recipe. For a wedding or other special celebration, you could cover the cake with crystallized flowers and leaves (see below).

CRYSTALLIZED FLOWERS AND LEAVES
The flowers will last for about 4 weeks so you can choose out of season flowers such as primroses, violets, small roses, hibiscus, geraniums and forget-me-nots (do not preserve bulb flowers as these are poisonous). Leaves such as mint and lemon balm look great as well as taste good if you should want to eat them. To crystallize flowers you will need plenty of castor sugar, but most of it is shaken off.

Quantities depend on number of leaves and flowers crystallized
egg whites
rose water
castor sugar
variety of leaves and flower petals (see note above)

1. Heat the oven to 200°F/100°C/Gas very low.
2. Beat some egg whites lightly with a fork and add 1 teaspoon of rose water for every 1 egg white.
3. Paint the leaves and petals with this mixture. Take care to coat thoroughly and thinly – any uncovered area will go mouldy.
4. Spread a thick layer of sifted castor sugar on a baking tray. Place coated leaves and flowers on this and sprinkle them liberally with more sugar. Shake off excess and

transfer to a wire rack covered with baking parchment.
5. Dry in the oven for about 24 hours, turning once after 40 minutes.
6. Store in an airtight tin.

CHRISTMAS PLUM PUDDING
Although I have included honey or sugar in the list of ingredients, you can make these puddings very successfully without. You can use polyunsaturated margarine instead of the vegetable suet but you will have to cream this with the honey, beat in the eggs then add all the other ingredients.

Makes 4 x 450g/1 lb puddings.
You will need 4 x 450g/1 lb pudding bowls.

225g/8 oz wholemeal flour, plain
225g/8 oz wholemeal breadcrumbs
1 level teaspoon freshly ground nutmeg
½ level teaspoon ground mace
1 level teaspoon ground cinnamon
½ level teaspoon ground allspice
1 level teaspoon ground ginger
¼ level teaspoon ground clove powder
¼ teaspoon sea salt
225g/8 oz shredded vegetable suet
225g/8 oz raisins
225g/8 oz sultanas
225g/8 oz currants
170g/6 oz almonds, chopped to a medium crumb mixture
170g/6 oz clear honey or Barbados sugar
4 large eggs
170g/6 oz carrot, grated
170g/6 oz cooking apple, grated with skin on
grated rind and juice of 1 lemon
grated rind and juice of 1 orange
1 level teaspoon natural vanilla essence
4 tablespoons brandy

1. In a large bowl mix flour, breadcrumbs, spices, salt and vegetable suet together.
2. Stir in dried fruit and sugar if using, then blend in the eggs. If using honey instead of sugar, beat the honey into the eggs first then stir this into the flour and fruit mixture.
3. Add the grated carrot, apple, lemon and orange rind and juice, vanilla essence and

the brandy and mix all well together.

4. Pack into four pudding basins, tie up and steam for 3 hours, as directed below.

Steaming puddings: The basins should be well greased and only three-quarters full of mixture. Cut out a circle of greaseproof paper or foil larger than the top of the basin and press this under the rim. Place a square of cotton sheeting over the top. Tie some string under the rim, collect the two opposite corners of the cotton square up over the top and tie together, then tie the other two opposite corners of the square to make a handle. Make sure that you have clean paper or foil and a dry, clean cloth on your puddings when storing them.

EGGLESS BOILED LIGHT FRUIT CAKE

This cake is a very good simple basic recipe for vegans. You can vary the fruit and spices. Do not use baking powder instead of bicarbonate of soda or the end result will be heavy.

You will need a 20 cm/8 inch round, loose-bottomed or spring back cake tin, greased and lined.

170g/6 oz clear honey
85g/3 oz carrot, finely grated
55g/2 oz sultanas or raisins
55g/2 oz dates, chopped
110g/4 oz polyunsaturated margarine
1/2 level teaspoon ground cinnamon
1/4 level teaspoon ground clove powder
1/4 level teaspoon freshly ground nutmeg
170ml/6 fl oz water
170g/6 oz wholemeal flour
2 level teaspoons bicarbonate of soda
55g/2 oz hazelnuts, chopped

1. Preheat the oven, 350°F/180°C/Gas Mark 4.
2. Put honey, carrots, raisins, dates, margarine, spices and water in a heavy-based saucepan, bring to boil, turn down heat and simmer uncovered for 5 minutes. Leave to cool for 15 minutes.
3. Mix flour, bicarbonate of soda and nuts together and stir this into the cooled mixture.

4. Mix gently but thoroughly together, do not beat.
5. Put the mixture into the prepared tin and bake in the centre of the oven for 1 hour. Leave to stand in the tin for 10 minutes then cool on a wire rack.

SCONES AND MUFFINS

WHOLEMEAL SCONES
Makes 10.
You will need 1 large baking sheet, greased.

225g/8 oz wholemeal flour, plain
1 level tablespoon baking powder
1/4 teaspoon sea salt
40g/1 1/2 oz polyunsaturated margarine
140ml/1/4 pt natural yoghurt or milk or half
* and half milk and yoghurt mixed*
little milk or beaten egg to glaze

1. Preheat the oven, 425°F/220°C/Gas Mark 7, and put the baking sheet in to warm 2 minutes before you need it.
2. Sieve flour, baking powder and salt together in a mixing bowl.
3. Rub in the margarine until the mixture resembles fine breadcrumbs.
4. Make a well in the centre, stir in the yoghurt and form into a soft dough.
5. Knead dough quickly and lightly to remove any cracks.
6. Roll out the dough, again lightly, to a thickness of 2 cm/3/4 inch.
7. Using a floured 5 cm/2 inch fluted or plain cutter cut out 10 rounds.
8. Brush with either milk or beaten egg and place on the hot baking sheet.
9. Bake in the centre of the oven for 10 minutes until lightly browned and well risen. Cool on a wire rack.

WHEATMEAL SCONES
Makes 10.

Simply use 81 per cent brown wheatmeal flour instead of wholemeal flour in the recipe for *Wholemeal scones* above.

RICH FRUIT SCONES
Makes 10.

Prepare as for *Wholemeal scones* above but use either wholemeal flour or 81 per cent brown wheatmeal flour, add 28g/1 oz demerara or raw cane castor sugar and 55g/2 oz dried fruit (either raisins, sultanas or finely chopped dates). Use 1 tablespoon less yoghurt and add 1 small beaten egg.

APPLE SCONE ROUND
A very tasty simple recipe.

Makes 8 pieces.
You will need a baking sheet greased and lightly floured.

225g/8 oz wholemeal flour or 81 per cent brown
  wheatmeal flour
1 level tablespoon baking powder
½ teaspoon sea salt
55g/2 oz polyunsaturated margarine
4 level tablespoons natural yoghurt or milk
55g/2 oz raw cane or demerara sugar
1 teaspoon mixed spice
170g/6 oz coarsely grated apple with skins on
  (weight when cored)
little milk and honey to glaze

1. Preheat the oven 400°F/200°C/Gas Mark 6.
2. Make a dough as in the *Wholemeal scones* recipe (see page 68), sieving the sugar and spice with the flour, salt and baking powder, and stirring in the apples with the yoghurt.
3. Knead the dough lightly and roll out, again lightly, to a 20 cm/8 inch circle. Place on the baking sheet.
4. Score into 8 pieces and brush with a little milk and honey liquid.
5. Bake in the centre of the oven for 20 minutes until well risen and golden brown.
6. Best served after 10 minutes while still warm. Spread with a little butter or polyunsaturated margarine.

CHEESE SCONES
Makes 10.

Prepare as for *Wholemeal scones* (see page 68) but use 81 per cent brown wheatmeal flour and add 85g/3 oz finely grated Cheddar cheese.

QUICK SCONE PIZZA
Prepare the dough for *Wholemeal scones* (see page 68), roll out to a circle to fit a 23 cm/9 inch or 25 cm/10 inch round shallow baking tin or pizza tray. Spoon on the delicious pizza sauce and topping from page 20. Bake at 350°F/180°C/Gas Mark 4 for 25 minutes. If not brown enough on top then grill until cheese is crisp and golden.

DROP SCONES
Makes 24.
You will need a heavy-based frying pan or even better, a griddle well greased.

225g/8 oz wholemeal flour, plain
1½ teaspoons baking powder
½ level teaspoon sea salt
1 level tablespoon either honey or soft brown
  sugar
1 large egg
250ml/just under ½ pt milk

1. Sieve flour, baking powder and salt together.
2. Whisk the honey or sugar with the egg and add this with half the milk to the flour. Mix to a smooth thick batter.
3. Gradually beat in the rest of the milk.
4. Heat the pan or griddle to hot and drop tablespoons of the batter onto it.
5. Cook on moderately hot heat until the scones are covered with bubbles then flip them over and cook on the other side for no more than 1 minute.
6. Keep warm by placing the cooked scones in a folded tea towel.
7. Serve warm spread with butter or margarine and no-sugar jam.

FRUITY DROP SCONES
Makes 24.

Prepare the batter for *Drop scones* above and add either 170g/6 oz of grated cooking apple, finely chopped fresh apricots or the same amount in dried fruit soaked, drained and chopped (weight of dried fruit is when drained and chopped). Cook in the same way as for *Drop scones.*

PLAIN WHOLEWHEAT MUFFINS
Makes 12.
You will need a muffin tin with 12 moulds, well greased.

*225g/8 oz either wholewheat flour or 81 per
   cent brown wheatmeal flour*
1 level tablespoon baking powder
28g/1 oz Barbados sugar
½ level teaspoon sea salt
1 large egg, lightly beaten
225ml/8 fl oz milk or yoghurt or half and half
55ml/2 fl oz sunflower or corn oil

1. Preheat the oven 400°F/200°C/Gas Mark 6.
2. Combine all the dry ingredients.
3. Combine all the wet ingredients.
4. Fold wet ingredients quickly into the dry ingredients and gently mix only until the flour is moistened. Do not over beat because the mixture should still be a bit lumpy.
5. Fill the muffin moulds two-thirds full.
6. Bake in the centre of the oven for 20 to 25 minutes until well risen. Turn onto a wire rack and serve immediately split and spread with butter or polyunsaturated margarine.

7. Any muffins left to get cold should be split and toasted as muffins are best eaten warm.

BANANA MUFFINS
Makes 12.

Prepare mixture for *Plain wholewheat muffins* above but use 170ml/6 fl oz of milk or yoghurt instead of 225ml/8 fl oz and add 2 good size bananas mashed into the liquid ingredients.

Note Any other finely chopped seasonal fruit can be used instead of bananas.

OAT, WHEAT AND APPLE MUFFINS
Makes 12.
You will need a muffin tin with 12 moulds, well greased.

140g/5 oz wholewheat flour .
55g/2 oz porridge oats
½ teaspoon sea salt
1 level tablespoon baking powder
1 level teaspoon ground cinnamon
225ml/8 fl oz milk
1 egg, lightly beaten
3 tablespoons sunflower or corn oil
3 level tablespoons clear honey
*170g/6 oz cooking apples, peeled, cored and
   grated (weight when grated)*

Follow method as for *Plain wholewheat muffins* above, stirring the apple into the mixture last.

Note Any other soft finely chopped fruit in season can be added instead of the apple.

ONION AND CHEESE MUFFINS
Makes 12.

Prepare mixture for *Plain wholewheat muffins* above, but use only 1 rounded teaspoon sugar and add 2 tablespoons of finely grated onion and 85g/3 oz of finely grated Cheddar cheese. Mix the cheese in with the dry ingredients distributing it well and stir the onion into the wet ingredients.

SAVOURY OR SWEET SOYA FLOUR AND WHOLEWHEAT MUFFINS
Makes 12.

Prepare as for *Plain wholewheat muffins* above, but use 140g/5 oz wholewheat flour and 85g/3 oz soya flour. Add fruit or cheese and onion as described in the recipes above.

BISCUITS

Biscuits are quick to prepare and if using wholesome ingredients are a nourishing and tasty treat.

Most biscuits are softish when they first come out of the oven, but usually harden on the baking sheets. If the centres remain soft after cooling then simply return to the oven and bake for 5 minutes longer.

A problem with biscuits is that they often stick to the baking sheets and break when removing. If this happens constantly then line the tin with lightly greased greaseproof paper or baking foil, then the biscuits will peel off more easily.

I sometimes use a mixture of butter and sunflower oil or just butter rather than margarine, as the results are better in some recipes. I will start you off with less sweet biscuits.

WHOLEWHEAT DIGESTIVE BISCUITS
These are delicious served with cheese, simply lightly buttered or just on their own.

Makes 15.
You will need 2 baking sheets, well greased.

225g/8 oz wholemeal flour, plain
110g/4 oz polyunsaturated margarine or butter
55g/2 oz raw cane castor sugar
1 medium size egg, beaten
2 level tablespoons natural yoghurt
1 level tablespoon clear honey or brown sugar
good pinch sea salt
few sesame seeds to top

1. Preheat the oven 350°F/180°C/Gas Mark 4.
2. Mix flour and salt together and rub in the margarine or butter until the mixture resembles fine breadcrumbs.
3. Blend sugar, beaten egg, yoghurt and honey or sugar together and pour into the flour mixture.
4. Form into a soft dough.
5. Roll out on a lightly floured surface to a thickness of 5 mm/¼ inch.
6. Using a 6 cm/2½ inch plain cutter cut out 15 rounds and place on the prepared baking sheets.
7. Prick the tops evenly in several places with a fork, brush tops with water and sprinkle on a few sesame seeds and bake for 25 minutes.
8. If baking two batches at a time then place one just above centre and one just below and change the trays around after 15 minutes.
9. Leave to cool slightly on the baking sheets for a few minutes before transferring to a wire rack to cool completely.

SAVOURY OATMEAL BISCUITS
Delicious served with cheese.

Makes 16.
You will need 2 baking sheets, well greased.

110g/4 oz fine oatmeal
85g/3 oz wholemeal flour, plain
1 very level teaspoon sea salt
½ teaspoon baking powder
pinch bicarbonate of soda
60g/2½ oz polyunsaturated margarine
4 tablespoons water

1. Preheat the oven 400°F/200°C/Gas Mark 6.
2. Mix dry ingredients then rub in the margarine until the mixture resembles very fine breadcrumbs.
3. Add water gradually (not all at once) and form a stiff dough.
4. Roll out to a thickness of 5 mm/¼ inch and using a plain 5 cm/2 inch cutter cut out 16 rounds.
5. Place on the prepared baking sheets and bake in the preheated oven for 15 minutes.

SWEET 'N' SIMPLE OATMEAL BISCUITS
Makes 16.

Add two level tablespoons of soft brown sugar to the dry ingredients, and proceed as for *Savoury oatmeal biscuits* above.

GINGERBREAD PEOPLE
These are a great favourite with children.

Makes 12.
You will need 2 large baking sheets, well greased.

225g/8 oz wholemeal fine milled pastry flour
½ level teaspoon bicarbonate of soda
½ level teaspoon baking powder
1 rounded teaspoon ground ginger
85g/3 oz polyunsaturated margarine
85g/3 oz soft brown sugar
3 tablespoons slightly warmed runny raw cane syrup
1 egg yolk beaten (optional)
few currants and glacé cherries to decorate

1. Preheat the oven 375°F/190°C/Gas Mark 5.
2. Mix flour, baking powder, bicarbonate of soda and ginger together.
3. Rub in the margarine lightly until the mixture resembles fine breadcrumbs.
4. Stir in the sugar.
5. Add the slightly warm cane syrup with the egg yolk and form into a soft dough.
6. Knead together until smooth and pliable.
7. Roll the mixture out to a thickness of 3 mm/⅛ inch. Using a gingerbread man cutter cut out 12 shapes.
8. Lift onto the baking sheet 4 cm/1½ inch apart.
9. Decorate using the currants for eyes, nose and buttons down the front and a thin curved piece of glacé cherry for the mouth.
10. Bake in the preheated oven for 12 minutes. These are best baking one tray at a time in the centre of the oven for perfect results.
11. Loosen from the baking sheet while still hot. Leave to sit for a few minutes then transfer to a wire rack to cool and harden completely.

TRADITIONAL OATMEAL DROP COOKIES
Makes 36.
You will need 4 baking sheets, lined and greased.

170g/6 oz porridge oats
55g/2 oz wheatgerm
110g/4 oz demerara sugar
55g/2 oz chopped almonds
55g/2 oz raisins
good pinch sea salt
1 teaspoon ground cinnamon
¼ level teaspoon ground clove powder
110ml/4 fl oz sunflower oil
2 medium size eggs
blanched and split almonds to decorate

1. Preheat oven 350°F/180°C/Gas Mark 4.
2. Mix oats with wheatgerm, sugar, nuts, raisins, salt and spices.
3. Beat oil and eggs together and stir this into the oat mixture.
4. Mix well together then drop teaspoons of the mixture onto the prepared baking sheets 5 cm/2 inch apart.
5. Place an almond half in the centre of each and bake each tray separately in the centre of the oven for 10 minutes until cookies are lightly golden.
6. When cooked remove from the baking sheet immediately and cool on a wire rack.
7. Store in an airtight tin between layers of greaseproof paper.

CAROB CHIP AND NUT COOKIES
Makes 36.
You will need 4 baking sheets, lined with foil and greased.

110g/4 oz polyunsaturated margarine or butter
110g/4 oz soft brown sugar or raw cane castor sugar
1 large egg, beaten
½ teaspoon natural vanilla essence
110g/4 oz wholemeal flour
good pinch of sea salt
40g/1½ oz porridge oats
85g/3 oz carob chips
40g/1½ oz medium finely chopped hazelnuts, almonds or pecan nuts

1. Preheat oven 350°F/180°C/Gas Mark 4.
2. Cream margarine or butter and sugar together until light and fluffy.
3. Gradually beat in the egg and vanilla essence.
4. Mix the flour with the salt and gradually fold this into the creamed mixture.
5. Mix the oats, carob chips and chopped nuts together and fold this into the mixture.
6. Drop teaspoons of the mixture onto the prepared baking sheets about 2.5 cm/ 1 inch apart.
7. Bake for 12 to 15 minutes until lightly browned. Leave on the baking sheets for 1 minute then ease off with a palette knife and cool on a wire rack.

COCONUT COOKIES
Makes 36.

Omit the carob chips and the nuts from the *Carob chip and nut cookies* recipe (see page 72) and add 55g/2 oz desiccated coconut instead.

CURRANT AND NUT COOKIES
Makes 36.

Omit the carob chips and the vanilla essence from the *Carob chip and nut cookies* recipe (see page 72) and use 85g/3 oz of currants and almond essence instead.

MALTED SESAME CRUNCHIES
These are very simple to prepare and are extremely popular.

As they are inclined to stick to the baking sheets, line the sheets with greased foil or greaseproof paper.

Makes 24.
You will need 3 baking sheets, lined and greased.

2 level teaspoons bicarbonate of soda
1 tablespoon hot water
125g/4½ oz polyunsaturated margarine
2 level tablespoons malt extract
85g/3 oz demerara sugar
85g/3 oz sesame seeds
110g/4 oz wholemeal flour, plain
85g/3 oz porridge oats
good pinch sea salt

1. Preheat the oven 325°F/170°C/Gas Mark 3.
2. Dissolve the bicarbonate of soda in the hot water.
3. Melt the margarine, malt and sugar on a very low heat until the margarine and sugar have melted (do not over heat).
4. Mix the dry ingredients together then pour the bicarbonate mixture into the malt mixture. Pour the lot into the dry ingredients.
5. Mix well.
6. Roll into 24 small balls and place 8 on each tray leaving 5 cm/2 inch between them. They will spread considerably while cooking.
7. Bake in the preheated oven for 20 minutes. If baking two trays at a time, then place one above centre and the other below centre and change the trays around after 10 minutes. If baking one tray at a time then bake in the centre of the oven.
8. Loosen from the trays then leave to sit for 10 minutes before removing to a wire rack to cool and harden completely.

MALTED ALMOND OR COCONUT CRUNCHIES
Makes 24.

Omit the sesame seeds from the *Malted sesame crunchies* recipe above and add 85g/3 oz of medium finely chopped almonds (do not blanch) or desiccated coconut instead.

PUMPKIN SEED, ALMOND AND HONEY CRUNCHIES
Makes 24.

Follow the recipe for *Malted sesame crunchies* (see page 75), but use honey instead of malt, 125 ml/4½ fl oz sunflower oil instead of margarine and 40g/1½ oz each of almonds and pumpkin seeds finely ground instead of the sesame seeds. Also add 2 level teaspoons of ground ginger (optional).

CASHEW AND CINNAMON CRUNCHIES

Follow the recipe for *Pumpkin, almond and honey crunchies* above but use 85g/3 oz of finely chopped cashew nuts and ground cinnamon instead of the pumpkin seeds, almonds and ginger.

CAROB, HAZELNUT AND ORANGE COOKIES

These are very similar to the *Malted sesame crunchies* (see page 75) and just as simple to prepare.

Makes 24.
You will need 3 large baking sheets, lined and greased.

2 level teaspoons bicarbonate of soda
1 tablespoon hot water
2 level tablespoons either honey or malt
85g/3 oz demerara sugar
125ml/4½ fl oz sunflower or corn oil
grated rind of 1 orange
85g/3 oz porridge oats
110g/4 oz wholemeal flour, plain
85g/3 oz hazelnuts, medium finely ground
1 level tablespoon carob powder, sieved
good pinch sea salt

1. Preheat oven 325°F/170°C/Gas Mark 3.
2. Dissolve the bicarbonate of soda in the hot water.
3. Melt honey or malt, oil and sugar over a very low heat until the sugar has dissolved.
4. Mix all dry ingredients together.
5. Pour the bicarbonate of soda mixture into the honey and malt mixture and then pour this into the dry ingredients. Mix well together.
6. Roll into 24 small balls and place 5 cm/2 inch apart on the prepared baking sheets.
7. Bake as for *Malted sesame crunchies* (see page 75).

PEANUT OR SUNFLOWER SEED BUTTER COOKIES

Makes 20.
You will need 3 baking sheets, greased.

110g/4 oz smooth peanut butter or sunflower seed spread
110g/4 oz polyunsaturated margarine
140g/5 oz soft brown sugar
1 large egg, well beaten
170g/6 oz wholemeal flour, plain
½ level teaspoon baking powder
½ level teaspoon bicarbonate of soda
good pinch sea salt
few unsalted peanuts to top

1. Preheat oven 375°F/190°C/Gas Mark 5.
2. Beat peanut butter or sunflower seed spread, margarine, sugar and egg together until well blended.
3. Mix flour, baking powder, salt and bicarbonate of soda together.
4. Add the egg mixture to the flour mixture and form into a dough.
5. Place dough in a polythene bag and chill for 30 minutes.
6. Shape into 4 cm/1½ inch balls and place 5 cm/2 inch apart on the prepared baking sheet.
7. Flatten slightly with the back of a teaspoon and sprinkle on a few unsalted peanuts.
8. Bake in the preheated oven for 20 minutes. If baking two trays at a time, then place one tray just above centre and one tray just below. Change the trays around after 12 minutes. If baking 1 tray at a time, then place in the centre of the oven.
9. Leave on the baking sheet to harden slightly for 5 minutes, then remove to a wire rack to cool completely and fully harden.

WHEATLESS OAT AND PEANUT OR SUNFLOWER SEED BUTTER COOKIES

These are not only wheat-free but without added fat.

Makes 30.
You will need 4 baking sheets, lined and greased.

70g/2½ oz peanut butter or sunflower seed
   spread
85g/3 oz clear honey
55ml/2 fl oz maple syrup
2 large eggs
1 teaspoon natural vanilla essence
225g/8 oz porridge oats
few peanuts or sunflower seeds to top

1. Preheat oven 350°F/180°C/Gas Mark 4.
2. Beat peanut butter or sunflower seed
   spread, honey, maple syrup, eggs and
   vanilla essence with a whisk until smooth.
3. Stir in the oats and mix well.
4. Spoon very slightly rounded
   dessertspoonfuls onto the prepared baking
   sheets 5 cm/2 inch apart.
5. Flatten slightly with fingertips.
6. Decorate with a few peanuts or sunflower
   seeds and bake in the preheated oven for
   10 to 12 minutes.
7. Remove from the baking sheets within 1
   minute of coming out of the oven. Cool on
   a wire rack.

MALTED SEED AND OAT FINGERS
Makes 32.
You will need a 20 cm/8 inch x 30 cm/12 inch
Swiss roll tin, greased and lined.

170ml/6 fl oz sunflower or corn oil
140g/5 oz malt extract
1 teaspoon natural vanilla essence
55g/2 oz Barbados sugar
170g/6 oz jumbo oats
170g/6 oz porridge oats
2 level tablespoons sunflower seeds*
2 level tablespoons sesame seeds*
2 level tablespoons pumpkin seeds*
*lightly roasted in moderate oven for 15
   minutes

1. Preheat the oven 350°F/180°C/Gas Mark 4.
2. Heat oil, malt and sugar on very low heat
   until warm (do not boil). Stir in the
   vanilla essence.
3. Mix all the dry ingredients and stir into
   the warm malt liquid.
4. Press into the prepared tin and smooth the
   top.
5. Bake in the centre of the oven for 30 minutes.

6. Cool in the tin for 2 minutes then cut into
   32 fingers, each 7.5 cm/3 inch x 4 cm/1½
   inch, making sure you cut right through
   to the lining paper. Leave to get
   completely cold in the tin then break into
   fingers and store between layers of
   greaseproof paper in an airtight tin.

MALTED FRUIT, SEED AND OAT FINGERS
Makes 32.

Simply use one tablespoon each of the seeds
instead of 2 tablespoons in the *Malted seed
and oat fingers* recipe above and add 1
tablespoon each of raisins, finely chopped
apricots and finely chopped dates.

PANCAKES AND FRITTERS

Pancakes can be used for a huge variety of
savoury and sweet dishes. They can be thick
or wafer thin and the batter can be enriched
with more eggs and made with a variety of
ground grains such as buckwheat flour,
cornmeal, brown rice flour and soya flour.
   I will give you a variety of basic pancake
mixtures in this lesson plus a few ideas for
fillings, but almost any seasoned mixture of
sautéd vegetables or sweetened fruit mixture
is ideal for stuffing pancakes.
   Pancake batters are best left to stand for at
least 1 hour then stirred before using. All
pancakes can be stacked on top of each other
as you take them out of the pan and, if not
using immediately, frozen when cold, wrapped
in polythene. They will not stick together.

It is best to use an 18 cm/7 inch crêpe pan but you can use any heavy-based frying pan or griddle. Brush it with oil before cooking each pancake.

WHOLEWHEAT PANCAKES
Makes 12.

110g/4 oz wholewheat flour, plain
good pinch sea salt
1 large egg, beaten
185 ml/¹/₂ pt milk
1 tablespoon sunflower, corn or virgin olive oil

1. If you have a blender, then process all ingredients until smooth.
2. If mixing by hand, then mix flour and salt together in a bowl, make a well in the centre and add the egg and half the milk.
3. Mix to a smooth thick batter, gradually adding the rest of the milk to make a smooth runny batter.
4. Brush the pan with oil and heat until hot.
5. Turn down heat to moderate, tilt the pan slightly and pour 1 tablespoon of the batter onto the raised pan and swerve the pan around so that the batter spreads in a rough circle.
6. Cook until the underside is lightly browned and the top is bubbling.
7. Flip over and cook the other side for 10 seconds only.

These are delicious served straight from the pan spread with either clear honey or maple syrup or a mixture of both, with a sprinkling of lemon juice.

If making to stuff with either savoury or sweet fillings then stack one on top of the other until ready to fill.

DATE AND APPLE STUFFED PANCAKES
Makes 12.

1 recipe quantity Wholewheat pancakes (see above)
1 recipe quantity of filling for Date and apple slice (see page 54)
little maple syrup

1. Follow the *Wholewheat pancakes* recipe above and stack pancakes ready for filling.

2. Spoon a generous tablespoon of the filling into the centre of each pancake while still hot. Roll up and trickle a little maple syrup over the top.
3. Serve with Greek yoghurt or *Vanilla yoghurt cream* (see page 191).

APRICOT, PRUNE AND APPLE STUFFED PANCAKES
Makes 12.

1 recipe quantity Wholewheat pancakes (see above)
1 recipe quantity of filling for Apricot, prune and apple slice (see page 54)
little maple syrup

Follow the same method as for *Date and apple stuffed pancakes* above, using the apricot, prune and apple filling instead.

BUCKWHEAT PANCAKES
Makes 12.

Prepare as for *Wholewheat pancakes* (see opposite) but use 70g/2¹/₂ oz of wholewheat flour and 40g/1¹/₂ oz buckwheat flour plus ¹/₂ level teaspoon of bicarbonate of soda.

These are delicious with the *Date and apple filling* or the *Apricot, prune and apple filling* used in the two previous recipes or for something simple try this:

Banana, lemon and cinnamon filling: For 12 pancakes mash 6 bananas with the juice of 2 large lemons and add ground cinnamon to taste. Spoon the cold filling into the centre of the piping hot pancakes. Roll up and trickle on a little maple syrup. Lovely!

PARSLEY PANCAKES
Makes 12.

Prepare either the *Wholewheat pancakes* (see opposite) or *Buckwheat pancakes* (see above) batter and stir in 55g/2 oz of fresh chopped parsley. Best to use a mixer so that the parsley merges with the ingredients and gives it a tint of green.

Parsley pancakes are really good stuffed with a mixture of leeks, mushrooms and asparagus (see below).

LEEK, MUSHROOM & ASPARAGUS STUFFED PARSLEY PANCAKES
Makes 12.

1 recipe quantity Parsley pancakes (see page
  76)
1 recipe Basic white sauce (see page 172)
340g/12 oz asparagus (weight when trimmed)
2 tablespoons sunflower oil
3 leeks trimmed and cut in thin rings
225g/8 oz button mushrooms
1 rounded teaspoon dried tarragon
4 tablespoons white wine
85g/3 oz Pecorino cheese, finely grated

1. Make *Parsley pancakes* (see above) and
   stack ready for filling.
2. Steam the asparagus until tender. Cut off
   the tips and chop the stems in small
   pieces.
3. Sauté the leeks in the oil for 5 minutes.
   Add the mushrooms and fry for 3 minutes
   more.
4. Blend the white sauce with the tarragon,
   chopped asparagus stems and the wine in
   a mixer until smooth.
5. Spoon half of the sauce into the leeks and
   mushrooms. Stir in the asparagus tips
   taking care not to break them.
6. Spoon equal amounts of the vegetable and
   sauce mixture into the centre of the
   pancakes. Fold over and place the filled
   pancakes in a large ovenproof dish.
7. Spoon over the rest of the sauce and
   sprinkle on the cheese. Bake in the centre
   of the oven, 375°F/190°C/Gas Mark 5, for
   25 minutes until the top is golden.

BROCCOLI PANCAKES
It is best to use a blender for this recipe.

Makes 12.

Prepare either the *Wholewheat pancakes* (see
page 76) or *Buckwheat pancakes* (see page 76)
batter, but add ½ level teaspoon of
bicarbonate of soda and 170g/6 oz broccoli
florets, which have been steamed until tender
then finely chopped. Add a little more salt if
you wish. Cook pancakes in the usual way
(see page 76).

These go well with a spicy bean filling (see
page 108 for *Chilli red bean stuffed pancakes*).
They are also delicious stuffed with the *Leek,
mushroom and asparagus* filling from the
previous recipe.

TORTILLAS (MEXICAN CORN PANCAKES)
It is best to use masaharina for perfect results
in this recipe. Masaharina is a special kind of
wholegrain cornmeal, which has been soaked
and boiled in lime water then roasted and
more finely ground than regular wholegrain
cornmeal. You can use regular wholegrain
cornmeal but the results will be heavier.

These are very simple to make and freeze
well if stacked on top of each other and
wrapped in foil. To defrost and warm, simply
open the foil and allow to defrost at room
temperature. As soon as you can, separate
them and lay them out individually. When no
longer cold to the touch pop each one into a
hot, heavy pan and heat on both sides for a
few seconds only. Stack, wrap in a warm thick
tea towel and then foil and keep in a very low
heated oven, 250°F/120°C/Gas Mark ½, until
ready to serve.

Makes 24.

225g/8 oz masaharina (precooked cornmeal)
285ml/½ pt water
little sea salt

1. Mix the flour, water and a good pinch of
   salt together in a mixing bowl. Form into
   a dough and knead for about 5 minutes,
   adding more flour if too sticky or more
   water if too dry.
2. Divide the dough equally into 24 pieces.
   Roll each piece into a ball and then roll
   out the balls between two sheets of
   greaseproof paper or polythene (do not use
   any flour to roll out) to approximately
   15 cm/6 inch round, flat pancakes, 3 cm/
   ⅛ inch thick.
3. Heat a lightly greased frying pan or
   griddle and fry the tortillas on a moderate
   heat for about 2/3 minutes until the edge
   curls a little. Flip over and cook on the
   other side still on a moderate heat for
   about 2 minutes.

4. Stack cooked tortillas on top of each other, wrap in a slightly damp, warm tea towel then wrap in foil and keep in a low heated oven, 250°F/120°C/Gas Mark ½ until ready to serve.

5. Serve with any spicy meal or stuff in the same way as for *Chilli red bean stuffed pancakes* (see page 108).

FRIED TORTILLA FINGERS

These are great to use as crudités for dips and pâtés.

Makes 48.

6 uncooked tortillas (see above)
soya oil for frying

1. Heat about 1.25 cm/½ inch soya oil in a large frying pan.
2. Cut tortillas into 8 strips (they will vary in length).
3. Test one in the hot oil – it should instantly sizzle and turn golden brown very quickly.
4. Fry a few at a time, until golden brown, then take out with a slotted spoon and drain on a double thickness of absorbent paper.
5. Serve immediately on a large platter surrounding a bowl of pâté or dip of your choice.

SWEETCORN AND CHEESE FRITTERS

Children love these and three fritters will provide them with a substantial meal if accompanied with a salad.

Makes 12.

85g/3 oz wholewheat flour and 28g/1 oz soya flour or all wholemeal flour
1 level teaspoon baking powder
1 large egg, beaten
½ teaspoon sea salt
225ml/8 fl oz milk
2 tablespoons very finely chopped onion
170g/6 oz sweetcorn (fresh off the cob or if frozen, cooked for 3 minutes and cooled)
85g/3 oz Cheddar cheese, grated
soya oil for frying

1. Mix flours, baking powder and sea salt together. Make a well in the centre and pour in the egg and half the milk. Blend with a fork until smooth.
2. Gradually add the rest of the milk.
3. Stir in the onion, corn and cheese and leave to stand for 30 minutes. Stir before using.
4. Heat 2 tablespoons of oil in a heavy-based frying pan on a moderate heat. Cook 3 fritters at a time using 1 tablespoon of batter for each. Spread each one gently with the back of a spoon and fry until the underside is golden and the edges curl and bubbles appear on top. Flip over and cook the other side on a slightly lower heat until golden brown.
5. Drain on absorbent kitchen paper and serve immediately.

SWEET PEPPER AND MUSHROOM FRITTERS
Makes 12.

Prepare batter as for *Sweetcorn and cheese fritters* above, but omit the sweetcorn and add with the onion, 2 tablespoons of finely chopped red or green pepper and 2 tablespoons of finely chopped mushrooms. You can also add fresh chopped parsley or herbs of your choice and freshly ground black pepper.

FRUIT FRITTERS
Makes 12.

Prepare the batter for *Sweetcorn and cheese fritters* above, but omit the onion, corn and cheese and add 170g/6 oz of any soaked, drained and chopped dried fruit, or chopped soft fruit or grated apple plus 1 dessertspoon of honey.

LESSON 4

WHOLEGRAINS, NUTS AND SEEDS

This lesson includes nutritional information on a wide range of wholegrains, nuts and seeds, most of which are easily available in health food stores and many supermarkets. I have also included a section on gluten (wheat protein), mainly used in Japan and China and some parts of India in a variety of savoury dishes.

SHOPPING LIST

Check all herbs and spices, vegetable bouillon powder or vegetable stock cubes used in the first three lessons. Replenish if necessary and add those on this list. Check that you have a good supply of the nuts and seeds used in the previous lessons.

short grain Italian brown rice	pine nuts*
long grain Italian brown rice	pistachio nuts*
long thin brown rice	black mustard seeds
wholegrain millet	celery seeds
bulgur	methi (fenugreek leaf)
buckwheat (ready-toasted)	paprika
corn meal (or maize meal)	turmeric
pot barley	good curry powder
chick peas (see page 100)	mixed herbs
	dried sage
	dried thyme
	dried lemon thyme

*These do not store well so buy when needed.

TYPES OF WHOLEGRAIN

All wholegrains contain 9 to 14 per cent protein with the exception of oats which contain 17 per cent and Triticale which contains 19 per cent. They are also rich in vitamins and minerals and high in fibre. Whole berries or grains will keep for up to one year if stored in a cool place, away from light and in airtight containers. Millet, which has a longer shelf life, will keep for two years if stored in these conditions.

RICE

Rice grain is similar in structure to wheat grain. It has seven layers which contain all the proteins, vitamins, minerals and fats essential for health. The centre contains carbohydrates and starches. It is an easily digestible food with a low gluten and high fibre content. In the process of making white rice the grains have the husk, fibre and germ removed and are polished with glucose or talc so most of the nutritional value is destroyed. Brown rice has only the indigestible husk removed.

There are several varieties of rice on the market which are suitable for particular types of dishes and need slightly different cooking times.

Long thin brown rice
This includes Surinam, Basmati (usually sold white, but is available brown), Australian and American brown rice. It is quick cooking, light in texture and a suitable complement to curries and oriental dishes. This variety is particularly good for fried rice (see below).

Basic cooking method – Measure dry rice grains in a cup before washing. Place rice in a sieve and let cold water run through the grains for 1 minute. Move the grains around with your fingers. Drain and put into a saucepan. To each cup of dry rice add 1⅔ cups

79

of cold water and a little sea salt. For yellow rice add 1 level teaspoon turmeric (children love this). Bring to boil, turn down to simmer and cover with a tight lid. If the lid is not tight then use a sheet of foil under the lid, pressing it over the rim of the saucepan to seal. Let simmer undisturbed on low heat for 25 minutes only. The water should all be absorbed and the grain separate. Take lid off and if not using immediately spread out on a baking sheet to let the steam off otherwise the rice will stick together. Reheat by steaming for a few minutes in a colander or if you want fried rice see below.

Fried rice – When rice is cooked as above spread out in a thinnish layer on a baking sheet (for 450g/1 lb you will need two baking sheets). Let it steam off and cool for 10 minutes. Stir fry briskly in a little oil on moderately high heat.

For a deliciously flavoured rice then sauté an onion until brown and very slightly burnt. Then fry the rice briskly in this stirring constantly to avoid sticking.

Freezing rice – Spread the cooked rice out in a thin layer on baking sheets to let the steam off. Let it get completely cold then spoon into polythene freezer bags. Fill the bags loosely and flatten them, easing as much air out as possible. The rice will defrost in 1 hour. For quick defrosting steam in a colander for a few minutes.

Italian long grain brown rice
This rice is chewy and has a delicious nutty flavour. It is particularly good for risottos and savoury rice bakes (see *Rice and toasted cashew nut bake,* page 84).

Basic cooking method – Measure dry rice grains in a cup then place in a sieve and let cold water run through the grains for 1 minute. Move the grains around with your fingers. Put the grains into a saucepan and to one cup of rice add two cups of cold water and a little sea salt. Bring to boil, turn down to simmer. Cover with a tight lid and simmer gently for 35 minutes. Turn off the heat and leave the lid on for 5 minutes more. The water should all be absorbed and the grains separate. If not serving immediately then spread out on a baking sheet to let the steam off or the grains will stick together.

Italian short grain brown rice
This has a similar chewy texture and flavour to Italian long grain rice, but when cooked it is slightly softer and a little sticky. This makes it very suitable for sweet rice pudding and rice balls – see recipes for *Curried rice and chick pea balls* (page 86) and *Sweet rice balls* (page 86).

Basic cooking method – This is the same as for Italian long grain brown rice (see above) if you want a simple boiled rice, but for rice balls and sweet rice pudding then follow the instructions in individual recipes.

Organically grown brown rice
All organically grown food is superior to non-organic varieties as there are no sprays or chemical fertilizers used. It is obviously more expensive but works out the same price as pre-packaged supermarket brown rice if bought in bulk from a health store. This rice goes through a more gentle process when the outer indigestible husk is removed which leaves the sensitive areas undamaged and it is therefore nutritiously more valuable.

Basic cooking method – Depending on the variety used, cook as directed for other types of brown rice.

Converted rice
This rice goes through a process whereby it is treated with steam under immense pressure. This forces the nutrients from the outer layers into the centre of the grain. The rice is then milled in the same way as white rice but does not lose too many nutrients. It is quick cooking and has a much lighter texture than all the other brown rice varieties. Although the labels do not say converted rice, much of the supermarket branded pre-packaged 'brown rice' goes through this process. Its nutritional value is not as high as regular brown rice but it is far superior to white rice and well worth buying if you have never tried brown rice before.

Basic cooking method – The instructions on most supermarket pre-packed brown rice labels tell you to cook the rice in far too much water and the cooking time is often unnecessarily long. Prepare as for long thin brown rice (see page 79) and you won't go far wrong (25 minutes is the maximum cooking time needed for any heat-treated rice).

Wild rice
Unfortunately this rice is not widely available. It is not botanically related to other rice grains as it belongs to a different species. Its protein content is much higher than ordinary brown rice and it has several times more vitamin B. It is also very expensive, but if you should come across it anywhere then treat yourself for those special occasions and dinner parties.

Basic cooking method – Prepare as for Italian long grain brown rice, adding no more than 2 cups of water to 1 cup of wild rice but cook for 30 minutes only with a tight lid on. Leave the lid on for 5 minutes after cooking then remove it. All the water should be absorbed and the grains separate. Serve as an accompaniment to special meals rather than mixed in with vegetables or rich sauces, otherwise you won't taste the delicious flavour of this very special grain.

MILLET (WHOLEGRAIN)
This tasty grain is widely used in Africa, India and Asia. It is balanced in amino acids, is rich in iron and its protein utilization value is greatly increased in the body by the addition of vegetables. It is also gluten-free. As the grain is slightly musty when boiled it is ideal for croquettes (see page 89). It is also great oven-baked with vegetables (see page 89).
Basic cooking method – Stick to cooking 225g/ 8 oz of millet at a time until you have

practiced a bit. I cook millet in a large heavy-based frying pan with a tight lid. This ensures the grains get evenly toasted and cooked.

Brush the pan with oil then toast the grains over a moderate heat stirring them with a wooden spoon to cook evenly. Do this until the grains begin to smell nutty and are very lightly browned (alternatively you can do this in the oven on a large baking tray – set oven to 325°F/160°C/Gas Mark 3 and bake for 12 minutes). Then to every cup of millet add 2½ cups of boiling water. Boil then simmer with the lid on for 20 minutes only.

MILLET FLAKES
Wholegrain millet flakes are great as an alternative to porridge oats in rissoles, flapjacks and various other recipes.

BULGUR
This is a wholewheat product which is highly nutritious and simple to prepare. It is sold parboiled, which cuts down the cooking time enormously. The structure of the seed is such that the wheatgerm and the bran (fibre) are retained even when the seed is milled. It is widely used in Middle Eastern countries and is the basis of a delicious salad called *Tabbouleh* (see page 90). I use bulgur instead of couscous in the Arabian recipe of the same name, as couscous is a processed wheat grain and not a wholegrain. It's like using brown rice instead of white (see page 90 for *Arabian 'couscous'*). I also use it in rissoles and bean or nut loaves instead of breadcrumbs.
Basic cooking method – To 110g/4 oz bulgur add 170ml/6 fl oz boiling water and a good pinch of sea salt. Cover and let stand for 20 minutes. The grains will swell up. Your bulgur is now ready to use in the suggested recipes above. For extra flavour you can add 1 rounded teaspoon vegetable bouillon powder instead of the salt.

BUCKWHEAT
This is not botanically a grain but is used as one. It has a very distinctive flavour and is rich in all the B vitamins and iron. It also contains rutic which is known to have a beneficial effect on the circulatory system. It is best to buy ready-toasted buckwheat which

takes only 15 minutes to cook. You can also buy buckwheat spaghetti which is thin, very light in texture and has a rich nutty flavour.
Basic cooking method – To one cup of pre-toasted buckwheat add 3 cups of boiling water and a little sea salt. Boil then simmer with a tight lid on for 15 minutes. The water will all be absorbed. The cooked grains are quite soft and fluffy.

CORNMEAL (OR MAIZE MEAL OR POLENTA)

It is important to get *wholegrain, stoneground* cornmeal, as it is often sold with the valuable germ removed. This grain is rich in vitamin A, phosphorous and potassium.

My favourite dish using cornmeal is *Italian polenta* (see page 92). The basic cooking instructions are given in the recipe. As the water content varies according to the recipe you are using it is not possible to give a basic cooking method for this grain. It is also good included in bread and cake recipes and in pancake batters.

BARLEY (POT BARLEY)

Pot barley is the wholegrain, but more commonly used in many places is pearl barley which is polished and lacks most of the nutrients and the fibre contained in the wholegrain. Barley is easily digestible and therefore good for babies and those with digestive disorders. Pot barley contains 12 per cent protein and a good supply of vitamins and minerals. It is mostly used in soups and stews but you can use it as you would rice. It takes a long time to cook if it is not pre-soaked so whether it is going to be added to soups, stews or instead of rice it is best to soak it first.

Basic cooking method – Wash well and soak for 6 hours. If adding to soups or stews then use the soaking water as part of the liquid in the recipe. Make sure it cooks (in the recipe) for 30 minutes. If using as you would rice then to 1 cup of barley add 2½ cups of water. Soak for 6 hours. Bring the lot to boil, add a little sea salt, cover with a tight lid and simmer for 30 minutes.

TRITICALE

This grain is produced by crossing wheat (*Triticum*) with rye (*Secale*), hence its name. It is nutritionally superior to wheat or rye as it contains 19 per cent protein and is richer in vitamins and minerals and has more of the essential amino acids (see *Protein* on page 11). It is delicious sprouted and can be used as you would rice but it has to be soaked overnight.
Basic cooking method – Soak the washed grains overnight. Drain and reserve the soaking water. Measure the grains in a cup. To every cup of grains add 1½ cups of water which includes the soaking water plus a little sea salt. Bring to boil and simmer with lid on for about 35 minutes.

NUTS AND SEEDS

Nuts are a high-protein food rich in the B vitamins and well worth making a regular ingredient in your diet. Although they have a high fat content, they are rich in linoleic acid which helps control the level of cholesterol in the body.

The majority of us, me included in the past, eat nuts only at Christmas or with drinks. Well, the Christmas nuts eaten straight from the shells are great but most of the pre-packed shelled and salted varieties should be avoided. They are often treated with preservatives, colourings and other inhibitors and roasted in saturated fats which can cause problems to our digestive systems. You can, however, obtain a good variety of assorted shelled and unsalted nuts all year round from healthfood shops and supermarkets. Buy them where the turnover is high for this particular food does not have a long shelf-life. They become soft and rancid if stored too long. I have included peanuts in this list but they are not strictly a nut. They belong to the bean family.

I add seeds to as many dishes as I can because they are bursting with goodness. They are an easily digested source of vitamins and minerals, are high in protein and very rich in linoleic acid.

ALMONDS

These delicately flavoured nuts are approximately 18.5 per cent protein. They impart a delicious taste to both savoury and sweet dishes. Almond oil was one of the earliest skin beautifiers and is still used today in many face creams. In the Middle East and India almonds are a common ingredient in savoury rice dishes and in sweet-making. Almond paste (marzipan) is very popular spread on cakes at festive times.

BRAZIL NUTS

Brazil nuts are approximately 33 per cent protein and are high in linoleic acid, but they have a very high calorific value so are to be avoided if you are on a slimming diet. I was amazed the first time I saw a picture of these nuts growing on a tree. What you see are large, coconut-type shells. Inside these shells are tightly packed brazil nuts as we know them.

CASHEW NUTS

These nuts are approximately 17 per cent protein. Like almonds they impart a lovely slightly sweet flavour when lightly toasted and added to savoury rice dishes. A native of Brazil, the cashews grow on the end of a pear-shaped fruit which is often eaten by the Brazilians, the nuts themselves being discarded.

HAZELNUTS (COB NUTS OR FILBERTS)

These are approximately 12.5 per cent protein. They are invaluable in sweet dishes, especially when lightly toasted (try the delicious *Coffee, maple and toasted hazelnut ice cream* on page 186). I love them in cakes, biscuits and sprinkled on breakfast cereals. You can now buy a delicious toasted hazelnut spread.

PEANUTS

As previously mentioned, these are not nuts but a member of the bean family. They grow in the ground, not on trees, which is why they are sometimes referred to as groundnuts. They are approximately 26 per cent protein and are rich in essential amino acids (see notes on protein on page 11) and linoleic acid, but have a high calorific content so should be eaten in moderation by weight-watchers. Peanuts also contain adverse substances which can under certain circumstances combine with iodine and prevent it from being absorbed by the blood. But as with any foods moderation is the best rule. Eat once or twice a week and not every day. Avoid the salted variety and toast your own sprinkled with a little soya sauce in a moderate oven for 15 minutes.

PECAN NUTS

Pecan nuts are approximately 9 per cent protein. The shelled pecans look similar to shelled walnuts but they are slightly sweeter and less bitter tasting. In America they are also called hickory nuts. They are delicious in fruit cakes, as an alternative to almonds. Another idea is to rub a little nutmeg and cinnamon into chopped pecans and sprinkle this on top of baked egg custard, or custard tarts or flans, just before baking.

PINE NUTS (PINE KERNELS)

These tiny cream-coloured nuts are approximately 30 per cent protein. They grow inside the hard cones of the Stone Pine tree, originally grown in Italy but now cultivated all around the Mediterranean. They are a delicious ingredient in savoury stuffings for dishes such as *Stuffed vine or cabbage leaves* (see page 87), in *Tabbouleh* (see page 90) and in sweet and sour sauces and stir-fry vegetables. They are also superb in sweet dishes. Make sure you buy these from a shop which has a good turnover and regular fresh supplies as when shelled they do not have a long shelf-life.

PISTACHIO NUTS

These are my favourite nut but are very expensive. Unfortunately you can only buy them slightly salted. They are approximately

19 per cent protein. Their wonderful flavour enriches any savoury or sweet dish they are put into.

WALNUTS
There are two types – English walnuts (European) which contain approximately 14 per cent protein and black walnuts (American) which contain approximately 20 per cent protein. These nuts vary in flavour and can sometimes be very bitter, so nibble one before you add them to a particular dish. I like them chopped up in chunks in salads dressed with mayonnaise. I also find they go well with ripe bananas (see *Banana and walnut cake,* page 61).

PUMPKIN SEEDS
These seeds are 29 per cent protein and richer in iron than any other seed. They are either light or dark green in colour and have a pleasant distinctive flavour. Tests indicate that they may be a powerful healing aid in cases of bladder disorder. They are delicious sprinkled on *Pizza* (see page 20) instead of olives, especially for children.

SESAME SEEDS
These calcium-rich seeds are approximately 18.5 per cent protein. *Tahini* is a marvellous paste made from ground sesame seeds. It is a common ingredient in Greek and Middle Eastern cookery (see *Falafel* on page 104 and *Hummous* on page 104). I use them in bread and biscuit making. They have to be baked, toasted or ground to be absorbed by the body. *Halva* is a sweet which is made with ground sesame seeds and sugar. Its sugar content is extremely high so eat in moderation. It is sometimes made with honey and has vanilla flavouring plus nuts, but it should still be eaten in moderation.

SUNFLOWER SEEDS
These seeds are not just for the gerbils. They are approximately 24 per cent protein and a rich source of vitamins E and B, as well as being well supplied with important minerals. Mix them into your cereals, fork them into savoury rice dishes or salads or see *Tamari or shoyu sunflower seeds* on page 92 for a tasty

and nutritious nibble – an alternative to a bag of crisps.

WHOLEGRAIN, NUT AND SEED RECIPES

RICE AND TOASTED CASHEW NUT BAKE
Serves 5.
You will need a large casserole dish without a lid.

280g/10 oz long or short grain Italian brown rice
110g/4 oz cashew nuts
3 tablespoons sunflower, corn or virgin olive oil
1 large onion, about 225g/8 oz in weight when peeled and chopped
1 large juicy clove garlic, crushed
2 medium carrots, scraped and cut into 2 cm/ 1 inch thin sticks
3 sticks celery, chopped
110g/4 oz courgettes, sliced (optional)
1 medium green pepper, deseeded and chopped
110g/4 oz mushrooms, sliced
2 generous tablespoons parsley, finely chopped
1 rounded teaspoon dried basil
1 level teaspoon dried tarragon
1 level teaspoon ground coriander
396g/14 oz can tomatoes, chopped
¼ teaspoon black pepper, freshly ground
2 tablespoons shoyu (naturally fermented soy sauce)
140g/5 oz Cheddar cheese, grated
sprinkling of dried herbs to top

1. Prepare and cook the rice as directed on page 80, but instead of cooking it for 35 minutes turn off heat after 30 minutes. Take the lid off immediately and place rice in a sieve while you prepare the rest of the ingredients.
2. While rice is cooking toast the cashews in the oven at 325°F/160°C/Gas Mark 3 for 12 minutes.
3. Sauté the onion, garlic, carrots and celery in the oil for 5 minutes on a moderate heat, stirring to cook evenly.
4. Add courgettes, peppers, mushrooms, parsley, herbs and coriander and fry for 3

minutes, again stirring briskly to ensure even cooking.

5. Add the tomatoes, black pepper and shoyu and cook on a gentle heat for 1 minute only.
6. Place cooked rice in the casserole dish, stir in the vegetables and toasted cashew nuts.
7. Sprinkle on the cheese and a little more dried herbs and bake in the centre of the oven, 375°F/190°C/Gas Mark 5 (no need to preheat) for 30 minutes until golden brown.
8. Serve with a fresh green salad for a delicious simple and nourishing meal.

Note for vegans: Top the rice and vegetable mixture with thin slices of tofu and sprinkle on wholemeal breadcrumbs mixed with a little vegetable bouillon powder and dried herbs.

MEDITERRANEAN SUMMER RICE PILAF

If you have fresh basil then this dish is a must. You can used dried – it will still be very tasty. The recipe is a rich, delicious mixture and perfect for lunch in the garden or as part of a buffet party.

Serves 6.
You will need a very large saucepan with a tight lid for the rice and a large frying pan to prepare the vegetables.

450g/1 lb Italian long grain brown rice
340g/12 oz onion, peeled and chopped
6 tablespoons virgin olive oil
1 litre/1¾ pt boiling water
1 rounded tablespoon vegetable bouillon
  powder
1 level teaspoon coriander powder
1 level teaspoon cumin powder
½ level teaspoon turmeric
85g/3 oz raisins
2 large juicy cloves garlic, crushed
170g/6 oz mushrooms, sliced
1 large red pepper, deseeded and chopped
2 tablespoons fresh basil, chopped (or 2 level
  teaspoons dried)
110g/4 oz spinach or chard, shredded
6 good sized tomatoes, skinned and mashed
170g/6 oz fresh peas, lightly cooked and
  drained (frozen will do)

8 black olives, minced or finely chopped
freshly ground black pepper
110g/4 oz pistachios or pine nuts
fresh flat leaf parsley to garnish

1. Wash the rice well and drain in a sieve. Sauté the onion in 3 tablespoons of oil for 5 minutes.
2. Add the rice and fry stirring constantly on moderate heat. Cook until the grains are golden.
3. Pour in the boiling water and add the vegetable bouillon powder and the spices. Stir well.
4. Bring to boil, turn down to simmer, cover and let simmer for 20 minutes.
5. Add the raisins and continue to simmer for 10 minutes more until the water is all absorbed and the grains are soft and separate (do not stir the rice during cooking time).
6. While rice is cooking, sauté the vegetables. Heat the remaining oil in a large frying pan and sauté the garlic for 1 minute.
7. Add the mushrooms and red pepper and stir-fry for 3 minutes on a moderate heat.
8. Add the basil and shredded spinach and cook briskly for 1 minute.
9. Add the mashed tomatoes and cook for 1 minute.
10. Stir in the peas and olives and heat through.
11. Season with the black pepper.
12. When ready to serve stir this vegetable mixture into the rice, then stir in the pistachios or pine nuts, saving a few to garnish.
13. Garnish with remaining nuts and chopped flat-leaved parsley (or ordinary parsley) and serve.

CURRIED RICE AND CHICK PEA BALLS

Make these the size recommended in the recipe if serving for a main meal (2 per person) or half the size if making as part of a buffet party. You can keep the mixture in the fridge for three days if not using all immediately. The mixture also freezes well.

These are delicious if served with *Dried peach chutney* (see page 177).

Makes 16 (or 32 buffet size).

110g/4 oz chick peas (dry weight) cooked (see
   page 100) – you can use canned chick peas
   but you will need at least 225g/8 oz in
   weight when drained
450g/1 lb short grain Italian brown rice
2 tablespoons sunflower oil
170g/6 oz onion, weight when finely chopped
1 large clove garlic, crushed
1 rounded tablespoon curry powder
1 rounded dessertspoon methi (fenugreek leaf)
1 tablespoon lemon juice
2 tablespoons shoyu (naturally fermented soy
   sauce)
110g/4 oz sunflower seeds, finely ground
1 egg beaten to bind
soya oil for semi-deep frying

1. Drain the chick peas well.
2. Cook the rice as instructed on page 80, but leave the lid on the saucepan for 10 minutes after cooking so that the rice becomes extra soft and more easily mouldable. Leave to cool.
3. Sauté the onion and garlic in the sunflower oil until soft.
4. Stir in the curry powder and methi and cook for 1 minute on gentle heat stirring constantly.
5. Stir in the lemon juice and shoyu.
6. In a large mixing bowl put the cooked rice (there must be no water in it), ground sunflower seeds and chick peas.
7. Stir in the onion and spice mixture, distributing it well.
8. Pour in the beaten egg and mould the mixture well together.
9. Form into 16 (or 32) balls then slightly flatten each.
10. Heat enough soya oil in a large frying pan to reach half-way up the rice balls.
11. Fry, a few at a time, briskly in hot oil, turning them over when the underside is crisp and golden brown. Drain on absorbent kitchen paper.

Note for vegans: Omit the egg and blend 1 tablespoon buckwheat flour with a little water to a smooth paste. Stir into the mixture to bind.

SWEET RICE BALLS

Other than for rice pudding, rice is very rarely used in the west as a dessert. Try these unusual and delicious sweet rice balls and experiment with other fruit and spices to add a variety of flavours to the mixture, e.g. dried apples soaked and chopped with cinnamon and a little clove powder instead of the apricots and ginger in the recipe.

Start this recipe the day before.

Makes 16.

225g/8 oz Italian short grain brown rice
110g/4 oz raisins
2 tablespoons lemon juice
2 knobs of stem ginger (bought in a jar), finely
   chopped
2 level tablespoons honey or no-sugar apricot
   jam
55g/2 oz dried apricots or dried mango pieces
110g/4 oz flaked almonds, toasted under a grill
   and crushed

1. Cook the rice as directed on page 80, but leave the lid on the saucepan for 10 minutes after cooking. The water should all be absorbed. Cool in a colander then put into a food processor and process for a few seconds to break up the grains a little. Scoop into a bowl, cover and leave to chill overnight in the fridge.
2. Put raisins, lemon juice, ginger and jam or honey in a small bowl and marinate overnight.
3. Soak apricots or mango pieces in water overnight.
4. Next day chop the soaked, drained apricots or mango pieces into smaller bits.
5. Knead and mould the cold rice and then add all the other ingredients, blending them well into the rice.

6. Form into 16 balls.
7. Chill before serving.

STUFFED CABBAGE, SPINACH OR VINE LEAVES
Delicious hot or cold.

Serves 5 (30 parcels).

340g/12 oz long thin brown rice, washed and
*   soaked in water for 2 hours*
1 level teaspoon sea salt
3 tablespoons sunflower or virgin olive oil
225g/8 oz onion (weight when peeled and finely
*   chopped)*
1 large clove garlic, crushed
170g/6 oz small mushrooms, chopped finely
3 tablespoons parsley, finely chopped
1 very level teaspoon allspice, finely ground
1 very level teaspoon ground cinnamon
¼ teaspoon cayenne pepper
1 level teaspoon dried tarragon or dill weed
2 rounded tablespoons tomato purée
85g/3 oz raisins, chopped
85g/3 oz pine nuts (use chopped, flaked
*   almonds if you can't get pine nuts)*
340g/12 oz vine leaves (soaked in boiling water
*   for 5 minutes, then rinsed in cold water) OR*
*   30 spinach leaves (blanched for 2 minutes in*
*   boiling water) OR 30 cabbage leaves*
*   (blanched for 5 minutes in boiling water)*
boiling water to just cover the stuffed leaves
*   when packed in the baking dish – to every*
*   570ml/1 pt water add 2 tablespoons lemon*
*   juice and 1 level dessertspoon vegetable*
*   bouillon powder*

1. Drain the rice and rinse in a sieve with cold water. Drain well again.
2. To each cup of soaked and drained rice add 1 cup of boiling water.
3. Bring back to boil, add 1 level teaspoon sea salt, turn down to simmer, cover with a tight lid and cook for 15 minutes.
4. Put rice in a sieve and leave on one side.
5. Heat oil in a frying pan and sauté the onion and garlic in the oil for 3 minutes only.
6. Add the mushrooms, parsley, spices and dill or tarragon and continue to sauté for 2 minutes more.

7. Stir in the tomato purée, raisins and pine nuts and stir, as you merge the ingredients together over the heat, for 30 seconds.
8. Put drained rice in a mixing bowl and stir in the sautéed mixture (taste and, if needed, add a little sea salt).
9. Place a dessertspoon of the mixture (according to the size of the leaf) in the centre of each prepared leaf (vine, spinach or cabbage). Fold over the sides of the leaf then roll up into a parcel.
10. Place these parcels, packed well together in a large heavy-based frying pan (with a lid). If you have two layers then separate the layers with a layer of unstuffed leaves.
11. Pour on enough of the seasoned boiling water to just cover the parcels.
12. Place a heat-proof plate bottom side up on top of the parcels, cover the pan with the lid and simmer very gently for 1 hour if using vine leaves and 30 minutes if using spinach or cabbage leaves.

SAFFRON RICE WITH NUTS AND SWEETCORN
Children and adults alike love this simple rice dish.

Serves 4.

340g/12 oz long thin brown rice (see page 79
*   for varieties of this rice)*
2 tablespoons sunflower oil
225g/8 oz onion, peeled and chopped
good pinch saffron or 1 level teaspoon turmeric
thin strip of lime or lemon peel
850ml/1½ pt boiling water
1 level tablespoon vegetable bouillon powder
120g/6 oz fresh (frozen will do) peas, lightly
*   cooked*
110g/4 oz sweet corn kernels, lightly cooked
85g/3 oz pistachio nuts (you can use cashew
*   nuts but toast lightly first)*
1 tablespoon lime or lemon juice
1 tablespoon shoyu (naturally fermented soy
*   sauce)*
2 tablespoons fresh parsley, finely chopped to
*   garnish*

1. Wash rice well by letting cold water run through the grains in a sieve for 1 minute. Drain well.
2. Heat the oil in a large heavy-based saucepan and sauté the onion in the oil for 10 minutes with the lid on.
3. Stir in the rice and saffron and cook on a low heat for 2 minutes, stirring to coat the grains evenly.
4. Add lime or lemon peel, boiling water and vegetable bouillon powder. Bring to boil, turn down to simmer and cook with the lid on for 25 minutes.
5. Turn rice into a colander and leave to steam off and cool.
6. Put cooled rice into a serving dish and fork in the peas, sweet corn, nuts, lime juice and shoyu.
7. Sprinkle on a little chopped parsley to garnish.

MEXICAN VEGETABLE RICE
This is a fiery and flavoursome rice dish, which is great for a buffet party.

Serves 12.

675g/1½ lb long grain Italian brown rice
4 tablespoons sunflower oil or virgin olive oil
450g/1 lb onion, finely chopped
4 fresh green chillies, finely chopped
curl of lime peel
2 level tablespoons tomato purée
1.7 litre/3 pt hot water
1 level tablespoon vegetable bouillon powder
170g/6 oz frozen sweetcorn, cooked for 2 minutes only
170g/6 oz frozen peas, lightly cooked
1 tablespoon fresh chopped coriander leaves or parsley, finely chopped
2 tablespoons lime juice
2 tablespoons shoyu (naturally fermented soy sauce)
twists of sliced lime and sprigs of either flat-leafed parsley or coriander leaves, to garnish

1. Wash the rice well and drain. Heat the oil in a very large heavy-based saucepan and sauté the onion for 10 minutes until soft and golden brown (not burnt).

2. Stir in the drained rice and cook on a low heat, stirring constantly, to coat all the grains.
3. Add the chillies, lime peel, tomato purée, hot water and vegetable bouillon powder. Bring to the boil, turn down heat and simmer with a tight lid on for 35 minutes, by which time all the water should have been absorbed.
4. Leave the lid on for 5 minutes after cooking then turn into a colander and leave for a further 5 minutes to let the steam off.
5. Transfer to a serving dish, stir in the sweetcorn, peas and chopped parsley or coriander.
6. Blend the shoyu with the lime juice and fork into the rice.
7. Garnish with the lime twists and the flat-leafed parsley or coriander leaves.

CHINESE RICE WITH ARAME, ALMONDS AND PEAS
A beautiful and simple dish to prepare. Arame is a seaweed (see page 145 for more information).

Serves 4.

14g/½ oz arame
225g/8 oz long thin brown rice, either Surinam, American or Australian, cooked (see page 79 on how to cook)
1 large onion, chopped
2 tablespoons either sesame, safflower or sunflower oil
1 level teaspoon ground coriander
75g/3 oz blanched whole or split almonds
110g/4 oz frozen peas, cooked for 2 minutes only and drained
1 tablespoon shoyu (naturally fermented soy sauce)
1 tablespoon lemon juice (optional)

1. Soak the arame in hot water for 15 minutes then squeeze.
2. Cook the rice as directed for 25 minutes. All the water should be absorbed (if not then drain). Spread rice out on a large baking tray to let the steam off.
3. Sauté the onion in the oil until soft and very lightly browned.

4. Add the coriander, almonds and arame and fry for 3 minutes.
5. Add the rice and stir as you fry for 1 minute then stir in the peas, shoyu and lemon juice and heat through.

MILLET AND CHEESE CROQUETTES

These are children's favourites. I've fed lots of finicky children but none have refused these yet.

Makes 12.

225g/8 oz millet, cooked (see page 81)
110g/4 oz Cheddar cheese, grated
1 level dessertspoon dried sage
1 medium onion, peeled, chopped, sautéed for 10 minutes
½ level tablespoon cayenne pepper (optional)
1 large egg yolk to bind
egg white well whisked to coat
soya oil for frying

1. When the millet is cooked and still hot add the cheese, sage, onion and cayenne pepper, if using.
2. Mix well together then add the egg yolk and press the mixture firmly together as you would a dough.
3. Form into 12 balls, flatten slightly and brush with a little well beaten egg white (this stops the millet breaking up and the oil spitting when frying).
4. Heat 5 cm/2 inch soya oil in a large non-stick or heavy-based frying pan. When hot (as for chips) fry the croquettes on moderate heat until golden on both sides.
5. Drain on absorbent kitchen paper.
6. Serve with one of the delicious chutneys on pages 176 to 178 and a fresh salad.

MILLET AND SEED CROQUETTES

Makes 12.

Omit the cheese and the egg from the previous recipe and add 110g/4 oz lightly toasted and very finely ground sunflower or sesame seeds. Add a rounded teaspoon of vegetable bouillon powder to the ground seeds before moulding into the millet and onion mixture.

Mould really well. Form into very flat rounds and fry in a large heavy-based pan a few at a time in about 4 tablespoons hot soya oil until golden on both sides. Drain and serve.

MILLET, VEGETABLE AND CHEESE PILAF

Serves 6.
You will need a large casserole dish well greased and with a tight lid.

2 tablespoons sunflower or corn oil
225g/8 oz millet
2 medium carrots, scraped and cut into 2.5 cm/ 1 inch thin slices
225g/8 oz onion (weight when peeled and chopped)
1 large clove garlic, crushed
1 small red pepper, deseeded and finely chopped
170g/6 oz button mushrooms, sliced
2 tablespoons parsley, chopped
1 rounded teaspoon dried marjoram or 1 rounded tablespoon fresh leaves chopped
1 teaspoon dried lemon thyme
½ level teaspoon cayenne pepper
850ml/1½ pt boiling water
1 rounded tablespoon vegetable bouillon powder or 1½ vegetable stock cubes
1 tablespoon lemon juice
110g/4 oz very thin slices of Farmhouse Cheddar cheese or Mozzarella
3 medium tomatoes, thinly sliced
sprinkling of dried oregano

1. Preheat oven to 325°F/160°C/Gas Mark 3.
2. Spread the millet out on a baking sheet and toast in the oven 325°F/160°C/Gas Mark 3 for 20 minutes. Turn heat off and leave millet in the warm oven until needed.
3. Heat the oil in a large heavy-based frying pan and sauté the carrots, onion and garlic for 5 minutes.
4. Add the red pepper and mushrooms and continue to fry for 3 minutes more.
5. Stir in the parsley, marjoram, lemon thyme and cayenne pepper and cook gently for 30 seconds.
6. Put the toasted millet in the casserole dish.
7. Dissolve the vegetable bouillon powder or stock cubes in the boiling water and pour this into the millet mixture.
8. Add the lemon juice.
9. Lay slices of cheese on top and then the slices of tomato (don't worry if they sink, they float to the top during cooking time).
10. Sprinkle on a little dried oregano, cover with a lid or foil sealing the edges well.
11. Turn oven up to 350°F/180°C/Gas Mark 4 and bake in the centre for 1 hour.
12. To crisp the top place under a moderately heated grill until golden brown.

TABBOULEH BULGUR SALAD

This wonderful Lebanese salad is great for buffet parties. It is best left for 24 hours to marinate in the dressing. Treble the recipe if catering for a large party.

Serves 6 to 8.

225g/8 oz bulgur
330ml/12 fl oz boiling water
2 level teaspoons vegetable bouillon powder
4 tablespoons virgin olive oil
2 tablespoons lemon juice
¼ teaspoon black pepper, freshly ground
2 cloves garlic, crushed
½ teaspoon honey
½ teaspoon dry mustard powder
4 tablespoons parsley, very finely chopped
110g/4 oz spring onions (use green ends as well), very finely chopped

1 dessertspoon fresh mint, finely chopped
6 tomatoes, cut in thin wedges
85g/3 oz pine nuts (save a few to garnish)
crisp lettuce leaves and mint sprigs to garnish

1. Place bulgur in a large mixing bowl and pour on the boiling water. Cover and allow to stand for 20 minutes.
2. Blend vegetable bouillon powder, oil, lemon juice, black pepper, garlic, honey and mustard powder. Shake the ingredients well together and stir into the bulgur.
3. When the mixture is cold then add the parsley, spring onions and mint.
4. Stir well together, cover and leave overnight to marinate.
5. One hour before serving stir in the tomatoes and most of the pine nuts.
6. Spoon the salad into a large shallow serving dish, sprinkle on the few pine nuts and dot with sprigs of mint. Surround the edges with crisp lettuce leaves.

ARABIAN COUSCOUS

This traditional Middle Eastern dish is usually made with couscous which is a grain similar to bulgur, but it is processed and not as nutritionally valuable as bulgur. A couscousier is used to cook the dish but a muslin-lined steamer or snug fitting muslin-lined colander placed on top of a deep saucepan will be just as good. Also the stew mixture usually includes meat but I think you will find the vegetable mixture with chick peas equally delicious. The list of ingredients is long but all are easily available and not expensive.

Serves 4 to 6.

340g/12 oz bulgur
2 tablespoons virgin olive oil or sunflower oil
good pinch sea salt
3 tablespoons virgin olive oil
225g/8 oz onion (weight when peeled and chopped)
2 large cloves garlic, crushed
3 medium carrots, scraped and cut into 1 cm/ ½ inch slanting ovals

1 kohlrabi or turnip (about the size of a tennis
   ball), peeled and coarsely chopped
small bulb of fennel, chopped
4 good size sticks celery, chopped
½ large red and ½ large green pepper,
   deseeded and cut in thickish strips
3 medium size courgettes, cut into 2 cm/¾ inch
   chunks
1 rounded teaspoon coriander seeds, ground
1 rounded teaspoon cumin seeds, ground
1 level teaspoon turmeric
½ teaspoon mustard seeds, crushed
1 scant teaspoon cayenne pepper
1 cinnamon stick
395g/14 oz can tomatoes (use fresh ripe
   tomatoes, skinned and chopped if in season)
1 rounded tablespoon tomato purée
110g/4 oz sultanas or raisins
425ml/¾ pt water
1 tablespoon lemon juice
1 rounded teaspoon vegetable bouillon powder
140g/5 oz dry weight chick peas, soaked,
   cooked and drained (see page 100)

1. Rinse the bulgur by putting in a sieve
   and letting cold water run through the
   grains. Drain well.
2. Put in a bowl and rub in the oil and a
   good pinch sea salt. Coat all the grains
   with the oil. Leave to one side.
3. Heat the oil in a large deep saucepan and
   stir-fry the onion, garlic, carrots and
   kohlrabi or turnip for 3 minutes, coating
   the vegetables well with the oil.
4. Add the fennel, celery, peppers and
   courgettes and stir-fry for 1 minute.
5. Make a well in the centre and drop 2
   teaspoons more oil into the pan. Fry the
   spices in this for 1 minute (do not burn).
   Add the cinnamon stick and stir the
   spices into the vegetables coating them
   well.
6. Stir in the chopped tomatoes, the tomato
   purée, raisins or sultanas, water, lemon
   juice, vegetable bouillon powder and the
   drained chick peas.
7. Bring to boil stirring as you do this, then
   turn down to simmer.
8. Place the oil-soaked bulgur into the lined
   steamer or colander and put on top of the
   stew-filled saucepan.

9. Cover and simmer for 30 minutes (if
   using a colander then make sure the
   edges are sealed. You can do this by
   placing foil over the colander and down
   the sides of the saucepan).
10. To serve spoon the bulgur onto a large
    shallow serving dish, make a big well in
    the centre and spoon in the stew.
    Cucumber, yoghurt and mint bowl cooler
    (see page 159) and a light green salad
    are superb accompaniments for a very
    special meal.

TOASTED BUCKWHEAT WITH PIQUANT SAUCE AND TAMARI SUNFLOWER SEEDS

Buckwheat has a very distinctive flavour and
it is greatly complemented by this piquant
vegetable sauce. Have the sauce cooked before
you cook the buckwheat.

Serves 4.

225g/8 oz ready-toasted buckwheat, cooked (see
   page 82)
225g/8 oz onion, peeled and finely chopped
1 large clove garlic, crushed
2 tablespoons sunflower or virgin olive oil
3 medium size courgettes, cut in thin 2 cm/
   ¾ inch sticks
1 good size green pepper, deseeded and finely
   chopped
1 level teaspoon celery seeds, crushed
1 large bay leaf
1 level teaspoon coriander seeds, ground
340g/12 oz ripe tomatoes, skinned and chopped
   (canned will do)
1 level teaspoon paprika
½ cinnamon stick
1 teaspoon Worcester sauce
1 tablespoon lemon juice
1 teaspoon chopped mint leaves (optional)
110g/4 oz Tamari sunflower seeds (see recipe
   on page 92)

1. Sauté the onion and garlic in the oil for 6
   minutes with the lid on.
2. Add the courgettes, green pepper, celery
   seeds, bay leaf, coriander and cook for 4
   minutes more.
3. Add tomatoes, paprika, cinnamon stick,
   Worcester sauce, lemon juice and mint.

4. Serve the buckwheat and the sauce in separate bowls. Also have the tamari sunflower seeds in a small bowl ready to be sprinkled on the individual servings.

Note: You can use many sauces with buckwheat such as *Tomato sauce* (see page 173), *Vegetable bolognese sauce* (see page 135) or even curry or sweet and sour vegetable sauces. In fact all sauces or vegetables that go with boiled rice will be good with buckwheat.

TAMARI (OR SHOYU) SUNFLOWER SEEDS

Make any quantity you wish.

Set oven at 325°F/160°C/Gas Mark 3. Put some sunflower seeds on a non-stick baking tray and toast in the centre of the oven for 10 minutes. Take out of the oven and sprinkle a little tamari or shoyu sauce over the hot seeds. Stir with a wooden spoon to coat all seeds. Then return to the oven and continue to toast for 10 minutes more.

Let get cold on the tray and store any you are not using immediately in a screw top jar. Children love these for snacks.

ITALIAN POLENTA

This is a lovely meal but you have to be careful not to make the polenta (cornmeal) base soggy, so measure the water content carefully.

Serves 4.
You will need large deep ovenproof dish, greased (square is best)

225g/8 oz cornmeal (polenta)
1 level teaspoon sea salt
285ml/½ pt cold water
570ml/1 pt boiling water
2 tablespoons sunflower oil
225g/8 oz onion, peeled and chopped
2 cloves garlic, crushed
1 large green pepper, deseeded and chopped
170g/6 oz aubergine, chopped
1 medium courgette, sliced
110g/4 oz mushrooms, sliced
1 level teaspoon dried mint
1 level teaspoon celery seeds, crushed

1 rounded teaspoon vegetable bouillon powder
¼ teaspoon black pepper, freshly ground
396g/14 oz can tomatoes, chopped
2 tablespoons tomato purée
55g/2 oz flaked almonds or sunflower seeds
140g/5 oz either Farmhouse Cheddar or Mozzarella cheese, grated

1. Preheat oven 375°F/190°C/Gas Mark 5.
2. Mix the cornmeal (polenta) with the salt and the cold water to a smooth paste.
3. Put the boiling water in a medium-size saucepan. Stir in the cornmeal mixture. Keep stirring until well blended and smooth.
4. Bring to boil stirring continuously and simmer on very low heat for 5 minutes. Stir once or twice while cooking to prevent sticking.
5. Spoon onto the base of the greased dish and smooth the surface with the back of the spoon.
6. Sauté the onion and garlic for 7 minutes with the lid on.
7. Add the green pepper, courgette, aubergine and mushrooms. Continue to fry for 3 minutes more.
8. Add the mint, celery seeds, vegetable bouillon powder and pepper. Stir well and cook for 2 minutes more.
9. Now add the tomatoes, purée and almonds or sunflower seeds.
10. Simmer for 15 minutes with the lid on. Spoon this mixture over the cornmeal (polenta).
11. Sprinkle on the cheese and bake for 30 minutes in the centre of the oven.

NUT, SEED AND BULGUR ROAST

This delicious roast can be eaten hot as a main dish, accompanied with the *Vegetable gravy* on page 170, roast potatoes, lightly steamed vegetables and *Brandied cranberry and apple sauce* (see page 178). You could also accompany it with either the *Tomato sauce* on page 173 or even better the *Leek and tarragon sauce* on page 173. If serving with roast potatoes then par-boil the potatoes in the vegetable gravy stock for 10 minutes before roasting. It adds flavour to the stock as well as the potatoes.

Serves 6.

110g/4 oz bulgur
170ml/6 fl oz boiling water
2 tablespoons shoyu (naturally fermented soy
   sauce)
110g/4 oz almonds
110g/4 oz cashew nuts
110g/4 oz hazel nuts
55g/2 oz pumpkin seeds
55g/2 oz sunflower seeds
170g/6 oz onion, peeled and finely chopped
3 tablespoons fresh parsley, finely chopped
1 teaspoon lemon thyme or marjoram
2 large eggs, beaten
3 tablespoons sunflower oil
few pumpkin seeds to top

1. Preheat oven 375°F/190°C/Gas Mark 5.
2. Put the bulgur into a small mixing bowl, add the boiling water and shoyu. Cover and allow to stand for 30 minutes.
3. Grind the nuts and seeds to a medium-fine crumb consistency (not too powdery).
4. Mix all the ingredients together except 1 tablespoon of the oil. Mould well with your hands and form into a loaf shape.
5. Place the loaf in an oiled roasting tin, sprinkle on the pumpkin seeds pressing them gently into the top of the loaf.
6. Prick the top with a fork and pour the remaining tablespoon of oil over the top.
7. Cap loosely with a foil hood.
8. Bake in the centre of the oven for 35 minutes. Take off hood and bake for 10 minutes more.

NUT, SEED AND BULGUR RISSOLES
Makes 12.

Make up the *Nut, seed and bulgur roast* ingredients moulding them well together. Form into 12 rissole shapes 1 cm/½ inch thick. Fry gently in a little soya oil for 5 minutes on each side until golden brown.

   Serve with either a *Tomato Sauce* (see page 173) or *Leek and tarragon sauce* (see page 173), jacket potatoes and lightly steamed vegetables or a salad.

Note for vegans: Omit the eggs in the mixture and blend 1 rounded tablespoon buckwheat flour with a little water to a smooth paste and blend in with the ingredients. It will bind together very well.

NUTTY STUFFED MARROW IN PIQUANT CHILLI TOMATO SAUCE

If you are fortunate enough to grow your own vegetables and have an overgrown courgette, especially the more tender golden variety, then you can use this instead of a marrow.

Serves 4.
You will need a large deep oval flameproof casserole dish.

1 recipe quantity Piquant chilli tomato sauce
   (see page 174)
2 x 900g/2 lb marrows or 2 overgrown
   courgettes
2 tablespoons cold pressed sunflower oil
2 medium size onions, finely chopped
4 level tablespoons fresh chopped parsley
170g/6 oz medium finely ground almonds
110g/4 oz medium finely ground cashew nuts
140g/5 oz wholemeal breadcrumbs
2 teaspoons vegetable bouillon powder
2 small eggs
110g/4 oz either grated Cheddar or Parmesan
   cheese
good pinch dried oregano

1. Preheat oven 375°F/190°C/Gas Mark 5.
2. Trim stalks off marrows. Cut each in half lengthwise and scoop out the seeds.
3. Bring half a large saucepan of water to boil and cook the marrows for 10 minutes.

4. Drain well on a wire rack, skin side up, while you make the filling and sauce.
5. Heat oil in a large frying pan. Sauté the onion for 5 minutes on low heat with the lid on. Put parsley, nuts, breadcrumbs, bouillon powder and eggs in a mixing bowl.
6. Stir in the sautéed onions and bind well together.
7. Put the drained marrow halves in a greased ovenproof dish. Divide the filling and stuff this into the hollows of each marrow.
8. Spoon over the tomato sauce and sprinkle on the cheese and the oregano.
9. Bake for approximately 25 minutes until the cheese is golden brown.
10. Serve with fresh salad.

Note for vegans: Omit the eggs from the filling and add 1 level tablespoon buckwheat flour, blended with a little water, to bind the nut mixture. Also omit the cheese and arrange thin slices of firm tofu on top instead.

NUTTY PATE
Great as a dip, stuffed in *Pitta bread* (see page 19) or in sandwiches with salad vegetables. The nuts and seeds can vary. For a more exotic pâté use some pistachios and pine nuts.

Serves 6 to 8.

340g/12 oz mixed nuts and seeds (basic choice is almonds, hazels, cashews, sesame, sunflower and pumpkin seeds)
4 tablespoons sunflower oil
4 rounded tablespoons Greek yoghurt
1 tablespoon shoyu or tamari
1 small bunch spring onions, finely chopped (use green ends as well)
1 level teaspoon celery seeds, finely ground
1 rounded teaspoon mixed dried herbs
1 rounded tablespoon very finely chopped red pepper
1 rounded tablespoon very finely chopped green pepper
freshly ground black pepper to taste

1. Toast the nuts and seeds in a wide heavy-based pan over moderate heat stirring

constantly with a wooden spoon for 6 minutes.
2. Grind toasted nuts and seeds to a powder in a processor or liquidizer and continue to process until they exude a little oil and begin to stick together.
3. Add the oil and yoghurt and blend until smooth.
4. Add the rest of the ingredients and blend for a few seconds until well merged. Scoop out and place in a serving dish. This will keep for several days in the fridge. Keep it covered. It will also freeze well.

MUSHROOM, HAZELNUT AND CHEESE PATE
Serves 6 to 8.

110g/4 oz hazelnuts
1 leek, trimmed and very finely chopped
1 clove garlic, crushed
2 tablespoons virgin olive oil
225g/8 oz button mushrooms, very finely chopped
1 rounded teaspoon vegetable bouillon powder
¼ teaspoon freshly ground black pepper
3 level tablespoons very finely chopped parsley
1 level teaspoon celery seeds, finely crushed
1 level teaspoon dried tarragon
1 level tablespoon agar agar flakes
2 tablespoons sherry
1½ tablespoons lemon juice
110g/4 oz Greek yoghurt
110g/4 oz quark
sprigs of watercress and dried mushrooms (marinated in lemon juice, soy sauce and honey) to garnish

1. Toast the hazelnuts in the oven 325°F/160°C/Gas Mark 3 for 20 minutes. Rub off as much of the skins as possible and grind the nuts to a smooth thick paste.
2. Sauté the leek and garlic in the oil on a very low heat with the lid on the pan for 5 minutes (do not burn).
3. Add the mushrooms and cook on a low heat for 2 minutes until soft.
4. Stir in the vegetable bouillon powder, black pepper, parsley, celery seeds and tarragon and continue to cook for 1 minute. Stir in the yoghurt, quark and hazelnuts. Take off heat.

5. Put sherry and lemon juice in a small saucepan and heat to boiling. Turn down heat and stir in the agar agar flakes then stir on a low heat until dissolved. Stir this into the mushroom mixture. Blend well in.
6. Spoon into individual ramekin or small brioche fluted moulds or one large mould.
7. Let get completely cold then chill for about 2 hours until set. Turn out onto a serving dish and surround with sprigs of watercress and marinated mushrooms. (If the pâté will not loosen from the mould then dip mould in hot water for a few seconds to loosen.)

MUSHROOM, HAZELNUT AND TOFU PATE
This is a vegan variation on the previous recipe.

Omit the yoghurt and quark from the previous recipe and stir in 225g/8 oz firm tofu plus 1 extra tablespoon lemon juice instead.

NUT, SEED AND FRUIT FINGERS OR BALLS
These are great as a sweet treat for packed lunches. Try to obtain rice paper for the fingers and wrap them in cellophane, screwing up each end like a large toffee. The balls are delicious rolled in either coconut or lightly toasted sesame seeds. You can use any dried fruit, nut and seed mixture – the recipe is just a guide-line.

225g/8 oz dates
110g/4 oz dried apricots, well washed
225g/8 oz raisins
225g/8 oz mixed nuts and seeds (hazels, almonds, sunflower seeds and pumpkin seeds)
a few toasted sesame seeds or rice paper

1. Steam the dates and apricots for twenty minutes (put the apricots at the bottom). Pat dry.
2. Put all the ingredients, except the toasted sesame seeds and rice paper, through a mincer then knead together for 1 minute.
3. If forming into fingers then lay one sheet of rice paper on a baking sheet. Spread the mixture on top about 15 mm/⅓ inch thick.

Lay another sheet of rice paper on top and press in gently.
4. If not using rice paper then cut the mixture into fingers and coat with lightly toasted sesame seeds. Wrap in cellophane and store in an airtight container in the fridge.
5. If forming into balls then roll the mixture into walnut size balls and roll in desiccated coconut, pressing the coconut in gently. Lay these on sheets of greaseproof paper in an airtight container and store in the fridge.

GOMASIO (TOASTED SESAME SEED AND SALT CONDIMENT)
This is a delicious condiment and much better than using neat salt on scrambled, poached or fried eggs or sprinkled on dishes such as shepherd's pie instead of cheese if your diet is vegan.

Some recipes for this say one part sea salt to ten parts toasted sesame seeds but I prefer one part salt to about sixteen parts seeds. You can vary this according to what you are using it for. Make a first batch using the following as a trial. You can add favourite dried herbs to make an extra tasty condiment.

10 rounded tablespoons sesame seeds
1 rounded dessertspoon sea salt

1. Toast the seeds in a wide bottomed heavy-based frying pan stirring constantly on moderate heat until the seeds start to pop and become a rich deep golden brown (do not burn).
2. Place in a blender with the salt and process on high speed until powdery. Store in an airtight container in the fridge. It will last 2 months in these conditions.

HERBY GOMASIO
Add ½ teaspoon each of dried basil, tarragon, marjoram and garlic powder plus 1 level teaspoon finely ground celery seeds to the previous recipe for a superb condiment.

GLUTEN (WHEAT PROTEIN)

Wheat gluten is a rich protein food which is mainly used in Japan and China. You can buy it canned in the West, disguised with fish and meat-type flavours, but I think this nutritious protein deserves to be recognised as a food in its own right and not as a substitute for other protein foods. It has a meat-like chewiness and its porous texture absorbs flavours from stock, vegetables, herbs and spices. For best results make using strong wholemeal flour. Strong flour comes from hard wheat which contains more protein than soft wheat. You can make gluten from white flour, but using 100 per cent wholemeal means that you not only get a rich protein food but one high in fibre and wheatgerm.

Although a high protein food, gluten is not a complete protein (see notes on complete protein, page 11), but as you are unlikely to eat it on its own it is easy to complement it with other protein-rich foods which will balance its amino acid content. Combined with legumes (dried peas, beans and lentils) nuts and seeds or cheese it will achieve the correct balance.

When extracted from flour, gluten, which feels sponge-like and should stretch like bubble-gum, is usually pre-cooked before using in a dish. This can be done by either frying, baking, boiling in a savoury stock or steaming. I prefer to fry or bake it as this gives a crispy coating and a firmer texture. It is important to break the gluten rather than cut it before you pre-cook, or the texture will become bread-like rather than chewy. Whatever pre-cooked gluten you do not require will freeze well in polythene bags, so make plenty at one time. To defrost, simply drop into hot savoury stock and cook for 4 to 5 minutes. After pre-cooking, the gluten is ready to either mince, slice or cut into bite-sized pieces to use in a variety of interesting and well-flavoured dishes.

RAW GLUTEN
This quantity will make enough gluten for three meals for four people. I use approximately eight to ten pre-cooked balls for four servings.

900g/2 lb strong wholemeal flour, plain
570ml/1 pt water

1. Put flour in a large mixing bowl, make a well in the centre and slowly pour water in, mixing as you do so to form a medium-firm unsticky dough.
2. Knead for about 12 to 15 minutes (the longer the better). Place in a clean bowl, cover and let stand for 45 minutes. Knead dough for a further 15 minutes.
3. Put back into the clean bowl and gently pour cold water over the dough to cover it completely. Let stand for about 4 to 6 hours (you can leave overnight).
4. Now begin to knead and squeeze it under the water as if it were a sponge, being careful to hold the gluten together as you extract the starch. Keep changing the water as it becomes milky from the starch. When the water is almost clear you will have a soft rubbery, pliable ball of raw gluten. Let this drain for 10 minutes.

FRIED GLUTEN BALLS
These balls are cooked for only 5 minutes after which they are ready to mince or cut, depending on which recipe you choose.

Makes approximately 30.

1 recipe quantity Raw gluten (see above)
soya or sunflower oil for deep frying

1. Pour oil into a wok or frying pan and heat gently.
2. Do not cut the raw gluten dough but break off pieces to mould into 2.5 cm/ 1 inch balls, making them as round and smooth as possible. When the oil is hot fry only 4 or 5 balls at a time allowing space for them to expand. Baste the balls continuously. They must cook for 5 minutes without browning too much. If cooked too quickly they will not expand, so keep heat at a fairly low temperature.

COUNTRY CASSEROLE WITH GLUTEN

Serves 4.

Follow the recipe for *Soya chunk and vegetable casserole* on page 138, but use 10 *Fried gluten balls* (see page 96) instead of the soya chunks. Cut the balls into bite-size pieces and fry these with the onion for 2 minutes.

CHILLI BEANS WITH MINCED GLUTEN
Serves 4.

Follow the recipe for *Chillied kidney beans* on page 107, but omit the bulgur and use 225g/ 8 oz *Fried gluten balls* (see page 96), minced, instead. Add this to the sautèed onion and garlic and fry for 2 minutes.

CURRIED GLUTEN
Gluten is delicious in any curry sauce. Try it with *Molee curry sauce* (see page 175), adding 10 *Fried gluten balls* (see page 96) to every 270ml/1 pt sauce. Slice the gluten into thinnish slithers and add to the sauce 10 minutes before the end of its cooking time. You can also make *Soya chunk korma* (see page 138) using 240g/12 oz *Fried gluten balls* instead of the soya chunks. Cut the balls into bite-size pieces and fry these with the onion for 2 minutes.

GLUTEN RIBS WITH BARBECUE SAUCE
Serves 4.

Raw gluten (see page 96) can be moulded with sautéed onion, herbs, spices and a little shoya (soy sauce), then fried or baked. Put 225g/8 oz raw gluten in a bowl. Add 2 level tablespoons sunflower seed spread, 110g/4 oz finely chopped onion, 1 crushed clove garlic and 1 tablespoon shoyu. Add herbs and spices if you wish and mould well together for 2 minutes. Break off pieces of the mixture and shape these into strips 2.5 cm/1 inch wide × 1.25 cm/ ½ inch thick × 7.5 cm/3 inch long. Place on a baking tray, sprinkle on a little oil and bake uncovered at 180°C/350°F/Gas Mark 4 for 35 minutes. Then pour over 570ml/1 pt *Barbecue sauce* (see page 174) and bake for a further 10 minutes.

LESSON 5

PULSES

This lesson includes a variety of dishes from all parts of the globe and will, I hope, bring many delightful flavours to your table. Read all the information about the individual pulses and follow carefully the instructions for soaking and cooking.

SHOPPING LIST

Check oils used in previous lessons, especially virgin olive and sunflower oil. Check all herbs and spices used in previous lessons as you will need most of them for this lesson. Also check vegetable bouillon powder or vegetable stock cubes and shoyu (naturally fermented soy sauce) as these are used extensively throughout the lesson. Now stock up on plenty of the following:

aduki beans	black eyed beans
butter beans (or Lima beans)	red kidney beans
	mung beans
chick peas	pinto beans
haricot beans	cider vinegar
lentils and split peas (see page 101)	miso soya bean paste (see page 116)
T.V.P. beef or natural flavour (see page 122)	

FACTS ABOUT PULSES

Beans, peas and lentils provide a good, cheap source of protein. The protein content ranges from 17 to 25 per cent with the exception of the soya bean which has approximately 38 per cent protein. I have devoted a complete lesson to the soya bean (see page 00) because of its outstanding nutritional qualities and variable uses. Pulses are also a very good source of vitamins and minerals, namely iron, calcium and vitamin B1, thiamine and niacin. Vitamin C is present only when the pulses are sprouted.

The protein in these wonderful dried vegetables used to be regarded as 'second-class'. Only soya bean protein contains all the amino acids which the body requires, but through much research it has been found that pulses used in combination with certain other foods will produce a complete protein with all the amino acids in balance (see page 11).

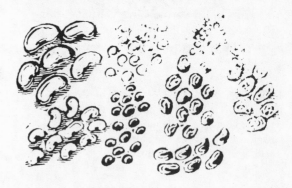

These foods are whole grains, nuts, seeds and all dairy produce. Using any of them with pulses will provide you with all the complete protein you need. If you make grains approximately 50 per cent of your main meal, nuts, seeds, beans or dairy produce 25 per cent and the remaining 25 per cent raw or steamed fresh vegetables, you will be eating enough well-balanced protein. This balancing is often instinctive and particularly apparent in traditional Eastern and Middle Eastern dishes. Unfortunately, with the increasing tendency to process wholefoods in the West, and to some extent in the East, we are in danger of clouding our instincts and our food is straying a long way from its natural state.

Eating more pulses and consequently a little less meat will help not only your purse and your health but our planet to survive. Remember that a harvest of soya beans from one acre of land will provide enough protein for one person for six years. The same harvest fed to animals will provide adequate protein for one human being for only eighty days.

SOAKING AND COOKING PULSES

All raw peas and beans (both fresh and dried) contain substances such as glycosides, saponins and alkaloids, which are harmful to digestion. When they are fresh just five minutes' cooking will be sufficient to render the substances harmless and when using the dried variety proper soaking, rinsing and cooking for the right length of time will stop any action of the poisonous substances.

As a general rule I soak all dried beans overnight, changing the water two or three times depending on the variety. I then drain off the water, rinse them well and add fresh water before cooking. This process inhibits the action of any adverse substances that could play havoc with your intestines. The cooking time will vary according to the size and variety of bean you are using. Lentils, and split peas other than whole brown lentils, do not need soaking but I pick them well over for small stones, as I do all beans, and wash them well. Do not add salt to beans until 10 minutes before the end of cooking time to prevent toughening of the outer skins. Never add bicarbonate of soda – it might soften the beans but it can kill valuable nutrients, as well as ruining their natural, individual and delicate flavours.

If beans are not stored properly in an airtight container away from direct sunlight, or are old stock, they will not only take ages to cook but will have absorbed moisture and smells from the atmosphere, which will make them unpleasant to taste. So be sure to get your pulses from a shop which has a quick turnover.

One last important point. Add pulses to your diet slowly. One new variety each week will help your body adjust to a new way of eating.

TYPES OF PULSE

ADUKI BEANS

'The King of Beans' is the grand title given to these little red beans by the Japanese. They originated in Japan and have been widely used there and in China for centuries, both for culinary and medicinal purposes. They are rich in protein, containing approximately 25 per cent, and have a good supply of the B vitamins, vitamin C, iron and calcium. The juice from the cooked bean is said to be a cure for kidney complaints and an aid to regulating the menstrual cycle. I found this variety comparatively easy to digest when I first began to incorporate pulses regularly into my daily diet, and its meaty taste went down well with the family.

Basic cooking method – Soak for four hours or overnight, changing the water once or twice. Rinse off the soaking water and add fresh water to cover before cooking. Boil for 10 minutes with the lid on, then simmer gently for a further 30 minutes. Add salt 10 minutes before the end of the cooking time. If these beans are very fresh they might take less time to cook as they are small and do not have a tough skin.

BLACK-EYED BEANS (OR PEAS)

These beans are a staple food in Africa. They have a distinctive, nutty flavour and go well in stuffed cabbage, spinach or vine leaves, as an alternative to the very expensive pine kernels which are often an ingredient in these recipes. They are also delicious in spicy dishes. They contain approximately 23 per cent protein and are well supplied with vitamins and minerals.

Basic cooking method – Soak overnight, changing the water twice, rinse and add fresh water to cook the beans. Bring to the boil and keep boiling with the lid on for 10 minutes, then simmer for a further 30 minutes or until soft. Add sea salt 10 minutes before the end of the cooking time.

BUTTER BEANS (OR LIMA BEANS – a smaller version)

As the name suggests, these beans originated

from Lima in Peru. I find they are very popular, probably because of their mild, buttery, potato flavour. They contain approximately 20 per cent protein and a good supply of vitamins and minerals.

Basic cooking method – It is very important to soak these particular beans overnight and change the soaking water three times. Rinse well after soaking and add fresh water to cook. Boil vigorously for 10 minutes then simmer for a further 40 minutes or until the beans are soft. They can go too mushy, so test after 35 minutes for softness.

The reason for extra care in cooking some beans such as these, red kidney beans and soya beans, is that some varieties have more adverse substances in them in their raw state than others. Do not be put off using them because of this. You will miss out, especially where the soya bean is concerned, on such a wonderful protein, vitamin and mineral boost to your diet. Just take care in the preparation and cooking and there will be no ill effects.

CHICK PEAS (OR GARBANZO PEAS)

These fabulous peas, thought to have originated in Western Asia, are one of my favourites. They are so versatile and tasty. Try the recipe for *Falafel* with a delicious sauce on page 104 and *Hummous* on page 104. They contain approximately 20 per cent protein and are well supplied with vitamins and minerals providing more iron and vitamin C than most other pulses.

Chick pea flour (gram flour) is fantastic used on its own or with soya and brown rice flour for battered vegetables (see page 169) or fish.

Basic cooking method – Soak overnight in plenty of water as they swell up more than most during soaking (change the water twice). Rinse well and add fresh water to cook. Boil for 10 minutes then simmer for 50 minutes. Add sea salt 10 minutes before the end of the cooking time. Taste one when they are cooked but don't let the family have any or you might find you have none left for your recipe!

FLAGEOLET BEANS

These are young kidney beans. They are delicate in flavour and absolutely delicious either eaten as a salad with French dressing or cooked in dishes. They contain reasonable amounts of protein, vitamins and minerals.

Basic cooking method – As these are not so widely used you have to be careful that these beans have not been on the shelf for too long a time. Soak overnight, change the water twice, rinse and add fresh water to cook. Boil for 5 minutes. Simmer for 40 minutes, but check after 30 minutes because if they are freshly dried they will cook quite quickly. Add only a very little salt just 10 minutes before the end of the cooking time. Search for these beans or pester your usual supplier. They are a real treat.

HARICOT BEANS (WHITE VARIETY)

These small, white, mild-flavoured beans are delicious as a replacement for soya beans in *Boston baked beans* (see page 123). I often use them in a mixed bean salad with red kidney beans but take care to cook them separately as they take longer than the red variety and take on a pinkish colour if cooked together, thus spoiling the look of the finished salad. They contain reasonable amounts of protein, vitamins and minerals.

Basic cooking method – Soak overnight or longer, change the water twice, drain, rinse and add fresh water to cook. Bring to the boil, let them boil for 10 minutes them simmer for 60 minutes more. Add sea salt 10 minutes before the cooking is finished.

KIDNEY BEANS (RED OR BLACK VARIETY)

These popular beans, often used in hot chilli dishes, have been cultivated in Mexico and South America for well over 7,000 years. Note the cooking instructions well as these beans contain more adverse substances than most pulses. Do not be put off using kidney beans because of this, however, as proper preparation and cooking will render the substances harmless. They contain approximately 22 per cent protein and are rich in vitamins and minerals.

Basic cooking method – Soak overnight, changing the water at least once. Rinse well and add fresh water to cook. Boil vigorously for 10 minutes, then simmer for a further 50 minutes. Sometimes these beans cook quite quickly so check after 40 minutes or you might find that they are overdone. You could end with mushy beans which are not good to use in salads. Salt the beans 10 minutes before the end of the cooking time.

MUNG BEANS

These are another of my favourite beans. They are great for sprouting – Chinese bean sprouts are mainly sprouted from mung beans. This bean originated in India and gradually spread throughout Asia. Like aduki beans they are easy to digest and need less soaking time than most beans. Their mild flavour makes them good beans to try if you are new to cooking pulses (see page 109 for a delicious *Mung bean shepherd's pie*). They contain approximately 24 per cent protein and a good supply of vitamins and minerals, particularly iron and vitamin C.

Green gram flour, made from mung beans, should not be confused with gram (chick pea) flour. It is great added to soups and in batter mixtures.

Basic cooking method – Soak for 4 hours or overnight changing the water once or twice. Rinse then cook in fresh water. Boil for 5 minutes them simmer for 30 minutes only.

PINTO BEANS

These lovely-flavoured, light brown, speckled beans are great in casseroles, bean salads and in the recipe for *Pinto bean and hazelnut loaf* (see page 110). They are similar in texture to butter beans but have a slightly stronger taste. They have been cultivated by North and South American Indians since prehistoric times. These beans contain reasonable amounts of protein, vitamins and minerals.

Basic cooking method – Soak overnight changing the water twice. Rinse well and cook in fresh water. Boil for 10 minutes then simmer for 40 minutes or until soft. Add sea salt 10 minutes before the end of cooking time.

LENTILS AND SPLIT PEAS

These types of pulse have no definite cooking times as they are invariably added to soups, rissoles and loaves or made into Indian dahl (thick or thin). Each recipe will give you cooking times and liquid amounts needed. There is a variety of types, of which some of the most common are:

Red split lentils – Most commonly used, this pulse lends itself to a huge variety of recipes including soups, rissoles, loaf bakes and Indian dhals. These were one of the first crops to be cultivated in the East and were introduced into America in the early twentieth century (about 1913). They contain approximately 25 per cent protein and a reasonable supply of vitamins and minerals.
Whole brown lentils – These lentils are unsplit and have their outer skins still on. I think they have much more flavour than the split lentils, but they need soaking before cooking. As long as you soak them you can cook and put into the same dishes as red split lentils. Simply soak for 2 hours in boiling water, drain, rinse well and cook as for red split lentils. They contain the same nutrients as red split lentils with just a little added fibre and a slightly spicy flavour.
Green lentils – These are sometimes more brown than green in colour. They are delicious made into a thick broth or used for a change of flavour when making dhal or any recipe where red split or whole brown lentils are used.

BEAN RECIPES

ADUKI BEAN BURGERS

These are a good alternative to beefburgers, served in wholemeal or wheatmeal baps with dollops of ketchup or *Barbecue sauce* (see page 174) and salad vegetables, or even better with *Mushroom sauce* (see page 173), baked jacket potatoes and lightly steamed vegetables or salad.

Makes 8.

85g/3 oz porridge oats
170g/6 oz aduki beans (dry weight), cooked (see page 99 for cooking instructions)
170g/6 oz onion, peeled and very finely chopped

*2 rounded tablespoons parsley, very finely
    chopped*
1 rounded teaspoon dried basil
1 large clove garlic, peeled and crushed
2 slightly rounded tablespoons tomato purée
*2 tablespoons shoyu (naturally fermented soy
    sauce)*
1 large egg, beaten
*½ very level teaspoon black pepper, freshly
    ground*
soya oil for frying the burgers

1. Spread the porridge oats on a baking tray
   and toast in the oven at 350°F/180°C/Gas
   Mark 4 for 10 minutes only.
2. Drain the cooked beans and mash them
   with a potato masher.
3. Mix all the ingredients together and
   mould well with your hands.
4. Form into 8 burgers 1 cm/½ inch thick.
5. Fry these in a little hot oil on moderate
   heat for 4 minutes on each side.

Note for vegans: Omit the egg and mix one
tablespoon buckwheat flour with a little water
and blend into the mixture.

ADUKI BEAN SHEPHERD'S PIE
Serves 4.

Follow the recipe for *Mung bean shepherd's
pie* (see page 109) but use cooked aduki beans
instead of mung beans.

ADUKI BEAN MOUSSAKA
Serves 4.

Follow the recipe for *Red bean moussaka* (see
page 108), but use cooked and drained aduki
beans instead of red kidney beans.

Also see the recipes for *Aduki bean pie* and
Aduki bean crumble on page 40.

SPICY BLACK-EYED BEANS
Serves 4.

*225g/8 oz black-eyed beans, cooked and
    drained (see page 99)*
3 tablespoons virgin olive oil or sunflower oil
225g/8 oz onion, peeled and finely chopped
2 large cloves garlic, crushed
1 large green pepper, deseeded and chopped
110g/4 oz mushrooms, chopped
1 rounded teaspoon ground coriander
1 level teaspoon ground cumin
½ teaspoon cayenne pepper
1 cinnamon stick
1 rounded teaspoon fresh ginger, finely grated
1 large bay leaf
1 rounded teaspoon methi (fenugreek leaf)
400g/14 oz can tomatoes, chopped
1 rounded tablespoon tomato purée
little sea salt to taste

1. Heat the oil in a large frying pan and
   sauté the onion and garlic for 7 minutes
   on low heat with the lid on.
2. Add the green pepper and the mushrooms
   and fry for 3 minutes more.
3. Add the spices, ginger, bay leaf and methi
   and cook for 1 minute stirring constantly.
4. Stir in the tomatoes and tomato purée and
   cook on very low heat with the lid on for
   15 minutes.
5. Taste and add a little sea salt if necessary.
6. Stir in the cooked and drained beans and
   heat through. Remove the bay leaf.
7. Serve on a bed of brown rice accompanied
   with a fresh salad.

BLACK-EYED BEAN MOUSSAKA
Serves 4.

In the recipe for *Red bean moussaka* (see page
108) use black-eyed beans instead of red
kidney beans.

BUTTER BEAN HOT POT
Serves 4.
You will need a casserole dish without a lid.

*225g/8 oz butter beans, soaked and cooked (see
    page 100 for cooking instructions)*
2 medium onions, peeled and finely chopped

3 sticks celery, finely chopped
2 tablespoons sunflower oil
1 tablespoon fresh parsley, chopped
1 level teaspoon dried rosemary or oregano
1 clove garlic, crushed
400g/14 oz can tomatoes, chopped
1 tablespoon shoyu (naturally fermented soy
*   sauce)*
freshly ground black pepper
900g/2 lb potatoes, steamed until cooked
110g/4 oz Cheddar cheese, grated

1. Set the oven to 375°F/190°C/Gas Mark 5. Cook the beans and reserve 140ml/¼ pint of the cooking liquid.
2. Put the cooked beans in the casserole dish with the cooking liquid.
3. Sauté the onion and celery in the oil for 5 minutes and add the parsley, rosemary or oregano and the garlic.
4. Stir well in, then add the tomatoes, shoyu and pepper.
5. Heat through and fork into the butter beans.
6. Slice the potatoes, leaving the skins on, and place, overlapping each other, over the bean mixture.
7. Sprinkle with the grated cheese. Bake for 30-35 minutes until golden brown.

Note for vegan: Omit the cheese but add 55g/2 oz reconstituted natural T.V.P. mince (see page 122) to the frying onions. Fry for 2 minutes and then proceed as directed above.

CURRIED BUTTER BEANS
Butter beans are delicious curried as they absorb the flavours easily.

Serves 4.

225g/8 oz (dry weight) butter beans, cooked (see
*   page 100 for cooking instructions)*
1 recipe quantity Basic curry sauce (see page
*   174) or Molee curry sauce (see page 175)*

1. Take care not to overcook the beans. Drain before they get mushy and reserve 225 ml/8 fl oz of the liquid to use in the curry sauce.

2. Make the curry sauce but add the cooked and drained beans 10 minutes before the end of cooking time.
3. Leave the lot to marinate for 1 hour at least then reheat when you want to serve. Even better is to marinate all day or overnight.
4. Serve with brown rice and lightly steamed vegetables or a side salad.

CHICK PEA, LEEK, WATERCRESS AND MINT SOUP
This is a refreshing Middle Eastern-style soup which can be made more spicy (even into a curried soup) by adding curry powder or a mixture of ground chilli powder, cumin, coriander and turmeric. In this recipe I have kept the flavour very mild and delicate. Fresh mint is essential.

Serves 6.

1 rounded teaspoon coriander seeds
225g/8 oz dry weight chick peas, cooked (see
*   page 100 on how to cook)*
2 tablespoons sunflower or corn oil
2 good size leeks, trimmed and finely chopped
1 large juicy clove garlic (optional)
2 tablespoons fresh parsley, chopped
1 rounded tablespoon fresh mint, chopped
2 tablespoons lemon juice
1 rounded tablespoon vegetable bouillon
*   powder or 1½ vegetable stock cubes*
2 bunches watercress, chopped (use stems as
*   well)*
freshly ground black pepper, to taste
few watercress leaves, to garnish

1. Dry-roast the coriander seeds in a pan for a few seconds then grind to a powder.
2. When cooked, drain the chick peas and reserve the cooking liquid. Measure the liquid and bring it up to the level of 1 litre 140 ml/2 pt, with more water if necessary.
3. Sauté the leeks and garlic for 3 minutes.
4. Add ground coriander, parsley, mint, lemon juice, the measured liquid, vegetable bouillon powder or stock cubes and the chick peas. Bring to boil then turn down to simmer and cook with the lid on for 10 minutes only.

5. Add the watercress and cook for another 4 minutes only.
6. Liquidize in several batches until completely smooth.
7. Taste and season with freshly ground black pepper.
8. When ready to serve reheat, pour into a serving bowl and garnish with a few twists of black pepper and a few watercress leaves.

FALAFEL (GROUND CHICK PEA BALLS)
A traditional Middle Eastern delight! Serve on a bed of fresh lettuce with pitta bread and yoghurt. This recipe is a real treat – well worth the bother.

Makes 30 to 40.

450g/1 lb (dry weight) chick peas, cooked and drained (see page 100 for cooking instructions)
1 heaped teaspoon ground coriander
4 tablespoons olive oil
2 tablespoons fresh parsley, finely chopped
3 large cloves garlic, crushed
2 tablespoons tahini (ground sesame seed paste, see page 84)
juice of 2 lemons (approximately 4 tablespoons)
½ teaspoon freshly ground black pepper
1 egg, beaten to bind
sea salt to taste
1 level teaspoon cayenne pepper or chilli powder (optional but adds that extra oomph!)
wholemeal flour, plain, for coating
vegetable oil for deep frying

1. Drain the chick peas well.
2. Discard the water and grate the chick peas through either a hand or electric cheese grater. Soft, powdery flakes will form. Do not add any water.
3. Add all the other ingredients, leaving the beaten egg until last.
4. Form into walnut-size balls, making approximately 40.
5. Roll each in wholemeal flour and deep fry for 3 minutes in hot oil. Do not use a basket to deep fry or the balls will stick to it. Take out with a slotted spoon. Drain on kitchen paper and keep warm in the oven.

Note: Delicious served with *Cucumber, yoghurt and mint bowl cooler* (see page 159) or with *Piquant chilli tomato sauce* (see page 174). You can add 110g/4 oz wholemeal breadcrumbs to this recipe to make a more complete protein meal.

HUMMOUS (MIDDLE EASTERN CHICK PEA DIP)
This freezes well so divide the mixture into several tubs and freeze until needed. Great for a buffet party but double the recipe.

Serves 6 to 8, as a starter.

225g/8 oz (dry weight) chick peas, cooked (see page 100 for cooking instructions)
4 tablespoons lemon juice
2 tablespoons tahini (ground sesame seed paste, see page 84)
2 large cloves garlic, crushed
2 tablespoons virgin olive oil (a must)
1 dessertspoon fresh mint, finely chopped (optional but great)
sea salt and black pepper, freshly ground to taste
sprig mint or parsley to garnish

1. Cook the chick peas for 15 minutes longer than instructed on page 100. Drain and reserve one cup of the liquid.
2. Put drained chick peas, lemon juice, tahini, garlic, olive oil and mint into a blender or liquidiser and purée until smooth, only adding a little of the chick pea cooking liquid to achieve a smooth, thick, scoopable consistency.
3. Scoop out into a serving bowl and add sea salt and black pepper to taste.
4. Swirl the top, sprinkle on a few twists of black pepper and decorate with a sprig of mint or parsley.

Note: Hummous is a wonderful party bowlful to dunk either crackers, *Fried tortilla fingers* (see page 78) or vegetable crudités in. Alternatively, stuff into *Pitta bread* (see page 19) with crisp lettuce leaves and watercress.

CHICK PEA AND SUNFLOWER SEED DIP
Serves 6 to 8, as a starter.

Follow the previous recipe for *Hummous,* but use sunflower seed spread instead of tahini (sesame seed spread). The results are equally delicious and enjoyed by those who find tahini too strong in flavour.

CHICK PEA RISSOLES
The ingredients are unspiced but you can add a little curry powder or a mixture of ground coriander, cumin, turmeric and cayenne pepper if you wish. You can also use fresh or dried herbs to vary the flavour of these tasty rissoles.

Makes 10.

225g/8 oz (dry weight) chick peas, cooked and
    drained (see page 100 for cooking
    instructions)
170g/6 oz onion, finely chopped
large clove garlic, crushed
2 tablespoons virgin olive or sunflower oil
2 tablespoons parsley, finely chopped
1 rounded teaspoon dried tarragon or
    marjoram
2 tablespoons sunflower seeds
55g/2 oz porridge oats or fine oatmeal
1 large egg, to bind (well beaten)
small dish of fine oatmeal or ground porridge
    oats to coat
little soya oil for frying

1. Put the drained chick peas through a hand or electric mincer (do not purée in a blender or the mixture will be too smooth). If you haven't a mincer then mash with a potato masher.
2. Sauté the onion and garlic in the oil for 6 minutes until soft but not brown.

3. Stir in the parsley and tarragon or marjoran (if adding extra spices then add at this stage) and fry over a gentle heat for 1 minute. Stir this into the minced chick peas.
4. Grind the sunflower seeds in a blender (if using porridge oats instead of fine oatmeal then grind these with the seeds to a powdery consistency).
5. Add seeds and oatmeal into the chick pea mixture and bind the lot together with the egg.
6. Form into flatish rounds 1 cm/½ inch deep and 6 cm/2½ inch in diameter. Dip in the fine oatmeal or the ground porridge oats and fry a few at a time in very shallow hot oil for 3 minutes on each side until golden. Take out with a fish slice and keep warm in a low heated oven.
7. Serve with fresh salad or any steamed vegetables.

Note for vegans: Omit the egg. The mixture should stay together but be extra careful to mould it well before frying.

CHICK PEA CASSEROLE
Serves 4 to 6.
You will need a large casserole dish with a lid.

225g/8 oz (dry weight) chick peas, cooked and
    drained (see page 100 for cooking
    instructions)
225g/8 oz aubergine, cut in thickish slices
225g/8 oz onion, peeled and finely chopped
2 cloves garlic, crushed
3 tablespoons either virgin olive oil or
    sunflower oil
1 large green pepper, deseeded and chopped
2 medium size courgettes, cut in chunks
110g/4 oz mushrooms, sliced
1 tablespoon vegetable bouillon powder or
    vegetable stock cube
1 rounded tablespoon gram (chick pea flour)
1 level teaspoon celery or fennel seeds, ground
1 level teaspoon dried rosemary
1 rounded teaspoon ground coriander
1 large bay leaf
140ml/¼ pt hot water
2 rounded tablespoons parsley, finely chopped

450g/1 lb either ripe skinned fresh tomatoes or
  canned, well chopped
1 rounded tablespoon tomato purée
freshly ground black pepper, to taste

1. Sprinkle a little salt on the aubergine
   slices, place in a colander, put a plate with
   a weight on top and leave for 15 minutes.
   Rinse well and pat dry and cut the slices
   into four.
2. Stir-fry the onion and garlic in the oil for
   2 minutes, add the aubergine, green
   pepper, courgettes and mushrooms and
   stir-fry for 1 minute only.
3. Blend the vegetable bouillon powder, gram
   flour, ground celery seeds, rosemary and
   ground coriander with the hot water.
4. Add this with the bay leaf, parsley,
   tomatoes and tomato purée to the stir-
   fried vegetables. Add freshly ground black
   pepper to taste.
5. Put the chick peas in the casserole dish.
   Stir in the tomato mixture. Cover with a
   tight lid and slow bake in the oven 300°F/
   150°C/Gas Mark 2 for 1½ hours.
6. Serve with bulgur (see page 81 on how to
   prepare bulgur) and a fresh green salad.

CHICK PEA SALAD WITH OLIVES AND TOMATOES
This is great for a buffet or casual
summertime lunch.

Serves 4 to 6.

225g/8 oz (dry weight) chick peas, cooked and
  drained (see page 100 for cooking
  instructions)
16 black olives, stoned and halved
double recipe quantity Basic oil and lemon
  dressing (see page 153)
10 medium size firm tomatoes, cut in thin
  wedges
½ teaspoon dried oregano
1 small red pepper, deseeded and chopped
1 small green pepper, deseeded and chopped
110g/4 oz small button mushrooms, sliced
1 small onion, peeled and cut in thin rings
4 hard boiled eggs, sliced
2 bundles watercress
1 level tablespoon fresh mint, finely chopped

1. To assemble the salad, put the drained
   and cold chick peas in a large mixing
   bowl.
2. Stir in two-thirds of the dressing, most of
   the olives, the tomatoes, red and green
   peppers, mushrooms and oregano. Gently
   coat with the dressing using a fork to
   avoid squashing the tomatoes.
3. Spread the watercress out on a large
   shallow serving dish, spoon in the chick
   pea mixture. Garnish the top with the
   sliced egg, onion rings and dot with a few
   olives. Pour on the remaining dressing
   and a sprinkling of fresh chopped mint
   (use parsley if you have no mint).

FLAGEOLET, AVOCADO AND ASPARAGUS SALAD BOWL
This is very simple to prepare once you have
cooked the beans. Definitely for a special
occasion buffet party or dinner party.

Serves 4 to 6.

225g/8 oz (dry weight) flageolet beans, cooked,
  drained and cooled (see page 100 for
  cooking instructions)
340g/12 oz asparagus spears, either fresh or
  frozen
2 tablespoons parsley, finely chopped
double recipe quantity either Basic lemon, lime
  or vinegar dressing (see page 153)
1 teaspoon dried tarragon
1 large ripe avocado, peeled and stoned
1 tablespoon lemon juice
1 head crisp lettuce
little chopped parsley to garnish

1. Put the cold beans in a mixing bowl and
   pour on two-thirds of the dressing, the
   tarragon and parsley. Leave to marinate.
2. Trim woody ends off the asparagus, if
   using fresh, and steam for 10 minutes or
   until tender. Do not over cook. If using
   frozen then steam for 5 minutes or until
   just tender. Cut off the tips and reserve for
   garnish. Chop the stems into small pieces
   and stir into the beans.
3. Cut the avocado into quarters lengthwise
   and then cut three of the quarters into
   small chunks. Cut the remaining quarter

into thin wedges for garnish. Sprinkle with lemon juice to stop browning. Stir the avocado chunks into the beans.

4. To assemble the salad spread the lettuce leaves onto a large shallow serving dish. Spoon on the bean mixture leaving a frill of lettuce leaves showing all around the edge.
5. Garnish the top with asparagus tips and slices of avocado.
6. Trickle on the remaining dressing and a little chopped parsley.

HARICOT BEANS, COURGETTE AND MUSHROOM AU GRATIN

You can use cooked flageolet beans (see page 100 on cooking these) instead of haricot beans in this recipe.

Serves 4.
You will need a casserole dish (not too deep) with a lid. Use foil if you have no lid.

225g/8 oz (dry weight) haricot beans, cooked and drained (see page 100 for cooking instructions)
3 tablespoons sunflower oil
225g/8 oz onion, peeled and chopped
2 cloves garlic, crushed
4 medium courgettes, washed and sliced in rings
225g/8 oz mushrooms, sliced
2 rounded tablespoons tomato purée
1 tablespoon shoyu (naturally fermented soy sauce)
1 teaspoon Worcester sauce
1 teaspoon dried oregano
¼ teaspoon black pepper, freshly ground
140ml/¼ pt water
1 large bay leaf
85g/3 oz grated cheese

1. Preheat the oven 325°F/160°C/Gas Mark 3.
2. Put the drained cooked beans in the casserole dish.
3. Sauté the onion and garlic in the oil for 5 minutes in a pan with the lid on.
4. Add the courgettes and mushrooms and stir-fry for 3 minutes only.
5. Blend the tomato purée, shoyu, Worcester sauce, oregano, black pepper and water together.

6. Add this with the bay leaf to the vegetables. Cook on gentle heat for 1 minute.
7. Pour this vegetable mixture over the beans in the casserole dish, cover and bake in the centre of the oven for 30 minutes.
8. Remove from the oven, take out bay leaf sprinkle on the grated cheese and grill for a few minutes until lightly browned.
9. Serve with either brown rice, buckwheat or boiled pot barley (see page 82 on cooking pot barley).

CHILLIED KIDNEY BEANS

Serves 4 to 6.

225g/8 oz (dry weight) red kidney beans, cooked (see page 100 for cooking instructions)
110g/4 oz bulgur
1 x 780g/1 lb 2 oz can tomatoes
1 level dessertspoon vegetable bouillon powder
340g/12 oz onion, chopped
2 large cloves garlic, crushed
3 tablespoons sunflower or virgin olive oil
1 large green pepper, deseeded and chopped
1 teaspoon ground cumin
1 teaspoon dried basil
1 slightly rounded teaspoon cayenne or chilli powder
1 heaped teaspoon paprika (this is not hot)
2 rounded tablespoons tomato purée
4 tablespoons dry red wine (optional)

1. Place bulgur in a small bowl. Strain 100 ml/just under 4 fl oz of tomato juice off the canned tomatoes, add 100 ml/just under 4 fl oz water and the vegetable bouillon powder. Heat this liquid to boiling then pour this over the bulgur. Cover and leave to soak while you sauté
2. Sauté the onion and garlic in the oil for 10 minutes. Add the green pepper and stir-fry for 3 minutes.
3. Stir in herbs and spices and cook for 1 minute more.
4. Chop the canned tomatoes and add these with the tomato purée and the wine if using and stir well together. Simmer gently with the lid on for 10 minutes.

5. Take off heat. Add the drained beans and the bulgur and leave to marinate with the lid on for 15 minutes.
6. Heat through just before serving.

Note: Delicious served with *Tortillas* (see page 77) or *Chapatis* (see page 28) and small bowls of thick yoghurt and cucumber.

RED BEAN MOUSSAKA
This dish is a typical Middle Eastern or Greek casserole of layered sliced aubergine (eggplant) with a delicate butter topping. Minced lamb or beef is usually added but using beans instead is equally delicious. I use less aubergine than is traditional and add some sliced courgettes with excellent results (if not using courgettes then use one extra aubergine).

You can use black-eyed beans or aduki beans instead of the red kidney beans in this recipe.

Serves 4.
You will need a large shallow baking dish.

225g/8 oz red kidney beans, cooked and drained (see page 100 for cooking instructions)
2 aubergines (approximately 280g/10 oz each in weight), thinly sliced
280g/10 oz onion, chopped
1 large clove garlic, crushed
virgin olive or sunflower oil for aubergines and sautéing the other vegetables
280g/10 oz courgettes, thinly sliced
400g/14 oz can tomatoes, mashed to a pulp
1 tablespoon tomato purée
½ level teaspoon ground cinnamon
¼ teaspoon black pepper, freshly ground
4 tablespoons dry red wine (optional but great)
2 rounded tablespoons gram flour (chick pea flour)
2 eggs
140 ml/¼ pt milk
140 ml/¼ pt thick yoghurt
little sea salt
freshly ground black pepper
½ level teaspoon ground nutmeg or mace
85g/3 oz Pecarino or Parmesan cheese, very finely grated

1. Make sure the beans are not overcooked and drain well.
2. Sprinkle a little sea salt over the aubergine slices, place in a colander and leave for 20 minutes to draw out moisture and bitter juices. Rinse well and pat dry with absorbent kitchen paper. Lay the slices on a lightly oiled baking sheet and sprinkle with a little more oil. Bake in the oven at 350°F/180°C/Gas Mark 4 for 10 minutes until tender (this cuts out frying the aubergine in lots of oil, which is the method traditionally used).
3. Sauté the onion and garlic in 2 tablespoons of oil until tender and just beginning to colour. Add the courgettes and fry for 3 minutes until just tender.
4. Stir in the tomato pulp, tomato purée, cinnamon, black pepper, wine and beans and cook on a gentle heat uncovered for 15 minutes until thickened.
5. Make the batter topping by simply blending the gram flour, eggs, milk, yoghurt, salt, pepper and nutmeg together in a food processor or liquidizer until smooth.
6. Preheat the oven to 350°F/180°C/Gas Mark 4.
7. To assemble the moussaka, oil the baking dish and line the bottom with aubergine slices. Spoon on the bean mixture and top with a layer of aubergine slices slightly overlapping each other. Pour on the batter topping and sprinkle on the grated cheese. Bake in the centre of the preheated oven for 40 minutes until lightly browned on top.

CHILLI RED BEAN STUFFED PANCAKES
You can use either the plain *Wholewheat, Buckwheat, Parsley* or *Broccoli pancake* batter mixture for this recipe (see pages 76 to 77). My choice is either *Broccoli* or *Parsley pancakes,* as these seem to complement the filling well. Make the pancakes and cook the beans the day before as this will cut down the preparation time enormously.

Serves 5.
You will need a large ovenproof dish, greased.

1 recipe quantity pancake mixture of your
   choice (see above)
225g/8 oz (dry weight) red kidney beans,
   cooked (see page 100 for cooking
   instructions)
250g/9 oz onion, chopped
1 large clove garlic, crushed
3 tablespoons sunflower oil
1 green eating apple, finely chopped
1 large green pepper, deseeded and chopped
1 teaspoon marjoram or oregano
1 bay leaf
1 level teaspoon cayenne or chilli pepper
few twists of black pepper, freshly ground
396g/14 oz can tomatoes, chopped
1 rounded tablespoon tomato purée
1 tablespoon shoyu (naturally fermented soy
   sauce)
140 ml/¼ pt bean cooking liquid
140g/5 oz grated cheese either Farmhouse
   Cheddar, Pecorino or Parmesan

1. Drain the beans and reserve 140ml/¼ pint
   of the liquid. Stack the pancakes on top of
   each other as directed on page 75, so they
   are ready to fill.
2. Preheat oven to 400°F/200°C/Gas Mark 6.
3. Sauté the onion and garlic in the oil for 7
   minutes with the lid on.
4. Add the apple and green pepper and
   continue to fry for 3 minutes more with
   the lid on.
5. Stir in the marjoram or oregano, bay leaf,
   cayenne pepper, black pepper, tomatoes
   and tomato purée and simmer with the lid
   on for 10 minutes then stir in the shoyu.
6. Put the drained beans into a bowl and stir
   in half the tomato mixture. Remove the
   bay leaf. Liquidize the other half of the
   tomato mixture with the 140ml/¼ pint of
   bean cooking liquid until smooth and a
   pouring consistency.
7. Divide the bean mixture between the 10
   pancakes, roll each one up and place in
   the ovenproof dish, side by side.
8. Pour on the liquidized mixture and
   sprinkle on the grated cheese.
9. Top with a sprinkling of oregano or
   marjoram and bake in the preheated oven
   for 25 minutes.

MUNG BEAN SHEPHERD'S PIE

This was the first meatless shepherd's pie I
made for the family and it is still, after 12
years, a favourite everyday meal.

Serves 4 to 6.
You will need a deep casserole dish (no lid
necessary).

170g/6 oz (dry weight) mung beans, cooked (see
   page 101)
55g/2 oz T.V.P. soya mince, either beef or
   natural flavour (or 55g/2 oz more cooked
   mung beans, if you wish)
1 rounded teaspoon vegetable bouillon powder
85ml/3 fl oz boiling water
2 tablespoons sunflower or corn oil
225g/8 oz onion, chopped
170g/6 oz carrots, scraped and finely diced
3 sticks celery, finely chopped
1 clove garlic, crushed
2 rounded tablespoons parsley, finely chopped
1 large bay leaf
1 rounded teaspoon basil
396g/14 oz can tomatoes, well chopped
1 rounded tablespoon tomato purée
1 tablespoon shoyu (naturally fermented soy
   sauce)
little black pepper, freshly ground
900g/2 lb potatoes, scrubbed, chopped with
   skins on, steamed and mashed
2 tablespoons natural yoghurt
good pinch sea salt
lump of polyunsaturated margarine
55g/2 oz Cheddar cheese, grated (optional)
thin slices of tomato to top
little sprinkling of dried herb

1. Do not overcook the beans. When beans
   are cooked drain and reserve 200ml/7 fl oz
   of the cooking liquid.

2. To reconstitute the soya mince (if using) place it in a small bowl, stir in the boiling water and the vegetable bouillon powder, cover and leave for 5 minutes to swell.

3. Sauté the onions, carrots, celery and garlic in the oil for 5 minutes until just soft.

4. Stir in the reconstituted soya mince (if using), bay leaf and basil and cook stirring constantly on moderate heat for 2 minutes.

5. Add the tomatoes, tomato purée, shoyu, parsley and a little black pepper. Heat through only (do not boil).

6. Stir this mixture into the cooked mung beans and the reserved 200 ml/7 fl oz bean cooking liquid. It might look too watery but it dries up when baked. Put this bean mixture into a deep casserole dish.

7. Blend the potatoes, salt, yoghurt and margarine together. Spread this out over the bean mixture. Sprinkle on the cheese, arrange the tomatoes on top of the cheese and sprinkle on a little dried herb.

8. Bake 375°F/190°C/Gas Mark 5 for 30 minutes or until the top is golden brown.

Note for vegans: Omit the yoghurt and the cheese from the topping and add a little more polyunsaturated margarine and sprinkle on a little *Gomasio* (see page 95) or even better *Herby gomasio* (see page 95).

Mung beans can also be used instead of lentils or split peas in soups or dhals (see page 112). Soak them for four hours, drain and rinse well, then use in the same way as lentils or split peas in those recipes. The soaking makes them more digestible and quicker to cook.

PINTO BEAN AND HAZELNUT LOAF

This loaf makes a very simple, tasty and nourishing meal served with either *Vegetable gravy* (see page 170) or a simple *Tomato sauce* (see page 173).

Serves 4 to 6.
You will need a baking tray, well greased, and a sheet of foil to loosely cap the loaf. Don't pack it into a loaf tin or you will end up having to spoon it out and it will not look very appetizing.

225g/8 oz (dry weight) pinto beans, cooked (see page 101 for cooking instructions)
4 tablespoons sunflower oil or corn oil
225g/8 oz onion, chopped finely
1 small green pepper, deseeded and chopped
110g/4 oz small button mushrooms, sliced
2 rounded tablespoons parsley, finely chopped
2 rounded tablespoons Greek yoghurt
110g/4 oz hazelnuts, medium finely ground
55g/2 oz wholemeal breadcrumbs or ground porridge oats
1 large egg, beaten to bind
little sea salt to taste
little black pepper, freshly ground to taste
little extra beaten egg, to glaze
2 tablespoons fine wholemeal breadcrumbs or ground porridge oats, for topping

1. Drain the cooked beans well and mash them with a potato masher.

2. Sauté the onion in 2 tablespoons of the oil for 7 minutes until soft.

3. Mince the green pepper and the mushrooms by putting in a food processor or liquidizer for a few seconds.

4. Add these to the sautéed onion and cook for 2 minutes only. Take off heat.

5. Stir in the parsley and yoghurt.

6. Spoon this mixture into the mashed beans. Add the nuts and 55g/2 oz wholemeal breadcrumbs or ground porridge oats.

7. Season with a little sea salt and black pepper to your taste.

8. Bind with the beaten egg.

9. Form into a loaf, shape on the greased baking tray. Brush with extra beaten egg and sprinkle on the 2 tablespoons of fine breadcrumbs or ground porridge oats.

10. Prick the top and trickle on the remaining 2 tablespoons of oil.

11. Cap loosely with the foil making a hood which does not stick to the loaf but still seals it in reasonably well.

12. Bake at 375°F/190°C/Gas Mark 5 for 30 minutes. Take off the cap and let brown in the oven for 15 minutes more.

LENTIL AND SPLIT PEA RECIPES

LENTIL AND MISO SOUP

This soup is a meal in itself, served with garlic bread and cheese. The combination of lentils, miso (a naturally fermented soya bean paste – see page 116) and vegetables makes a complete protein food (see page 11). As miso contains salt there is no need for added salt in this recipe.

Serves 4 to 6.

3 tablespoons sunflower or corn oil
1 level teaspoon fennel seeds (optional)
2 medium onions, chopped
2 cloves garlic, crushed
4 sticks celery, chopped
2 large carrots, scraped and chopped
140g/5 oz red split lentils, well washed
1 litre 140ml/2 pt boiling water
2 rounded tablespoons tomato purée
2 rounded tablespoons parsley, chopped
little freshly ground black pepper
2 rounded tablespoons miso

1. Heat the oil in a large heavy-based saucepan and fry the fennel seeds for a few minutes.
2. Add the onion, garlic, celery and carrots and stir-fry over a moderately high heat for ½ minute only.
3. Add the lentils, boiling water, tomato purée, parsley and black pepper.
4. Stir well, bring to boil, turn down to simmer, cover and cook gently for 20 minutes.
5. Purée in a blender, four ladlesful at a time, adding the parsley and the miso as you blend.
6. Pour the lot back into the saucepan and heat through (do not boil) just before serving.

LENTIL BURGERS

For this recipe you can use either red split lentils, green or whole brown lentils. You will have to soak the whole brown lentils for 1 hours before cooking and cook both them and the green lentils for 5 to 10 minutes longer than you would red lentils.

Makes 10.

225g/8 oz (dry weight) red split lentils
300 ml/just over ½ pt boiling water
1 very level tablespoon vegetable bouillon powder
1 bay leaf
1 rounded teaspoon ground coriander
1 level teaspoon cumin
good pinch cayenne pepper (optional)
curl lemon rind
2 tablespoons lemon juice
1 large onion, finely chopped
1 clove garlic, crushed
1 tablespoon sunflower or corn oil
2 tablespoons parsley, finely chopped
40g/1½ oz each of sunflower and sesame seeds
1 egg to bind
little sea salt and freshly ground black pepper, to taste
85g/3 oz fresh wholemeal breadcrumbs, to coat
little soya oil for frying

1. Wash lentils and pick over for stones. Drain.
2. Put lentils, water, vegetable bouillon powder, bay leaf, coriander, cumin, cayenne (if using), lemon rind and juice in a saucepan and simmer gently for 20 minutes with the lid off until the lentils are tender and all the water is absorbed. Take out bay leaf and rind and spoon into a large bowl to cool.
3. While lentils are cooking sauté the onion and garlic for 5 minutes until softish.
4. Dry roast the sunflower and sesame seeds in a heavy-based pan until lightly browned and the seeds are popping (stir all the time). Finely grind in a liquidizer or small mill. Mash these with the sautéed onion and the parsley into the cooked and cooled lentils.
5. Season with a little sea salt, if needed, and freshly ground black pepper. Form into ten burgers, coat each with breadcrumbs and fry a few at a time in a little hot oil on moderate heat until golden brown on both sides.
6. Serve with either *Tomato sauce* (see page 173) or *Mushroom sauce* (see page 173).

LENTIL LOAF
Serves 4 to 6.

Prepare recipe mixture as for *Lentil burgers* above. Line a 675g/1½ lb capacity loaf tin with baking parchment, grease this well and sprinkle on breadcrumbs. Spoon the lentil mixture into the tin and level the top. Bake uncovered in a moderate oven for 50 minutes until golden brown and crisp on top (it is important to prepare the tin as instructed or the mixture will stick to the tin).

Serve with a *Leek and tarragon sauce* (see page 173), baked potatoes and lightly steamed vegetables or a fresh salad.

Note for vegans: Both the *Lentil burgers* and the *Lentil loaf* can be made without egg. Simply add 1 rounded tablespoon cold water to the rest of the ingredients just before you mould together.

LENTIL AND MUSHROOM SLICE
Serves 6.

You will need a 5 cm/2 inch deep, 20 cm/8 inch square baking dish or a 23 cm/9 inch round dish very well greased and thickly coated with breadcrumbs.

280g/10 oz red split lentils
400 ml/14 fl oz boiling water
1 level tablespoon vegetable bouillon powder
2 small bay leaves
1 curl of lemon rind
3 tablespoons sunflower or corn oil
1 large onion, finely chopped
110g/4 oz button mushrooms, sliced
1 clove garlic, crushed
1 rounded teaspoon ground coriander
1 level teaspoon cumin
2 rounded tablespoons parsley, finely chopped
1 tablespoon lemon juice
1 tablespoon shoyu (naturally fermented soy sauce)
¼ teaspoon black pepper, freshly ground
55g/2 oz sunflower seeds
55g/2 oz sesame seeds
55g/2 oz porridge oats
1 large eeg
55g/2 oz wholemeal breadcrumbs
55g/2 oz Cheddar cheese, grated (optional)

1. Wash the lentils and pick over for small stones.
2. Put lentils, water, vegetable bouillon powder, bay leaves and lemon rind in a saucepan. Bring all to boil stirring as you do this. Simmer on very gentle heat for 20 minutes until lentils are soft and all the water is absorbed. Spoon into a large bowl. Remove bay leaves and lemon rind.
3. Preheat the oven to 375°F/190°C/Gas Mark 5.
4. Sauté the onion and garlic in the oil for 5 minutes, add the mushrooms, coriander and cumin and fry for 2 minutes more on medium heat stirring as you do this.
5. Stir in the parsley, lemon juice, shoyu and black pepper and cook briskly for 1 minute more, still stirring until the liquid is all absorbed. Spoon into the cooked lentils.
6. Dry-roast the sunflower and sesame seeds in a heavy-based pan on a moderate heat stirring constantly until lightly browned and the seeds are popping.
7. Grind these seeds with the porridge oats in a blender until powdery. Stir into the lentil mixture.
8. Blend in the beaten egg and mould the mixture well together.
9. Spoon mixture carefully into the prepared dish, smooth the top and sprinkle on breadcrumbs and the grated cheese (mix these together first).
10. Bake in the preheated oven for 40 minutes until the top is golden brown and crisp.
11. Cut into portions and serve hot with *Tomato sauce* (see page 173), jacket potatoes and *Limed hot onion rings with stir-fry cabbage* (see page 168) or cold with a fresh salad.

Also see recipe for *Lentil and mushroom pie* on page 41.

DHAL
Dhals can be either thin and runny or have a very thick soup consistency. In India they are often eaten with chapatis or rice as a main meal or as an accompaniment to a main

vegetable or meat curry dish, again with rice or chapatis.

You can either use red split lentils, green lentils, yellow or green split peas, mung beans or whole brown lentils but it is advisable to pre-soak all varieties, other than the red split lentils, for a few hours before cooking. Drain well and follow the instructions for cooking given below.

Serves 4 to 6.

225g/8 oz red split lentils (or other type if
preferred – see note above)
800ml/1¼ pt water
little sea salt
225g/8 oz onion, finely chopped
2 tablespoons sunflower or corn oil
1 fresh chilli, finely chopped or ½ level
teaspoon cayenne or chilli powder
1 level teaspoon black mustard seeds
½ level teaspoon cumin seeds, crushed
½ level teaspoon coriander seeds, crushed
1 level teaspoon turmeric
1 rounded teaspoon fresh ginger, grated
1 level teaspoon methi (fenugreek leaf)
(optional)
2 tablespoons lemon or lime juice

1. Wash lentils well and drain.
2. Put in a saucepan with the water and a little sea salt. Bring to boil. Stir a few times, cover and let gently simmer for 30 minutes. The mixture should be quite thick and mushy.
3. Meanwhile sauté the onion until lightly browned but not burned.

4. Make a space in the centre of the onion and fry the other ingredients, except for the lemon and lime juice, for 1 minute. Then stir everything together and continue to fry for 1 minute more on a low heat.
5. Take off heat and stir in the lemon or lime juice.
6. Stir this mixture into the cooked lentils.
7. Reheat gently just before serving. The flavour is even better if the dhal is made the day before.

LENTIL AND TOMATO DHAL

As in the previous recipe you can use a variety of pulses here, but remember to pre-soak any pulse, other than red lentils, for a few hours before cooking.

Serves 4 to 6.

40g/1½ oz tamarind
225g/8 oz red split lentils (or other pulse if
preferred – see note above)
800 ml/1¼ pt water
little sea salt
1 cinnamon stick
1 medium onion, finely chopped
1 large juicy clove garlic, crushed
2 tablespoons sunflower or corn oil
1 level teaspoon black mustard seeds
½ teaspoon ground cumin
1 level teaspoon ground coriander
½ level teaspoon turmeric
½ level teaspoon cayenne pepper (more if you
wish)
1 teaspoon methi (fenugreek leaves)
1 rounded teaspoon fresh ginger, grated
110g/4 oz mushrooms, sliced
4 good size ripe firm tomatoes, peeled and
diced
chopped coriander leaves or parsley to garnish

1. Soak the tamarind in just enough boiling water to cover for 1 hour. Press through a sieve. You should have a thickish slightly runny paste.
2. Wash lentils well and put in a saucepan with the water, the cinnamon stick and a little sea salt.

3. Bring to boil, turn down to simmer, cover and cook on a gentle heat for 30 minutes.

4. Meanwhile sauté the onion and garlic in the oil until very lightly browned.

5. Make a space in the middle and fry the spices, methi and ginger on very low heat for 1 minute.

6. Add the mushrooms and fry for 2 minutes more. Stir everything together and take off heat.

7. Stir in the tamarind paste, then stir this mixture into the cooked lentils.

8. Just before serving, stir in the diced tomatoes.

9. Cook on gentle heat for 5 minutes so that the tomatoes are soft but not mushy. Take out cinnamon stick.

10. Garnish with the coriander leaves or parsley and serve with brown rice and *Cucumber, yoghurt and mint bowl cooler* (see page 159).

Note: You can add other vegetables to this, such as lightly steamed cauliflower florets or shredded white cabbage. Stir-fry these in the spices and then cook in the lentils for 5 minutes only before serving. This makes a sort of lentil and vegetable curry.

This dahl can also be turned into a delicious soup by adding 285ml/½ pint more water, a tablespoon tomato purée and a little sea salt. Liquidize the lot in a blender, heat and serve.

LESSON 6

THE VERSATILE SOYA BEAN

This to me is the most vital lesson in the book as it covers the soya bean in all its versatility. Read all the information about this miraculous bean and its by-products and you will understand why it is valued so highly in Eastern cuisine.

SHOPPING LIST

You can buy soya milk and tofu in most health food stores and some supermarkets. Tempeh is often available ready-made too. You will find, however, detailed instructions in this lesson on how to make all three products from the soya bean. Tofu and tempeh do not have a long shelf-life so buy or make when needed.

Check your store cupboard for cooking oils, all spices, herbs and vegetable bouillon powder or stock cubes and replenish if necessary. Your store cupboard should now be well stocked if you have followed the previous lessons, but here are just a few more items you might have to add:

soya beans	wholewheat or
tamarind (see page 166)	spinach lasagne
	wholewheat spaghetti
T.V.P. (texturized vegetable protein) chunks, beef or natural	several other wholewheat pasta shapes
	garam masala
	five spice

FACTS ABOUT THE SOYA BEAN

The soya bean is approximately 38 per cent protein, equal to that of beef. Unlike meat, however, it contains unsaturated fat and a high level of lecithin which reduces the level of cholesterol in the blood, thus lessening the possibility of heart attacks. The soya bean is also an alkaline food which corrects acidity in the body and it is the cheapest source of minerals and 'complete protein' (see page 11) available today.

A one-acre harvest of this wonderful bean will provide enough protein for one human being for six years. The harvest from the same amount of land fed to animals will yield only enough protein for one human being for approximately 80 days. What better reason for experimenting with this 'miracle bean' by making some of the delicious, highly nutritious foods which are traditional in Chinese, Japanese and Indonesian cuisine and will add an exciting dimension to your diet?

As mentioned in the previous chapter, it is important to note that proper soaking and cooking of pulses is vital because they all contain to a greater or lesser degree substances which are harmful to digestion. This applies even more so to the soya bean, which contains a trypsin inhibitor that prevents the body assimilating an important amino acid called methionine. The bean, the flour from the bean and sprouted soya beans must be cooked to render these substances harmless.

BASIC COOKING METHOD FOR SOYA BEANS

Soya beans need even more soaking and cooking time than other legumes. Soak them for 15 hours in summer time and for about 20 to 24 hours in winter time, changing the water 3 to 4 times. Rinse them afterwards and boil them vigorously in fresh water for 10 minutes, then simmer for approximately 3 hours. If using a pressure cooker, the beans will only take 30 minutes to cook, but they must be pre-soaked for the same amount of time.

SOYA BEAN PRODUCTS

SOYA FLOUR

This flour is even higher in nutritional value than the beans and is approximately 50 per cent protein. There are several varieties on the market varying in degrees of fat content – full-fat flour contains 20 per cent fat and medium-fat flour approximately 7 per cent fat. There is also a cooked highly nutritious soya flour called soylk, which can be added to drinks or used in cooking in the same way as uncooked soya flour. As an extra protein booster add soya flour when making bread or other bakes in the ratio of 55g/2 oz to 450g/ 1 lb flour. It is great for thickening soups, casseroles and sauces especially if you are on a gluten-free diet, as soya flour contains no gluten (see notes on gluten, page 96).

SHOYU AND TAMARI (NATURALLY FERMENTED SOY SAUCE)

There are many brands of soy (or soya) sauce on the market. Many are synthetically compounded with additives such as caramel and syrup to give colour and flavour. These products are to be avoided. They are cheaper to manufacture as they are made within a few days, but they do not produce the protein yield of the naturally fermented soy sauces – shoyu and tamari. These two naturally produced sauces differ slightly. Shoyu is produced from soya beans, roasted wheat and sea salt, whereas tamari is wheat-free and produced from soya beans and salt only and is slightly thicker and stronger than shoyu. Tamari is useful for those on a gluten-free diet (see notes on gluten, page 96).

Both shoyu and tamari are naturally brewed over a period of one year to eighteen months (traditionally this period sometimes lasted three years). This fermentation process produces a source of vitamin B_{12}, the one vitamin rare in plant food (see notes on B_{12}, page 13). When added to foods such as whole grains, pulses, nuts and seeds, shoyu and tamari increase the amount of protein that can be digested. It is important to add natural soy sauce towards the end of cooking time so that its nutritional properties are not destroyed.

MISO

This is another wonder food! I don't say that flippantly, because just two good teaspoons of miso will give you enough complete protein for one day. How about that!

Miso is a soya bean paste produced by lactic fermentation. The process is lengthy, during which a culture is added to cooked soya beans and cooked rice. Salt is gradually added until the mixture achieves a paste-like consistency. The paste comes in various shades. The darker miso contains up to 90 per cent soya bean while the lighter miso contains more rice and thus less protein. Not only is miso a high-protein food but it is also free of cholesterol. In addition it is an aid to digestion, is claimed to help develop a strong resistance to disease and, most incredible of all, it is claimed that it can remove radioactive substances from the body, but I wouldn't like to have to test this.

Cooking with miso

Don't cook it, or at least let it simmer for only one minute in your soup or casserole. Cooking destroys the culture and flavour. Also very important, is not just to dollop a lump of miso into your prepared meal. Mix the miso with a little of the hot stock or some warm water to a smooth paste, then stir this with a fork into the prepared food. Remember that miso is salty and it is not necessary to include salt in any dish to which you will be adding miso.

I basically use it as an extra protein booster and always in vegetable soups or less complete protein bean stews. When I say vegetable soups, I means hearty ones with root vegetables, not leek or asparagus based soups, as miso is strong tasting and would destroy the delicate flavour of these vegetables. Try the *Lentil and miso soup* on page 111. It is a very tasty recipe to start off with if you have never used miso before.

SOYA MILK

Soya milk is low in calories, low in saturated fats and has no cholesterol or sodium (salt). It contains more iron and slightly more protein than cow's milk, with equal amounts of the B vitamins. It is also easy to digest and has an alkaline reaction in the body. For those who have a lactose intolerance or allergy to cow's milk it is invaluable.

Of course mother's milk is by far the best for infant feeding, but for various reasons this is not always available. In such circumstances medically approved, infant soya milk formulas are available and will give your child a healthy substitute.

You can use soya milk in any recipe where cow's or goat's milk is called for. It makes delicious sauces, custards, ice creams and milk shakes, and is great chilled with just a dash of honey. It will also make very good yoghurt (see page 118) using the same culture as for goat's milk or cow's milk yoghurt.

How to make soya milk
Home-produced soya milk is less than one third the price of cow's milk and one fifth the price of goat's milk.

Makes approximately 3 litres/5¼ pints.
You will need the following equipment:

5 litre/9 pt capacity, heavy-based saucepan (stainless steel, copper bottomed or cast-iron enamelled lined pots are ideal)
food processor or heavy duty liquidiser
large stainless steel colander
large deep bowl (or saucepan) 3½ litres/6 pints capacity, in which the colander fits snugly into the rim
double thickness of muslin, 50 cm/20 inch square
long-handled spoon for stirring the milk
cup for measuring
clean rubber gloves (vital for squeezing the pulp)
340g/12 oz soya beans
water as directed in the method

1. Wash the soya beans and soak for 24 hours. Change the water three times during soaking.
2. Rinse the beans well after soaking and to each cup of soaked beans add 1 cup of boiling water. Using a food processor or liquidizer, blend the beans and water cup by cup. Leave the motor on for 1½ minutes each time to achieve a reasonably smooth, runny batter consistency.
3. Grease the 5 litre/9 pt saucepan.
4. Bring 8 cups of fresh water to the boil and pour in the liquidized bean purée. Bring to the boil, stirring constantly. Keep on a moderate heat and leave to simmer for 20 minutes. The mixture will be frothy, so spoon back some of the froth to make sure that the liquid is gently bubbling underneath. Stir occasionally.
5. Line the colander with the muslin, leaving plenty hanging over. Place the colander over the clean 3½ litre/6 pt bowl to catch the milk
6. Put on the rubber gloves. Pour the boiled bean liquid into the muslin-lined colander. The soya milk will slowly filter through.
7. Rinse the cooking pot out with 1 cup of boiling water and pour this rinsing water into the muslin-lined colander. When most of the milk has filtered through, pick up the overhanging ends of the muslin to form a bag. Squeeze the bag to extract as much milk as possible.
8. Open the bag and let the muslin fall back over the colander again. Pour in 570ml/ 1 pt of boiling water, form muslin into a bag again and squeeze. The soya milk in the bowl is now ready.

The milk will freeze well after it is cooled. The quicker you cool the milk, the longer it will keep, so if you don't want to make tofu from it (see page 119), cool it by immersing the bowl in a sink of cold water, changing the water as it warms. Soya milk will keep fresh in the refrigerator for up to four days. Frozen, it will be good for at least 3 months.

OKARA

This is the pulp left after you have squeezed all the milk from the beans when making soya milk. It is a high-fibre food and contains 3.5 per cent protein, similar to the amount in unskimmed milk. It can be used in toppings for savoury and sweet crumble dishes by mixing it with the wholemeal flour in the sweet and savoury crumble mixes on pages 39 and 49, and in granola (toasted breakfast cereal). It can also be used in bean or nut burgers instead of breadcrumbs.

SOYA MILK YOGHURT

You can make yoghurt out of soya milk in exactly the same way as you would using goat's or cow's milk. The same culture starter, *Lactobacillus bulgaricus*, is used. (For more information on the nutritional value of yoghurt see page 180.)

You can buy a yoghurt-making kit or use wide-rimmed thermos flasks to keep your yoghurt at the right temperature, but I use preserving jars which I incubate in the airing cupboard at around the temperature of 43°C/110°F (just above body temperature).

For perfection, when testing the temperature of the milk before adding the culture, it is best to have a dairy thermometer which floats on the surface of the liquid. You can use a jam-making thermometer which can be bought from most chemists but you have to hold it in the liquid until the right temperature is reached. If you are using the finger test then the milk should still feel warm but not burn your finger.

The best soya milk yoghurt is achieved by using a thick soya milk (see *How to make soya milk* on page 117, follow all instructions but use 850 ml/1½ pints less water).

How to make soya milk yoghurt
It is important to sterilize all equipment and containers. Do this by immersing in a pan of water, bringing to the boil and boiling for a few minutes.

Makes 4 x 285 ml/½ pt pots of yoghurt.
You will need the following equipment:
3 litre/5¼ pt capacity, heavy-based saucepan
4 x 285 ml/½ pt hot, sterilized jars, with lids
plastic fork or spatula
tablespoon for stirring
dessertspoon

1.1 litres/2 pt soya milk
2 tablespoons natural yoghurt (or dry
commercial culture – see instructions on
packet for using this)

1. Bring soya milk to boil and boil for ½ minute stirring constantly.
2. Pour 285 ml/½ pt into each of the 4 hot sterilized jars, cover and let the milk cool to 43°C/110°F. To test without a dairy- or jam-making thermometer, the milk is ready when the jars feel comfortably hot to your wrist but not burning.
3. Spoon 1 dessertspoon of natural yoghurt into each jar. Stir briskly with a plastic fork or spatula, cover and leave to stand in the airing cupboard or suitable warm place for 3 to 4 hours or until set. Check the temperature with a room thermometer because the culture needs a constant temperature of around 43°C/110°F to grow properly.
4. When set, refrigerate.

How to make soya milk yoghurt cheese
This thick, creamy cheese is delicious for making cheesecake mixed with tofu and lemon. You can also use it in salad dressings (see pages 154 to 155) instead of tofu, but you will need a little less lemon juice as the yoghurt does not have the bland flavour of tofu.

It is also good on baked potatoes, mixed with chives, paprika and a pinch of salt, and as a topping to fresh or stewed fruit.

Makes 340g/12 oz.

You will need:
large stainless steel colander
double thickness of muslin, 50 cm/20 inch
    square
large deep bowl (or saucepan) in which the
    colander fits snugly into the rim
cord for tying

1. Spread the muslin over the colander, pour
    the fresh yoghurt into this. Pull up the
    overhanging ends of the muslin to form a
    bag, twist and tie with the cord and hang
    over the large bowl.
2. Leave to drip for 4 hours. This will give
    you a soft cheese – for a firmer, thick
    creamy cheese let it drip overnight.

TOFU

Tofu is a high quality complete protein-rich
food and a good source of minerals such as
iron and calcium. It contains potassium,
phosphorous and a good supply of the B and E
vitamins. It is also low in sodium (salt),
compared to meat and all dairy produce, and
has approximately a quarter of the calories to
be found in an equal portion of meat. Tofu has
no cholesterol and is low in saturated fats,
both of which in excess have been found to be
contributory factors in heart disease.

Most protein foods have an acid reaction in
the body whereas tofu has an alkaline effect.
Although tofu has only one-third of the
protein of meat, what is more important
where all protein is concerned is its Net
Protein Utilization (NUP). The protein content
might well be high in a particular food before
it is eaten, but if there are inhibiting factors
which make it difficult to digest, then the
body is not able to benefit fully from that high
percentage of protein. Surprisingly, research
has revealed that the NUP of tofu is actually
higher than chicken and just slightly lower
than beef. Research has also shown that the
NUP of tofu can be increased by combining it
with whole grains.

To make a balanced meal, add tofu to fresh
or lightly cooked vegetables or blend it with
herbs and garlic and spread on wholemeal
bread or use as a stuffing for pitta bread. You
can also use it in lasagne instead of curd or
Ricotta cheese. My favourite way is to add it
to stir-fried vegetables with sweet and sour
sauce.

How to make tofu (soya bean curd or cheese)
You can make tofu with Epsom salts or lemon
juice, but I find the best results, a higher yield
and greater firmness, are achieved by using
nigari, now available in health shops. Rich in
minerals, nigari is the residue left after the
salt (sodium chloride) and water are removed
from sea water. The residue is sun-dried and
bought as crystals. I also use a Japanese tofu
press which is made from Japanese cypress
wood (iroki).

Makes approximately 500g/1 lb 2 oz
You will need the following equipment:
5 litre/9 pt capacity, heavy-based saucepan
long-handled spoon for stirring
tofu press (or colander and bowl – see method
    below)
double thickness of muslin, 50 cm/20 inch
    square
1 kg/2 lb weight (you can use a jar of beans of
    this weight)

*3 litres/5¼ pt soya milk (see page 117 for how
    to make this)*
*2 teaspoons nigari dissolved in 200ml/7 fl oz
    water*

1. Pour soya milk into the saucepan and heat
    to just under boiling point. The milk must
    reach at least 85°C/185°F.
2. Remove milk from the heat and stirring
    briskly, *slowly* pour in one-third of the
    nigari liquid. Continue to stir for half a
    minute, making sure you stir in milk from
    the sides and bottom of the pan.

3. Let the movement of the liquid stop then using the back of your stirring spoon, pour a further third of the nigari liquid on to the surface of the milk. Cover and leave for 3 minutes, then stir again.

4. Using the back of the spoon, trickle the remaining nigari liquid over the surface of the milk, then slowly and gently stir only about 1 cm/½ inch of the surface of the milk as you count to 20. Cover and leave for another 3 minutes, then uncover and stir the liquid again. You should now have a mixture of curds and whey. The curds will be cream-coloured and the whey a clear yellow colour.

5. Line the tofu press with the muslin, draping it over the edge as it will be folded over the tofu later. If you have no press just place the cloth over a colander which is on top of a bowl to catch the whey (do not throw this away – see below).

6. Ladle the curds and whey into the press or colander. The curds (tofu) will stay in the muslin and the whey will drip through. The tofu will be quite soft at this stage.

7. Fold the cloth over the tofu, place the lid of the press on top and the 1 kg/2 lb weight on top of this. Leave to stand for 20-30 minutes. This will give you a firm tofu which is easy to slice. Uncover the tofu.

8. To store the tofu, if not using immediately, fill a bowl with cold water, ease the tofu into it and place in the fridge. Change the water every day and it will last for 6 days. You can freeze it, but the texture alters and it is then only good for soups and stews.

Whey

Don't throw away the whey which trickles gently from your tofu press as the curds mould together to form tofu. It contains a little protein, B vitamins and the natural sugars of the soya bean. Use it in bread-making – the natural sugar content helps yeast to rise more quickly and the result is a much lighter loaf. It is also great added to soups.

Another use is as a cleansing agent for dishes instead of detergent, as it breaks down fats and grease. For this you will only need about half a cupful to a large bowl of hot water.

SILKEN TOFU

Silken tofu is sometimes suggested for certain recipes such as salad dressings or light puddings.

To make silken tofu, you simply make a thick soya milk, using approximately 850ml/1½ pt less water than stated in the instructions for making soya milk on page 117. Then use this to make tofu by following the instructions on page 119, but keep the curds and whey together, pour them into a bowl and let them cool. This produces a considerably larger quantity of soft tofu as the curds and whey are not separated. You can freeze this in several containers and defrost as required for blended dishes.

Silken tofu is available ready-made in health food stores.

YUBA

Yuba is the name for the skin which develops on top of soya milk when it is heating. (Similar to the skin which forms on cow's or goat's milk). In China and Japan yuba is considered a delicacy and can be bought either fresh or dried. It is a very nutritious high energy food which contains at least 50 per cent protein and is rich in minerals, unsaturated oils and natural sugars. It is a great food for babies mixed with fruit purées, for pregnant and nursing mothers and of course for all sportsmen and women.

Freshly made yuba is delicious either as a savoury spread or as a sweet dish mixed with fruit. My favourite way of eating it is adding a few fresh chopped mixed herbs, black pepper or paprika, a little sea salt and a touch of garlic. Spread this on wholemeal toast or use for open sandwiches topped with sliced red pepper.

The dried variety can be stored in the refrigerator for several weeks. It is great chopped up in soups and added to stir-fried vegetables and rice dishes because of its high protein content.

How to make yuba

Yuba is very simple to make and dry. A double boiler is useful but you can use a shallow saucepan placed over a pan of hot water over a low heat. This is necessary because the yuba takes approximately 8 minutes to form and the milk has to be kept at a steady temperature of about 79°C/175°F. A cooking thermometer is necessary to test the temperature. The best yield is obtained by using a thick soya milk (made by using 850ml/1½ pt less water than stated in the instructions for making soya milk on page 117).

1. Pour soya milk into the double boiler or saucepan to a level of about 5 cm/2 inch and heat to a temperature of 79°C/175°F. Do not boil. Keep at this temperature (test using a cooking thermometer) until a thick skin forms. This takes approximately 8 minutes.
2. Cut the skin with a sharp knife all round the edge then lift it up carefully by sliding a long thick knitting needle or chopstick under the middle. This is the first sheet of yuba.
3. Top up milk to the 5 cm/2 inch level and repeat the process until you have several sheets of yuba.
4. If you wish to dry the yuba, hang it until it is brittle.

TEMPEH

Tempeh is a most delicious complete protein food, which originates from Indonesia where it has been a staple food for hundreds of years. It is made with a natural culture similar to those used in cheese and yoghurt making. Partially cooked and split soya beans are mixed with the culture which ferments slowly over approximately 24 to 30 hours. During the fermentation period the soya bean protein is broken down, making the tempeh formed an easily digestible food.

As well as being high in protein and easily digestible, tempeh is low in fat, has no cholesterol and is rich in iron and vitamins B_{12} and B_6. It has a chicken-like flavour, smells like fresh mushrooms and is good for barbecuing, baking in casseroles, adding to vegetable sauces or simply deep fried. By combining tempeh with grains, fresh vegetables and cheese, the amount of complete protein made available to the body is increased by approximately one third. You can also eat tempeh with meat using half meat and half tempeh.

Tempeh is now obtainable frozen from some healthfood stores and can be made at home. The process of making tempeh is quite a lengthy one and worth doing in big batches which can be frozen. Before freezing, it is best to steam pieces of freshly made tempeh for 5 minutes. Let cool, place in polythene bags and freeze. Refrigerated tempeh will last for 4 days, but do not stack pieces of uncooked tempeh on top of each other as the culture continues to grow and produces heat which ruins the tempeh. Once you make tempeh you will want, I'm sure, to prepare and eat this food often. Children seem to like the savoury taste which is a boon as many young children have rather temperamental eating habits.

How to make tempeh

You will need a large wire cooling rack and polythene bags which you perforate with a needle so that the upper and underside holes are approximately 2.5 cm/1 inch apart.

450 g/1 lb dry weight soya beans
water to soak, rinse and cook the beans
1½ tablespoons cider vinegar
1 teaspoon tempeh starter (obtainable from healthfood stores)

1. Bring beans just to boiling point in the water. Remove from heat, cover and let stand at room temperature for 12 hours.
2. Pour off the water and rub the beans vigorously to loosen the hulls.
3. Pour on fresh water, stir and skim off as many of the hulls as you can. Pour off the water and repeat this process several times until the hulls have been removed. (A few left will not matter but the tempeh has a better flavour without them.)
4. After rubbing, the beans will be split in half and ready to cook.
5. Pour on 1.7 litres/3 pints of hot water and the vinegar. Bring to boil and cook

uncovered for 45 minutes making sure that the water is gently bubbling all the time.

6. Now drain the beans and towel dry, massaging excess moisture away. (If the beans are wet you are likely to fail in making edible tempeh.)

7. When cool and easy to touch, which takes about 7 minutes, place in a mixing bowl, stir in the culture and mix well. Leave for 1½ to 2 hours, stirring regularly.

8. Now stir then spoon the bean mixture into the perforated plastic bags until half full. Seal the open ends and flatten mixture to 1.5 cm/½ inch thickness.

9. Put flattened bags on a cooling rack so that air can circulate all around, because the growing culture needs oxygen.

10. Put the rack in a warm place (about 30°–32°C/86°–90°F is ideal) to incubate for 20 to 30 hours. A south-facing sunny window, a warm shelf in the kitchen or an airing cupboard which has a light are ideal places for the incubation period, but check the temperature occasionally as the tempeh produces its own heat and many failures occur through overheating.

11. A white mould begins to appear after the first 12 hours. This white mould looks like frost after 20-25 hours.

12. At the slightest tinge of grey your tempeh is done.

For storing and freezing see notes on page 121. Carefully note the condition of your tempeh before using.

Perfect tempeh is when the beans are tightly bound by a whitish grey mycelium or mould which spreads branch-like throughout the cake. It smells fresh and faintly of mushrooms and does not crumble when sliced.
Imperfect tempeh is characterized by the mycelium or mould being pure white and not filling the areas between the beans snugly. This can be caused by either too short an incubation period, or an uneven distribution of the starter which means there is an uneven heat during fermentation. This tempeh crumbles when cut, has a harder texture and lacks flavour when cooked.

Over-ripe tempeh is when the mycelium or mould is grey/black. This is due to sporulation. The tempeh is still safe to eat but it is stronger in taste and smells slightly of ammonia.
Ruined tempeh smells very strongly of ammonia or other unpleasant odours and can have a slimy surface. This should be discarded. If the mould is any colour (eg red, green or yellow), other than white, grey or grey/black it is unsafe to eat.

T.V.P. (TEXTURIZED VEGETABLE PROTEIN)

T.V.P. is a much maligned and misused, valuable product of the soya bean. Just 140g/5 oz when reconstituted is equal in 'complete' protein (see page 11) to that contained in approximately 450g/1 lb lean beef. Yet that 140g/5 oz of T.V.P., if not wrapped in a fancy packet, will cost you one third of the price of 450g/1 lb of the cheapest mince meat.

Besides being cheap and nutritionally valuable, it is also cholesterol-free and high in fibre. You can buy many different flavours (which are expensive), but I have stuck to simple mince and chunks in this lesson, which can be easily obtained beef-flavoured or natural.

To hydrate (reconstitute) T.V.P. mince, add 1½ cups boiling water to 1 cup of dry mince and let stand for ten minutes. To hydrate the chunks use double the volume in boiling water and let stand soaking for at least 1 hour.

SOYA BEAN RECIPES

SPROUTED SOYA BEAN PUREE
This highly nutritious purée is worth making in bulk and freezing in portions ready for particular recipes. It can be used as a drip with crudités (see *Sprouted soya bean lemon and parsley soup* on page 123) or as a spread

in sandwiches or *Pitta bread* (see page 19) with salad.

The recipe is very simple to prepare but you have to start sprouting the beans 4 days in advance (see Lesson 7). You can make the purée with ordinary cooked soya beans but the nutritional value and digestibility is greatly improved when the beans are sprouted.

225g/8 oz soya beans
1 very level teaspoon sea salt

1. Sprout the beans as directed on page 143.
2. Put the sprouted beans in a large saucepan and add three times their volume of cold water (no salt at this stage). Bring to boil and boil vigorously for 5 minutes, then simmer for 2 hours until soft.
3. Add a very level teaspoon sea salt to the cooked beans and their cooking liquid. Purée the beans, until smooth, in just enough of the cooking liquid to achieve a thick creamy consistency. Add the water gradually so that the purée does not become too runny.

Note: To freeze, divide mixture into three small plastic containers and seal with lids. Before using, defrost completely (at least 12 hours). Do not refreeze.

SPROUTED SOYA BEAN, LEMON AND PARSLEY SOUP
This soup is not only nutritious but quite delicious.

Serves 4.

1 recipe quantity Sprouted soya bean purée (see page 122)
1 litre 300 ml/2½ pt hot water
1 good size bunch spring onions, chopped
110g/4 oz button mushrooms, sliced
1 rounded tablespoon vegetable bouillon powder
1 rounded teaspoon dried tarragon
55g/2 oz parsley, chopped
juice of 2 lemons
freshly ground black pepper, to taste

1. Bring all ingredients to boil in a large heavy-based saucepan.
2. Stir well, turn down to simmer and cook on gentle heat for 10 minutes only.

Note You can add many other vegetables to this soup and vary the flavour with a variety of spices and herbs. Curried it's delicious, or with any added fresh herbs.

SPROUTED SOYA BEAN DIP WITH SWEET AND SOUR MANGO SAUCE

Serves 4 to 6.

1 recipe quantity Sprouted soya bean purée (see page 122)
½ large cucumber, cut in small pieces
1 bunch radishes, chopped
2 tablespoons each chopped red and green pepper
6 good size spring onions, finely chopped
sea salt and freshly ground black pepper, to taste
1 large mango, peeled and chopped
1 level teaspoon fresh ginger, finely grated
1 level teaspoon clear honey
1 dessertspoon shoyu (naturally fermented soy sauce)
1 tablespoon lemon juice

1. Mix the cucumber, radishes, peppers and spring onions together with the sprouted soya bean purée. Season lightly with the sea salt and black pepper.
2. To make the mango sauce, purée the mango, ginger, honey, shoyu and lemon juice in a blender until smooth.
3. To serve, spoon the mango sauce over the sprouted soya bean mixture and stir together just before eating. Serve with vegetable crudités.

BOSTON BAKED BEANS
This recipe will keep well in the fridge for a few days. Serve on wholemeal toast for a quick lunch or with jacket potatoes and salad for a very wholesome meal.

Serves 4 to 6.

225g/8 oz soya beans (dry weight)
2 tablespoons tomato purée
1 level tablespoon Barbados or muscovado
  sugar
1 level tablespoon molasses
½ level teaspoon dry mustard powder
285ml/½ pt hot water
1 teaspoon Worcester sauce
1 level tablespoon vegetable bouillon powder
1 large clove garlic, crushed
2 bay leaves
½ teaspoon mixed dried herbs

1. Soak and cook the soya beans as directed
   on page 116, until the beans are soft but
   not mushy.
2. Drain well and discard the cooking liquid.
   Stir all the other ingredients into the
   drained beans, place in a casserole dish,
   cover and bake in the oven 300°F/150°C/
   Gas Mark 2 for 2 hours.

Note: You can use haricot beans for this recipe
with equal success. Follow *Basic cooking
method* for haricot beans on page 100. Oven
baking time as above.

SOYA BEAN BURGERS

Makes 12.

225g/8 oz soya beans (dry weight)
1 level teaspoon sea salt
1 large onion, finely chopped
2 tablespoons sunflower oil
1 large clove garlic, crushed
1 rounded teaspoon oregano
1 rounded tablespoon fresh chopped parsley
1 medium size green pepper finely chopped

1 tablespoon lemon juice
85g/3 oz porridge oats
freshly ground black pepper to taste
1 egg beaten
soya oil

1. Soak and cook the beans as directed on
   page 116, adding sea salt 10 minutes
   before end of cooking time.
2. Drain well and mash with a potato
   masher.
3. Sauté the onion in the oil with the garlic
   for 7 mins with the lid on, until soft. Mix
   all the ingredients well together, blending
   the egg in last to bind. Mould mixture
   well with your hands.
4. Form the mixture into flattish rounds 1
   cm/½ inch thick and 7.5 cm/3 inch in
   diameter. The thinner the burgers the
   crisper they will be. Fry in shallow hot oil,
   on moderate heat, until golden on both
   sides. Take out with a fruit slice or slotted
   spoon and drain on absorbent kitchen
   paper.
5. Serve with *Mushroom* or *Tomato sauce*
   (see page 173), jacket potatoes and salad
   or in wholemeal or wheatmeal baps with a
   dollop of ketchup, salad leaves and spring
   onions.

Note: For vegans you can omit the egg but
press the mixture well together so that it
doesn't break up when cooking.

TOFU (SOYA MILK AND SOYA MILK YOGHURT) SAVOURIES

Tofu is extremely versatile. Throughout the
book, I have indicated how to adapt many
recipes by using tofu, usually to make them
suitable for vegans. However, tofu is delicious
enough to try whatever your diet and I hope
the recipes given below will tempt you to
make more use of this highly nutritious source
of protein.

You will also find below recipes using soya
milk and soya milk yoghurt, but these two
ingredients can be used at any time as
alternatives to goat's or cow's milk and
yoghurt.

SAVOURY SAUTEED TOFU

I usually marinate, coat and sauté small chunks of tofu before adding to soups, casseroles, stir-fry vegetables or vegetable sauces.

340g/12 oz firm tofu
3 tablespoons shoyu (naturally fermented soy sauce)
85g/3 oz wholemeal flour, plain
1 large clove garlic, crushed with a pestle and mortar with ½ teaspoon sea salt
freshly ground black pepper
1 rounded teaspoon sweet mixed herbs
sunflower, corn or sesame seed oil for frying

1. Cut tofu into 2 cm/¾ inch cubes.
2. Sprinkle half the shoyu in a large shallow bowl and place the tofu cubes in this. Pour the rest of the shoyu on top. Let tofu pieces marinate for a few minutes while you prepare the other ingredients.
3. Mix flour with garlic and salt, or garlic salt, pepper and mixed herbs, in a shallow bowl.
4. Shake off excess soy sauce from the tofu pieces and dip each one, coating well, in the flour mixture.
5. Heat 6 mm/¼ inch of oil in a frying pan and fry the tofu, turning it until golden brown on all sides.
6. Drain on absorbent kitchen paper and keep warm in a low heated oven until needed.

CHINESE LEEK AND WATERCRESS SOUP WITH TOFU

This delicate flavoured soup is quick to prepare and a delicious starter to any entertaining meal.

Serves 6.

850 ml/1½ pt water
1 rounded tablespoon vegetable bouillon powder
1 strip kombu (see page 146)
2 good size leeks, trimmed, washed and cut into thin rings
110g/4 oz button mushrooms or chanterelles (see page 148), sliced

1 good size bunch watercress, chopped (use stems)
225g/8 oz firm tofu cubed or Savoury sautéed tofu (see above)
freshly ground black pepper, to taste
1 tablespoon lemon juice

1. Bring water to boil with vegetable bouillon powder and kombu (break up kombu into small pieces).
2. Add leeks and cook for 10 minutes only.
3. Add mushrooms and continue to cook for 3 minutes more.
4. Add the chopped watercress, tofu, black pepper and lemon juice and simmer for a few minutes only until the tofu is warmed through.
5. Serve in individual small bowls, piping hot.

ORIENTAL SPICED VEGETABLES WITH TOFU

Serves 4.

40 g/1½ oz piece of tamarind (see page 166)
½ cup boiling water, to soak tamarind
285ml/½ pt boiling water
1 large bay leaf
1 cinnamon stick
170g/6 oz onion, cut into very thin rings
170g/6 oz green pepper, deseeded and coarsely chopped
110g/4 oz small button mushrooms, sliced
2 tablespoons sesame or sunflower oil
1 slightly rounded tablespoon either wholewheat or unbleached white flour
1 teaspoon methi (fenugreek leaf)
1 rounded teaspoon medium curry powder
340g/12 oz ripe tomatoes, skinned and chopped
little sea salt to taste
1 recipe quantity Savoury sautéed tofu (see above)

1. Soak the tamarind in the ½ pt boiling water for 1 hour. Then press the lot through a sieve.
2. Place the 285 ml/½ pt boiling water in a saucepan with the tamarind syrup, bay leaf, cinnamon stick, onion rings, chopped peppers and mushrooms. Bring

3. Heat oil in a pan, stir in the flour, methi and curry powder and cook on low heat for 2 minutes only. Take off heat.

4. Drain vegetables, placing stock water that drains off in a jug. Remove the bay leaf and cinnamon stick and place vegetables in a casserole dish, cover and place in a very low oven to keep warm.

5. Put pan with spices and flour in it back on heat and gradually pour in the hot stock, stir constantly and cook on gentle heat until a smooth sauce is achieved.

6. Add the chopped tomatoes and cook for 3 minutes more, stirring as it cooks.

7. Sieve this sauce, pressing as much through as possible. The sauce will be a rich warm brown colour and the consistency of a thickish gravy.

8. Take out three-quarters of the sauce and reserve. Heat the rest and pour over the hot vegetables in the casserole dish.

9. Just before serving, warm the tofu pieces in a pan over a gentle heat, place on top of the vegetables in the casserole dish, reheat the reserved sauce and pour over the top of the tofu.

10. Serve with brown rice or *Spiced ginger and sesame potatoes* (see page 168) and a fresh salad.

TOFU TEMPURA WITH SWEET AND SOUR SAUCE

Tempura is a Japanese dish which is simply sliced vegetables, sea food or chunks of meat dipped in batter and deep-fried. Tofu is also delicious cooked in this way. Have the sweet and sour sauce ready before you fry the tofu.

Serves 6.

3 tablespoons sesame seed or sunflower seed oil
1 medium size onion, peeled and finely chopped
2 cloves garlic, crushed
1 medium size carrrot, scraped and thinly sliced in slanting ovals
1 small tin bamboo shoots, well drained or 1 small turnip, thinly sliced
1 small green pepper, cut in thinnish rings then quartered
1 level teaspoon finely grated root ginger
½ level teaspoon five spice (mixture of star anise, fennel, cinnamon, clove and pepper) or allspice
110g/4 oz fresh pineapple, finely chopped (or used canned)
1½ tablespoons clear honey
3 tablespoons cider vinegar
2 tablespoons shoyu (naturally fermented soy sauce)
2 tablespoons tomato purée
1 tablespoon arrowroot
225ml/8 fl oz water
55ml/2 fl oz dry sherry
28g/1 oz soya flour
28g/1 oz brown rice flour
110g/4 oz unbleached white flour
¾ teaspoon sea salt
1 level teaspoon baking powder
1 egg and 285ml/½ pt water or 330 ml/12 fl oz water
450g/1 lb firm tofu, cut into 2 cm/¾ inch cubes
little shoyu (naturally fermented soy sauce)
small bowl wholemeal flour, for coating
soya oil for deep-frying

1. Stir-fry quickly in hot oil the onions, garlic, carrots and bamboo shoots or turnip for 3 minutes only.

2. Add the peppers and continue to stir-fry for 2 more minutes.

3. Stir in the grated ginger, five spice or allspice and chopped pineapple. Set aside while you mix the honey, vinegar, 2 tablespoons shoyu, tomato purée, arrowroot and sherry in a medium sized bowl, gradually adding the water.

4. Pour this liquid over the vegetables.

5. Return to gentle heat and let cook until the mixture thickens slightly, stirring all the time.

6. Set this sweet and sour sauce aside to reheat when the tofu tempura is ready.

7. Sieve the soya, rice and white flour with the baking powder and sea salt into a large bowl.

8. Beat the egg with the water, make a well in the centre of the flour mixture and gradually stir in the liquid, mixing to form a smooth, creamy batter.

9. Cover batter and leave to stand for 1 hour before using.
10. In a shallow dish, sprinkle some shoyu over the cubed tofu and leave to marinate for 1 hour. Turn the pieces in the shoyu a few times to coat well.
11. When the batter is ready and the tofu well marinated, heat 6 cm/2½ inch soya oil in a wide frying pan until hot.
12. Drain the tofu, roll in the wholemeal flour to coat.
13. Stir the batter and dip two pieces of tofu at a time on a slotted spoon into the batter (coating well).
14. Lift the tofu out of the batter and plunge into the hot fat, still on the slotted spoon. Deep-fry until golden brown. Repeat until all the tofu is used.
15. Drain tofu tempura on absorbent kitchen paper.
16. Reheat the sweet and sour sauce and spoon it into a serving dish.
17. Lay the crisp tofu tempura on top.
18. Garnish with a little chopped parsley and serve immediately with any thin, long grain brown rice, such as Surinam (see page 79).

TOFU BURGERS

Children like these in baps smeared with tomato sauce for a light lunch. Give them an apple afterwards and they will have had a pretty wholesome midday meal.

Makes 8.

55g/2 oz bulgur
2 tablespoons shoyu (naturally fermented soy sauce)
1 onion, very finely chopped
1 tablespoon sunflower oil
340g/12 oz firm tofu
2 tablespoons fresh chopped parsley
2 tablespons green pepper, very finely chopped
freshly ground black pepper
1 level tablespoon arrowroot or 1 medium sized egg
soya oil for frying

1. Put bulgur in a small mixing bowl and stir in the shoyu.

2. Add enough boiling water to just cover and let stand for 20 minutes.
3. Sweat the onion in the oil for 5 minutes with lid on until soft.
4. Stir into the bulgur mixture with all the other ingredients. Blend well, taste and add more shoyu if necessary.
5. Mould well together with hands and form into 8 burgers 1cm/½ inch thick. Fry in hot oil for 3 minutes on each side until golden.
6. Drain well on kitchen paper and serve hot with a tomato sauce and steamed green vegetables, or cold with salad.

Note For vegans omit the egg and mould ingredients well together.

LEEK, TOMATO AND TOFU QUICHE

Instead of eggs, milk and yoghurt as the liquid in this quiche (and the following variations on the recipe), I have used tofu and soya milk with a little soya flour as a slight setting agent. This produces a delicious non-dairy quiche, suitable for those on a vegan diet. It is also very low fat and great if you are slimming.

Serves 4 to 6.
You will need a 25cm/10 inch quiche or flan dish, greased.

¾ recipe quantity of Basic wholemeal shortcrust pastry (see page 38), chilled
225g/8 oz leeks (weight when trimmed and thinly sliced)
2 tablespoons sunflower or virgin olive oil
140ml/¼ pt soya milk
1 tablespoon lemon juice
340g/12 oz firm tofu
½ level teaspoon ground mace
1 level teaspoon dried tarragon
1 level teaspoon oregano
¼ teaspoon mustard powder
¼ teaspoon black pepper, freshly ground
2 level teaspoons vegetable bouillon powder
1 level tablespoon soya flour or arrowroot
3 medium sized tomatoes, thinly sliced
2 level tablespoons pumpkin seeds, roughly ground
2 level tablespoons wholemeal breadcrumbs
little more dried herbs

1. Preheat oven to 375°F/190°C/Gas Mark 5.
2. Roll out the pastry to fit the quiche dish and line the dish with it. Trim the edges, prick the base and bake blind for 12 minutes. Leave to cool.
3. When pastry case is almost cold, set oven again to 375°F/190°C/Gas Mark 5.
4. Sauté the leeks in the oil for 7 minutes until just tender. Leave to cool.
5. In a blender or liquidizer blend together the soya milk, lemon juice, tofu, mace, tarragon, oregano, mustard, black pepper, vegetable bouillon powder and soya flour or arrowroot until smooth. Pour this onto the leeks and stir to mix well.
6. Spoon this mixture into the baked pastry case and gently press the tomato slices on top (do not submerge them).
7. Mix the pumpkin seeds, breadcrumbs and dried herbs together and sprinkle over the filling.
8. Bake in the preheated oven for 30 minutes.

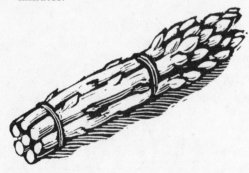

ASPARAGUS, TOMATO, TARRAGON AND TOFU QUICHE
Serves 4 to 6.
You will need a 25 cm/10 inch quiche or flan dish, greased.

¾ recipe quantity of Basic wholemeal shortcrust pastry (see page 38), chilled
225g/8 oz asparagus (fresh or frozen)
2 tablespoons sunflower or virgin olive oil
170g/6 oz onion, peeled and finely chopped
1 small clove garlic, crushed
1 level tablespoon soya flour or arrowroot
½ level teaspoon ground mace
¼ level teaspoon mustard powder
1 level teaspoon dried tarragon

340g/12 oz firm tofu
140ml/¼ pt soya milk
1 tablespoon lemon juice
2 level teaspoons vegetable bouillon powder
¼ teaspoon black pepper, freshly ground
3 medium sized tomatoes, thinly sliced
2 level tablespoons pumpkin seeds, roughly ground
2 level tablespoons wholemeal breadcrumbs
little more dried herbs

1. Preheat oven to 375°F/190°C/Gas Mark 5.
2. Roll out the pastry to fit the quiche dish and line the dish with it. Trim the edges, prick the base and bake blind for 12 minutes. Leave to cool.
3. When pastry case is almost cold, set oven again to 375°F/190°C/Gas Mark 5.
4. If using fresh asparagus, then trim off woody ends and steam for 7 minutes only. If using frozen then steam for 4 minutes only.
5. Cut off the tips and reserve. Roughly chop the stems. Let cool.
6. Sauté the onion and garlic for 10 minutes with the lid on until soft. Let cool.
7. In a blender or liquidizer mix soya flour or arrowroot, mace, mustard, tarragon, tofu, soya milk, lemon juice, vegetable bouillon powder, pepper and chopped asparagus stems until smooth. Pour this onto the onions and stir to mix well.
8. Spoon this mixture into the pastry case and arrange the asparagus tips and sliced tomato on top pressing them gently in (do not submerge).
9. Mix the pumpkin seeds, breadcrumbs and dried herbs together and sprinkle over the filling.
10. Bake in the preheated oven for 30 minutes.

COURGETTE AND MUSHROOM QUICHE
I use dried mushrooms in this recipe because the flavour is stronger than fresh mushrooms and I think much better in tofu quiches. You can use 110g/4 oz fresh sliced mushrooms instead.

Serves 4 to 6.
You will need a 25 cm/10 inch quiche or flan dish, greased.

¾ recipe quantity of Basic wholemeal
    shortcrust pastry (see page 38), chilled
4 medium sized dried mushrooms or 110g/4 oz
    fresh, sliced
225g/8 oz courgettes, thinly sliced
170g/6 oz onion (weight when finely chopped)
1 clove garlic, crushed
3 tablespoons sunflower or virgin olive oil
1 very level teaspoon celery seeds, finely ground
1 tablespoon lemon juice
1 rounded teaspoon dried marjoram
1 level teaspoon vegetable bouillon powder
1 level tablespoon finely chopped parsley
140ml/¼ pt soya milk
340g/12 oz firm tofu
1 extra teaspoon vegetable bouillon powder
1 level teaspoon soya flour or arrowroot
¼ teaspoon black pepper, freshly ground
2 level tablespoons pumpkin seeds, roughly
    ground
2 level tablespoons wholemeal breadcrumbs

1. Preheat oven to 375°F/190°C/Gas Mark 5.
2. Roll out the pastry to fit the quiche dish
   and line the dish with it. Trim the edges,
   prick the base and bake blind for 12
   minutes. Leave to cool.
3. When pastry case is almost cold, set oven
   again to 375°F/190°C/Gas Mark 5.
4. If using dried mushrooms, then soak in
   boiling water for 15 minutes. Cut off
   woody stems and discard. Chop the heads
   in small pieces.
5. Fry the courgette slices in a little of the
   oil over a moderate heat until lightly
   browned on both sides. Take out with a
   fish slice or slotted spoon and leave to
   cool.
6. Sauté the onion and garlic with the lid
   on the pan until tender. Take out with a
   fish slice or slotted spoon and leave to
   cool.
7. Fry the dried chopped or fresh sliced
   mushrooms on a moderate heat, stirring
   constantly for 3 minutes.
8. Add the crushed celery seeds and fry for
   1 minute then stir in the lemon juice,
   marjoram and vegetable bouillon powder
   and parsley and fry for one minute more.
9. In a blender or liquidizer blend soya
   milk, tofu, one teaspoon vegetable

bouillon powder, soya flour or arrowroot
and black pepper until smooth.
10. Pour into a bowl and stir in half the fried
    courgettes and the onion and the
    mushroom mixture. Spoon into the pastry
    case.
11. Arrange the remaining fried courgettes
    on top of the filling, pressing them gently
    into the mixture (do not submerge).
12. Mix the pumpkin seeds, breadcrumbs and
    dried herbs together and sprinkle on the
    topping.
13. Bake in the preheated oven for 30
    minutes.

Note Other vegetables for the filling could
include steamed, chopped broccoli with onion
or simply stir in a mixture of sautéed onion,
garlic, basil, aubergine, peppers, mushrooms
and tomato, making sure the mixture is not
too wet.

TOFU (AND SOYA MILK) DESSERTS

TOASTED HAZELNUT, COFFEE, MAPLE TOFU ICE CREAM
Serves 6.

2 level teaspoons agar-agar powder
570ml/1 pt soya milk
225g/8 oz firm tofu
4 tablespoons maple syrup
4 tablespoons clear honey
1 level teaspoon decaffeinated instant coffee
    granules
1½ teaspoons natural vanilla essence
5 tablespoons sunflower or corn oil
85g/3 oz chopped toasted hazelnuts

1. Warm the milk, stir in the agar-agar and
   keep stirring vigorously as you bring the
   milk to boil. Then remove from the heat.
2. Put all the ingredients in a blender except
   for the oil. Blend well together on high
   speed then, still on high speed, dribble in
   the oil.
3. Stir in the chopped hazels.

4. Pour the mixture into a freezer container, cover and freeze for 1 hour until firmish at the edge and softish in the middle.
5. Scoop out and blend until smooth. Freeze for a further hour.
6. Scoop out and blend again, then freeze completely.

Note: Watch the freezing process the first time you make this as the times will differ according to the depth of your mixture and the temperature of your freezer.

SOFT SUMMER FRUIT TOFU ICE CREAM
Serves 6.

2 level teaspoons agar agar
285ml/½ pt soya milk
225g/8 oz either fresh strawberries, raspberries, apricots (skinned) or blackcurrants
225g/8 oz tofu
2 rounded tablespoons clear honey
4 tablespoons either pure strawberry, raspberry, exotic fruit or blackcurrant juice concentrate (see page 184)
140ml/¼ pt water
good pinch sea salt
1½ teaspoons natural vanilla essence
5 tablespoons sunflower or corn oil

1. Heat the milk and add the agar agar stirring vigorously as you bring to boil. Take off the heat.
2. In another saucepan heat the fruit at very low heat with the honey, fruit juice concentrate and water. Simmer on lowest heat for a few minutes until all the fruit is soft.

3. Press the lot through a sieve extracting as much purée as possible. Put this runny purée in a blender.
4. Add all the other ingredients except the oil. Blend on high speed until smooth.
5. Then, still on a high speed, dribble in the oil.
6. Freeze and blend as instructed in stages 4, 5 and 6 of the previous recipe.

TOFU, CAROB, BANANA AND APRICOT CREAM PIE
Serves 6.
You will need a 23 cm/9 inch flan dish greased and lined.

¾ recipe quantity Wholemeal or wheatmeal sweet pastry (see page 48)
4 good size ripe bananas
small can apricot halves in natural fruit juice
340g/12 oz firm tofu
55g/2 oz honey
1 teaspoon natural vanilla essence
2 level tablespoons carob powder
1 level teaspoon cinnamon
2 tablespoons agar-agar flakes
few flaked almonds to top

1. Preheat oven to 350°F/180°C/Gas Mark 4.
2. Roll out the pastry to fit the flan dish and line the dish with it. Trim the edges, prick the base and bake blind for 12 minutes. Leave to cool.
3. When pastry case is almost cold, reset the oven to 350°F/180°C/Gas Mark 4.
4. Mash the bananas and drain the apricots, reserving the juice. Roughly chop the apricot halves.
5. Blend tofu with honey, vanilla, carob and cinnamon in a bowl. Stir in chopped apricots and mashed bananas.
6. Heat 140ml/¼ pt of the apricot juice in a small saucepan to boiling. Take off heat. Stir in the agar-agar flakes and keep stirring until dissolved.
7. Pour this onto the other ingredients and mix well.
8. Pour this mixture into the pastry case and sprinkle on a few flaked almonds.
9. Bake in the centre of the preheated oven for 40 minutes.

TOFU, BANANA AND RASPBERRY OR STRAWBERRY CREAM PIE
This filling does not have to be baked but bake the pastry case blind as in the previous recipe.

Serves 6.
You will need a 23 cm/9 inch flan dish, greased and lined.

¾ recipe quantity Wholemeal or wheatmeal
  sweet pastry (see page 48)
4 good size ripe bananas
225g/8 oz fresh raspberries or strawberries
3 tablespoons fruit sugar
340g/12 oz firm tofu
1 teaspoon vanilla essence
3 level tablespoons agar agar flakes
few toasted chopped hazelnuts or flaked
  almonds to top

1. Prepare and bake the pastry case as in stages 1 and 2 of the previous recipe.
2. Mash the bananas and place in a bowl. Heat the raspberries or strawberries in a heavy-based saucepan with the sugar until sugar has dissolved and the fruit is surrounded in syrup (do not boil).
3. Drain and reserve the syrup.
4. Stir the fruit into the mashed bananas.
5. Blend the tofu and vanilla essence together and stir into the fruit.
6. Heat the syrup to boiling then turn down heat and add the agar agar flakes. Stir on a low heat until dissolved. Pour this over fruit and tofu mixture and blend in well.
7. Pour mixture into the baked pastry case, sprinkle on the toasted nuts and chill for 2 hours until set.

TOFU FRUIT FOOLS
For these you can use any soft fruit such as blackcurrants, raspberries, strawberries or cranberries. Add more honey if the mixture is not sweet enough for your taste.

Serves 4 to 6.
340g/12 oz soft fruit of your choice
juice of half lemon
2 rounded tablespoons clear honey
285ml/½ pt boiling water

20g/¾ oz agar agar flakes
225g/8 oz firm tofu

1. Place fruit, lemon juice, honey and half the water in a saucepan. Bring to boil and simmer for 4 minutes.
2. Dissolve the agar-agar flakes in the remaining hot water. Stir into the fruit mixture and cook for 1 minute until well mixed.
3. Purée the fruit mixture in a food processor or liquidizer until smooth. Let cool then blend in the tofu until smooth.
4. Chill in individual dishes until set.

TOFU CAKES

You can make a huge variety of cakes using tofu and no eggs. In fact, you can make some of the cakes in Lesson 3 without eggs and still get good results (light sponge must be made with eggs).

I will give you three basic recipes plus a few ideas for variations, so experiment with different ingredients, keeping the proportions the same as in the recipes and you can't go far wrong.

TOFU, CAROB AND PECAN NUT CAKE
No eggs, sugar, margarine or butter are needed in this recipe. It makes a very tasty and nutritious cake and is very simple to make.

You will need a 23 cm/9 inch round cake tin, oiled and lined.

170g/6 oz clear honey
140ml/¼ pt sunflower oil
340g/12 oz firm tofu
½ teaspoon sea salt
1 teaspoon natural vanilla essence
110g/4 oz pecan nuts (chop 85g/3 oz, leave 28g/
  1 oz in halves to decorate)
280g/10 oz wholemeal flour, self-raising
55g/2 oz carob powder
1 very level teaspoon cinnamon

1. Preheat oven to 300°F/150°C/Gas Mark 2.
2. Blend honey, oil, tofu and sea salt and vanilla essence well together.

131

3. Stir in the chopped pecans.
4. Sift the flour, carob powder and cinnamon together, and gradually add to the tofu mixture. Mix well.
5. Spoon mixture into the oiled and lined cake tin and dot on top with the pecan nut halves.
6. Bake for 30 to 35 minutes. Test centre by inserting a sharp knife. If it comes out clean then your cake is done.

TOFU, DRIED MANGO AND GINGER CAKE

Omit the pecans, carob powder and cinnamon from the previous recipe and add 85g/3 oz fresh ginger peeled and finely grated, 85g/3 oz dried mango pieces soaked for 1 hour in boiling water then drained and chopped and 1 teaspoon mixed spice, and use 340g/12 oz wholemeal self-raising flour instead of 280g/10 oz.

Stir the grated ginger and the chopped mango into the mixture at stage 3 and proceed with the method in the previous recipe.

TOFU LIGHT FRUIT CAKE

You will need a 25 cm/10 inch round cake tin, oiled and lined.

140ml/¼ pint sunflower oil
340g/12 oz firm tofu
½ teaspoon sea salt
170g/6 oz clear honey
few drops natural vanilla essence
310g/10 oz wholemeal self-raising flour
1 level teaspoon fresh ground nutmeg
½ teaspoon ground cinnamon
55g/2 oz ground almonds
55g/2 oz sultanas
55g/2 oz raisins
55g/2 oz pre-soaked dried apricots, chopped and soaked in apple juice for 1 hour
30g/1 oz blanched almonds and a few glacé cherry halves to decorate

1. Preheat oven to 300°F/150°C/Gas Mark 2.
2. Blend oil, tofu, salt, honey and vanilla in a large mixing bowl.
3. Sift flour with spices and gradually add to the tofu mixture, mixing well in.
4. Stir in the ground almonds and the dried fruit, making sure the soaked apricots

have all surface moisture removed on absorbent kitchen paper.
5. Spoon into the prepared tin, arrange blanched almonds and glacé cherries on top and bake for 40 to 45 minutes. Test centre with a sharp knife; if it comes out clean then the cake is done.

TOFU RICH FRUIT CAKE

Simply double the fruit content in the previous recipe by adding 55g/2 oz chopped dates, 55g/2 oz finely chopped dried apple and 55g/2 oz chopped dried pineapple.

TEMPEH RECIPES

Tempeh can be served in a variety of exciting ways. Its delicate flavour enhances as well as absorbs the flavours of other foods including herbs and spices. It is also quick to use for preparing almost instant meals, once you have a stock of it in the freezer.

Just like tofu, it can be used as a source of protein in so many recipes. Use it instead of meat or fish or with it. Try adding sautéed tempeh to savoury pies, curries or risotto. Experiment and you will find it well worth the effort, both in terms of taste and nutritional value.

CRISPY FRIED TEMPEH

These are delicious added to either soup, stir-fried vegetables or sauces, such as curry or sweet and sour sauce, or in a goulash instead of other forms of protein.

Serves 4.

225g/8 oz tempeh
1 tablespoon shoyu (naturally fermented soy sauce)
1 tablespoon sherry
1 clove garlic, minced
gram flour (chick pea flour) or wholemeal flour for dusting
oil for deep frying

1. Cut tempeh into 2 cm/¾ inch cubes. Blend shoyu, sherry and garlic together and place in a shallow bowl. Marinate the

tempeh in this for 15 minutes or longer, turning occasionally to coat all sides.

2. Shake off any marinade of the tempeh cubes and roll each in the flour, then let stand on a clean plate for 5 minutes.
3. Heat oil in a frying pan.
4. Carefully place the floured tempeh pieces into the hot oil. Do not crowd the pan.
5. Fry, turning when necessary, until golden brown and crisp on all sides. Drain on absorbent kitchen paper.

TEMPEH, MUSHROOM AND NUTTY PATE

This rich pâté has a smooth texture and will keep for one week in the fridge. It is just perfect for a buffet party. You will need a food processor or a blender.

Serves 6 to 8.

55g/2 oz whole almonds
55g/2 oz hazelnuts
4 tablespoons virgin olive or sunflower oil
1 clove garlic, crushed
1 medium onion, finely chopped
225g/1/2 lb sliced button mushrooms
225g/8 oz tempeh, cut into 2.5 cm/1 inch pieces
good pinch sea salt
1 teaspoon sweet mixed herbs
1 tablespoon shoyu (or more, to your taste)
55g/2 oz pistachio nuts
3 tablespoons sunflower oil (to grind nuts with)
freshly ground black pepper to taste

1. Toast the almonds and hazelnuts in the oven at 170°C/325°C/Gas Mark 3 for approximately 20 minutes until lightly browned.
2. Heat the 4 tablespoons of sunflower oil in a pan and sauté garlic, onion and mushrooms until soft – about 5 minutes.
3. Add the tempeh, pinch sea salt and mixed herbs and cook gently for 10 minutes with lid off to let the liquid evaporate.
4. Stir in the shoyu.
5. Grind toasted almonds and hazelnuts with the pistachio nuts in a blender or food processor until powdery.
6. Add 3 tablespoons of sunflower oil and blend well together.
7. Gradually add the sautéed tempeh

mixture and blend until mixture is smooth and thick.
8. Scoop out, place in a serving dish and sprinkle freshly ground black pepper over the top.

TOMATO BROTH WITH TEMPEH DUMPLINGS

This soup is a meal in itself.

Serves 4 to 6.

1 large onion, finely chopped
1 large clove garlic (more if you wish)
3 tablespoons sunflower oil
110g/4 oz short grain brown rice (dry weight), washed and drained
1 litre/1 3/4 pt hot water
1 vegetable stock cube
1 bay leaf
2 medium sized potatoes, scrubbed and diced
2 medium sized carrots, scrubbed and diced
3 sticks celery, chopped
1 level teaspoon basil, dried
1/2 teaspoon dried tarragon
450g/1 lb ripe soft tomatoes, skinned
1 tablespoon tomato purée
1 tablespoon shoyu (naturally fermented soy sauce)
freshly ground black pepper
225g/8 oz tempeh, chopped into small pieces
1 egg
140ml/1/4 pt soya milk, goat's milk or cow's milk
1/4 teaspoon freshly ground black pepper
1/4 teaspoon mustard powder
110g/4 oz wholemeal flour
1 level teaspoon baking powder
1/2 teaspoon sea salt
1 litre/1 3/4 pt stock (or hot water to which you have added 1 tablespoon vegetable bouillon powder)

1. Sauté onion and garlic in the oil in a large heavy-based saucepan until soft, about 6 minutes.
2. Stir in the brown rice and fry gently for a few minutes more.
3. Pour in the hot water, stock cube and bay leaf.
4. Bring to boil and simmer with lid on for 20 minutes.

5. Add the potatoes, carrots, celery and herbs and cook for 10 minutes more with lid on.

6. Purée the skinned tomatoes and add these with the tomato purée. Continue to cook for 5 more minutes.

7. Stir in shoyu and freshly ground black pepper. Set aside to reheat when dumplings are ready.

8. To make the dumplings, blend the tempeh, egg, milk, pepper and mustard in a food processor or liquidizer until smooth.

9. Sift flour, baking powder and sea salt together and blend with other ingredients. You will end up with a thick batter.

10. In a deep frying pan bring the stock to boil and, using a tablespoon, drop four to five spoonfuls of the mixture into the boiling water. Make sure that you give the spoonfuls enough space to expand without touching each other.

11. Cover pan and simmer for 5 minutes, turn the dumplings over and cook for a further 5 minutes with lid off. Keep warm in a large covered dish in the oven. (Note: save the stock water and use for sauces, gravies or soups).

12. Finally, reheat the tomato broth and gently place the dumplings in. Do not boil but let dumplings absorb the flavour of the broth before serving.

TEMPEH OSSO BUCO STYLE
Serves 4.

340g/12 oz tempeh, cut into 6 portions
1 tablespoon flour for coating, with a little sea salt added
3 tablespoons olive or sunflower oil
3 medium sized carrots, very finely chopped
2 sticks celery, very finely chopped
1 good sized onion, very finely chopped
2 cloves garlic, crushed
200ml/⅓ pt dry white wine
200ml/⅓ pt hot water, to which you have added 1 tablespoon vegetable bouillon powder
396g/14 oz can tomatoes, liquidized
freshly ground black pepper

½ teaspoon honey (optional)
½ teaspoon dried rosemary or 1 small sprig of fresh rosemary
3 tablespoons finely chopped parsley
grated rind of 1 large lemon
1 clove garlic, crushed

1. Coat the tempeh in a little seasoned flour.

2. In a large heavy-based saucepan sauté the floured tempeh in hot oil until just lightly golden on both sides, about 2 minutes. Take out and leave to one side.

3. Sauté the very finely chopped carrot, celery, onion and garlic for 7 minutes with lid off, until lightly browned.

4. Put tempeh back into the pot with vegetables.

5. Pour over the wine, stock and tomatoes.

6. Season with freshly ground black pepper, the honey and rosemary. Simmer over low heat with lid on for 25 minutes. Uncover and cook gently for 5 more minutes.

7. Mix garnish ingredients together.

8. Using a slotted spoon or fish slice, remove tempeh carefully and place on a warm serving dish. Pour sauce over this and sprinkle on the garnish.

9. Serve with a tagliatelle pasta or rice and a fresh salad for a truly delightful dinner-party dish.

ORIENTAL TEMPEH STEW
Serves 4 to 6.

340g/12 oz tempeh
wholemeal flour for coating, seasoned with sea salt and freshly ground black pepper

3 tablespoons sunflower oil
1 good sized carrot
6 large spring onions, including green stems
570ml/1 pt hot water
1 vegetable stock cube
1 small clove garlic, crushed
115g/4 oz button mushrooms
1 level tablespoon tahini (sesame seed paste)
1 level tablespoon tomato purée
2 star anise
½ teaspoon freshly grated ginger root
1 tablespoon shoyu (naturally fermented soy
* sauce)*
2 tablespoons rice wine or sherry
1 level dessertspoon honey

1. Cut tempeh into 2.5 x 5 cm/1 x 2 inch strips.
2. Roll these in the seasoned flour.
3. Heat oil in a frying pan and sauté the tempeh until lightly browned on both sides. Take out with a fish slice and drain on kitchen paper.
4. Slice the carrot in very thin slanting ovals.
5. Cut spring onions in thin slanting strips.
6. Bring hot water plus the stock cube to boil and add tempeh, sliced carrot and garlic. Cover and simmer for 5 minutes.
7. Add spring onions and mushrooms, cover and continue to simmer for 5 minutes more.
8. Add all other ingredients. Stir well, cover and let cook for 10 minutes.
9. Take out star anise and serve the stew with plain boiled brown rice and a fresh salad.

TEMPEH WITH BARBECUE SAUCE
Serves 5.
You will need a large shallow baking dish.

450g/1 lb tempeh
4 tablespoons sunflower oil
285ml/1 pint Barbecue sauce (see page 174)

1. Cut tempeh into 2 cm/¾ inch wide x 5 cm/ 2 inch strips and fry in hot oil until golden brown all over. Drain on absorbent kitchen paper.
2. Spread a thin layer of the barbecue sauce over the bottom of the baking dish.

3. Place the tempeh strips on top then spoon a generous amount of barbecue sauce on top.
4. Leave to marinate for 30 minutes to let the tempeh absorb the flavours of the sauce.
5. Bake in the centre of the oven 350°F/ 180°C/Gas Mark 4 for 15 minutes until the mixture bubbles.
6. Serve with rice and salad or stuffed in *Pitta bread* (see page 19) with crisp lettuce leaves.

TEMPEH TEMPURA WITH SWEET AND SOUR SAUCE
Serves 6.

Follow the recipe for *Tofu tempura with sweet and sour sauce* (see page 126), but use tempeh instead of tofu.

T.V.P. (TEXTURIZED VEGETABLE PROTEIN) RECIPES

VEGETABLE BOLOGNESE SAUCE
This mixture freezes well, so if you want to have a few quick meals ready in the freezer double the recipe quantity and freeze what you don't want to use immediately. It will defrost easily on very low heat while you prepare the rest of the meal. For children I always liquidize the cooked sauce for a few seconds (take care not to make it too smooth).

Makes 4 to 6 servings.

100g/3½ oz T.V.P. soya mince, either natural
* or beef flavour*
boiling water to reconstitute (see page 122)
1 rounded teaspoon vegetable bouillon powder
3 tablespoons either virgin olive oil or
* sunflower oil*
1 large onion, peeled and chopped
2 large cloves garlic, crushed
4 tender stalks celery
1 medium size green pepper
110g/4 oz button mushrooms, sliced
3 tablespoons fresh parsley, chopped

1 rounded teaspoon basil
2 bay leaves
1 level teaspoon tarragon (optional)
794g/1 lb 12 oz can tomatoes, chopped before
    adding
2 rounded tablespoons tomato purée
½ level teaspoon black pepper, freshly ground
1 tablespoon lemon juice (optional)

1. Put soya mince into a small bowl.
2. Measure out 1½ times the volume of the
   soya mince in boiling water. Stir in the
   vegetable bouillon powder and dissolve.
3. Pour this over the mince and leave to
   stand for 10 minutes.
4. Sauté the onion, garlic and celery in the
   oil for 10 minutes with the lid on. Add the
   soya mince and fry stirring constantly for
   3 minutes.
5. Add peppers, mushrooms, parsley, basil,
   bay leaves and tarragon (if using) and fry
   for 2 minutes more.
6. Add tomatoes, tomato purée, black pepper
   and lemon juice. Bring to boil stirring
   constantly.
7. Turn down heat, cover and let simmer for
   25 minutes.
8. Liquidize the sauce for a few seconds in a
   blender, to a texture that is still a little
   rough. This enhances the flavour and, as
   previously mentioned, is advisable for
   children.
9. Serve on a bed of wholewheat spaghetti,
   tagliatelle, brown rice, buckwheat
   spaghetti or noodles, topped with a little
   grated Parmesan, Pecarino or Cheddar
   cheese.

LASAGNE
This recipe is good enough to serve for an
informal dinner party or casual buffet. For
speed I use wholewheat or spinach precooked
lasagne.

Serves 6 to 8.
You will need a deep baking dish, oiled.

1 recipe quantity Vegetable bolognese sauce
    (see page 135)
1 small glass red wine (optional)
225g/8 oz wholewheat or spinach precooked
    lasagne

225g/8 oz quark or cottage cheese
1 recipe quantity Basic white sauce (see page
    172)
55g/2 oz Parmesan, Pecorino or Cheddar
    cheese, finely grated
1 very level teaspoon oregano to top

1. Preheat the oven to 350°F/180°C/Gas Mark
   4.
2. Heat the sauces and keep hot while
   assembling the dish.
3. Line the dish with a layer of pasta. Spoon
   on half the Bolognese sauce. Dot with half
   the quark or cottage cheese.
4. Top with another layer of pasta and spoon
   on half of the white sauce. Spoon on the
   other half of the Bolognese sauce, dot
   again with the rest of the quark or cottage
   cheese and top with a layer of pasta.
5. Finally, pour on the rest of the white
   sauce and sprinkle on cheese and a little
   oregano.
6. Bake in the centre of the oven for 1 hour.
Serve with one bowl of fresh green salad and
one bowl of grated raw salad (see page 00) for
a delicious and satisfying meal.

STUFFED MARROW
This dish is great to prepare if you have any
left-over Bolognese sauce and cooked rice.

Serves 4 to 6.

2 medium sized marrows (900g/2 lb each in
    weight)
½ recipe quantity Vegetable bolognese sauce
    (see page 135)
110g/4 oz brown rice cooked and drained if
    necessary (see page 80 on how to cook)
1 recipe quantity Basic white sauce (see page
    172)
2 rounded tablespoons Greek yoghurt
85g/3 oz Parmesan, Pecorino or Cheddar
    cheese
1 teaspoon mixed dried herbs to top

1. Preheat the oven to 400°F/200°C/Gas Mark
   6.
2. Cut the marrows in half lengthwise and
   scoop out the seeds and soft middle pulp.
3. Steam marrow halves for 15 minutes
   (boiling in water makes them too soggy).

Let drain in a colander then pat dry with absorbent kitchen paper. Place hollow side up in a large baking dish.

4. Mix the Bolognese sauce with equal amounts in volume of cooked rice. Spoon into the four hollows piling the filling a little above the rims of the hollows.

5. Whisk the yoghurt into the hot white sauce and spoon on top of the stuffed marrows. Sprinkle on the grated cheese and a little dried mixed herbs.

6. Bake in the preheated oven for 25 minutes.

STUFFED COURGETTES
Serves 4.

Use 6 medium size courgettes, about 15 cm/ 6 inch long instead of the marrows in the previous recipe. Blanch in boiling water for 2 minutes only. Immerse in cold water, wipe dry and cut in half lengthwise. Scoop out a shallow hollow in the centre of each half. Save pulp and mash with the mixture of Bolognese sauce and rice. Place courgette halves in an oiled baking dish. Spoon the rice mixture into the hollows piling it high. Spoon over the white sauce and yoghurt mixture, sprinkle on the grated cheese and dried herbs. Bake for 25 minutes at 400°F/200°C/Gas Mark 6.

GOULASH WITH SOYA CHUNKS
This is simple and quick to prepare once you have soaked the chunks.

Serves 4 to 6.

110g/4 oz soya chunks, beef-flavoured
1 large onion, peeled and chopped
1 large clove garlic, crushed
3 tablespoons sunflower oil
1 large green pepper, deseeded and chopped
1 large bay leaf
2 level teaspoons paprika
1 rounded teaspoon vegetable bouillon powder
1 rounded tablespoon tomato purée
794g/1 lb 12 oz can tomatoes, chopped
¼ teaspoon black pepper, freshly ground
1 tablespoon unbleached white flour
140g/5 oz Greek yoghurt

1. Soak the soya chunks in boiling water for 2 hours. Drain and squeeze out liquid.

2. Sauté the onion and garlic in the oil for 10 minutes with the lid on. Add the soya chunks and fry for 3 minutes stirring the mixture continuously to coat the chunks well.

3. Add green pepper and continue to fry for 2 minutes. Add bay leaf, paprika and vegetable bouillon powder and fry for 2 minutes more again stirring to cook ingredients evenly.

4. Add tomato purée, chopped tomatoes and black pepper and stir in well. Simmer with the lid on for 40 minutes.

5. Blend flour with the yoghurt (this stops the mixture curdling) until smooth.

6. Pour this into the rest of the ingredients and blend well. Bring to boil stirring then simmer for another 10 minutes.

7. Serve with long grain brown rice and steamed broccoli and French beans or a fresh green salad.

SOYA CHUNK STEAK AND VEGETABLE PIE
The first time I made this, I added 55g/2 oz finely chopped kidney and fried it at the same time as the chunks in the method. No one knew that the chunks were soya. In fact I had made more effort to enrich the sauce than I usually did in our traditional steak and kidney pie, with the result that it tasted even better! The kidney is not necessary (so don't worry if you're a vegetarian) but it's a good idea to include it if your family is used to the traditional flavour, at least the first time you try.

Serves 6.
You will need a 25 cm/10 inch deep pie dish.

110g/4 oz soya chunks, beef-flavoured
1 medium size onion, peeled and chopped
1 large clove garlic, crushed
2 medium size carrots, scraped and cut into
    thin 2.5 cm/1 inch sticks
3 tablespoons sunflower or corn oil
3 stick celery, chopped
1 medium size leek, trimmed and chopped
1 small green pepper, deseeded and chopped

2 tablespoons parsley, finely chopped
1 level teaspoon mixed dried herbs
1 slightly rounded teaspoon wholemeal flour
1 level teaspoon vegetable bouillon powder
¼ teaspoon black pepper, freshly ground
1 generous tablespoon tomato purée
1 tablespoon shoyu
1 recipe quantity either Basic wholemeal
    shortcrust pastry (see page 38) or
    Wholemeal cheese shortcrust pastry (see
    page 39), chilled
little beaten egg or milk to glaze

1. Soak the soya chunks in boiling water for
   2 hours. Drain and squeeze out excess
   liquid.
2. Sauté the onion, garlic and carrots in the
   oil for 5 minutes. Add the chunks and
   continue to fry for 3 minutes.
3. Add the celery, leeks, green pepper,
   parsley and herbs and fry for 2 minutes
   more.
4. Stir in the flour and vegetable bouillon
   powder and cook for 1 minute stirring
   the ingredients so that they do not stick
   to the pan.
5. Gradually pour in 570ml/1 pt boiling
   water, stirring as you do this. Add
   pepper, tomato purée and shoyu and mix
   well.
6. Bring to boil then simmer with the lid on
   for 15 minutes only.
7. Put into the pie dish and let the mixture
   cool before topping with pastry.
8. Preheat the oven to 350°F/180°C/Gas
   Mark 4.
9. Roll out the pastry to fit the dish (use all
   the pastry as this topping is best thick).
   Lay on top of the filling, trim edges and
   patter with a fork to crimp. Prick top
   with a fork, and brush with beaten egg
   or milk. You can use cut-out pastry
   leaves to decorate the centre of the
   pastry topping – seal these on with the
   egg or milk glaze.
10. Bake in the preheated oven for 30
    minutes until golden brown.

SOYA CHUNK AND VEGETABLE CASSEROLE
Serves 6.

Simply omit the pastry topping and follow
instructions for preparing the filling in the
previous recipe, but add 140ml/¼ pint more
water and a little more shoyu to taste. Cook
on top of stove for 5 minutes only. Place in a
casserole, cover with a tight lid or seal in with
foil. Bake for 45 minutes at 350°F/180°C/Gas
Mark 4.

SOYA CHUNK KORMA

This delicious curry is best if the soya chunks
can marinate in the yoghurt and spice
mixture for at least 3 hours, so prepare well in
advance. Korma is a method of braising,
usually after marinating the meat or fish used
in a mixture of yoghurt and spices. The
marinade and spices vary according to the
meat, fish or alternative protein you use. If
you are interested in tempeh (see page 00) or
tofu (see page 00) then these protein foods are
absolutely delicious marinated and cooked in
the same way as the soya chunks. To make
the dish hotter add more cayenne, but not
until final tasting.

Serves 4 to 6.

140g/5 oz soya chunks, beef-flavoured or
    natural
225g/8 oz thick natural yoghurt or Greek
    yoghurt
200ml/8 fl oz water
good pinch sea salt

1 rounded teaspoon fresh ginger, grated
4 cardamom pods, crushed
¼ very level teaspoon clove powder
1 large bay leaf
stick of cinnamon
1 very level teaspoon turmeric
½ teaspoon of cayenne or chilli powder
1 teaspoon ground coriander
1 teaspoon ground cumin
225g/8 oz onion, peeled and chopped
2 large cloves garlic, crushed
3 tablespoons sunflower oil
1 tablespoon fresh chopped parsley or coriander
   leaves
794g/1 lb 12 oz can tomatoes, chopped
1 dessertspoon methi (fenugreek leaves)
1 dessertspoon garam masala
little chopped parsley or coriander leaves to
   garnish

1. Soak the soya chunks in boiling water for
   2 hours. Drain and squeeze out all liquid
   (discard soaking water).

2. Mix yoghurt, water, salt, ginger,
   cardamom pods, clove powder, bay leaf,
   cinnamon stick, turmeric, cayenne,
   coriander and cumin together until well
   blended. Stir into the squeezed soya
   chunks and leave to marinate for 3 hours.

3. Sauté the onion and garlic in the oil for 5
   minutes on moderate heat with the lid off.
   Stir in the parsley or corriander leaves,
   tomatoes, methi and the garam masala
   and fry for 2 minutes more on gentle heat
   (do not burn).

4. Stir in the soya chunks and marinade and
   simmer on very gentle heat for 40
   minutes.

5. Serve with Surinam or Basmati brown
   rice (see page 79) or chapatis (see page
   28).

Note You can add other vegetables when
frying the onion if you wish. A chopped green
pepper and a small chopped aubergine would
make a nice addition.

LESSON 7

SPROUTING BEANS, GRAINS AND SEEDS

This short lesson will show you how to sprout some of the beans, grains and seeds mentioned in previous lessons. Easy to grow all the year round, sprouted beans, grains and seeds are a marvellous convenience food packed with protein, vitamins and minerals. You can use them in an enormous range of dishes – they are great fresh tossed into salads or lightly cooked in stir-fries. There are no recipes given in this lesson, but numerous recipes given in the other lessons of this book will show just how versatile sprouted beans, seeds and grains can be.

Bean sprouts have also been an important part of the diet in the East for around 5000 years. In the West we seem to have virtually ignored this valuable food, except for odd spurts of interest. For instance, in the eighteenth century a Dr David MacBride experimented with sprouted barley seeds to form a wort which was found to cure scurvy, a disease that sometimes killed half the crew on long sea voyages. Captain Cook served this wort to his crew on board the *Endeavour* with the result that not one sailor died from scurvy on its three voyages from 1768 to 1771. Unfortunately, this effective cure was soon ignored when it was found that lemons could also prevent and cure scurvy.

During the Second World War, there was revived interest in sprouting seeds. The British and American governments advised the use of sprouted seeds because of their high protein content. In America, especially in the early 1940s when a protein shortage was imminent, the government mounted a nationwide campaign to educate people, not only about sprouting seeds but also to extol the virtues of the soya bean. When the expected shortage did not occur, interest in sprouting seeds and the soya bean sadly dwindled.

Up until the last few years, the majority of us in the West had probably only eaten bean sprouts in Chinese restaurants, cooked and doused in soy sauce and monosodium glutamate. But there is at present a growing interest in sprouting seeds and one can now buy fresh sprouts in most supermarkets and greengrocer shops at an amazingly cheap price. Commercially sold bean sprouts are usually sprouted from the mung bean, but there is a huge variety of beans, grains and seeds which can be easily sprouted at home. Each has its own particular flavour and texture and will not only enhance your cooking but enrich the body with nature's fresh goodness.

As sprouted beans, seeds and grains are eaten while still growing there is no nutritional loss – all the minerals and vitamins are still intact. When vegetables such as spring greens or lettuces are picked they lose approximately 25 per cent of their vitamin C within half an hour. All vegetables gradually lose their nutritional value during storage, so freshness is of prime importance. You can't eat any vegetables fresher than bean sprouts.

Sprouted beans, grains and seeds are more readily digestible and higher in food value than the dormant bean, grain, seed or plant, because of the complex changes which occur on germination (sprouting). The proteins, carbohydrates and oils are broken down into more digestible amino acids, natural sugars and fatty acids and there is a huge increase in the quantity of vitamins and amino acids already present.

Another important change takes place in the sprouting beans, grains and seeds which is useful for slimmers – the calorific content is drastically reduced. Fattening starches are changed into less fattening substances. Soya beans which have the highest protein content of all sprouting beans contain 115 calories per 28g/1 oz before sprouting and only about 12 calories when sprouted.

SPROUTING BEANS

ADUKI BEANS
See page 99 for more information about aduki beans. The sprouted seeds contain around 25 per cent protein and are rich in vitamin C and the B vitamins, iron and calcium.

ALPHATOCO BEANS
These beans, which look like aduki beans, are offered by seed merchants especially for sprouting. They are particularly rich in vitamin E, are a good source of vitamins C and B and contain a good supply of minerals.

CHICK PEAS
See page 100 for more information on chick peas. The sprouted chick pea is rich in vitamin C and contains almost double the iron of most beans and peas. These are best lightly cooked when sprouted and delicious in stir-fry dishes.

FLAGEOLET BEANS
See page 100 for more information on these beans. They are delicious sprouted, being eaten either raw or lightly stir-fried with other vegetables. These are one of my favourite beans and contain reasonable amounts of protein, vitamins and minerals.

LENTILS
See page 101 for further information on lentils. You must buy whole, not split, lentils for sprouting. The common tiny orange lentils are split but when in their whole state they have a brown skin. These whole brown lentils have a pleasant nutty flavour when sprouted as do the green lentils which are brownish/green in colour and flatter in shape. Take care to pick lentils over well, discarding broken ones and small stones. Sprouted lentils are a good source of protein, contain vitamins A, B, C and E and good amounts of iron, calcium and phosphorous.

MUNG BEANS
Many people are familiar with these bean sprouts as they are the most commonly sprouted. In India these are sometimes sprouted and are eaten raw or cooked as soon as the tiny shoots appear. This means they are chewier than the Chinese bean sprouts which are sold commercially and used extensively in Chinese cuisine. The Chinese variety are usually 7.5 to 10 cm/3 to 4 inch long and are plump, crisp and juicy. They are a good source of protein, vitamins and minerals including vitamins A, C and E, iron, calcium and phosphorous.

SOYA BEANS
See Lesson 6 for more information on the soya bean. When sprouted the beans are more easily digested and they contain lecithin which helps lower the level of cholesterol in the blood. They are also rich in vitamins A, B, C and E, calcium, iron and phosphorous. They are well worth sprouting, but they need more attention than most sprouting seeds because they ferment quickly. To keep them cool, I change the soaking water three times before sprouting then keep them in a cool place. I also rinse them four times daily. But the resulting, highly nutritious sprouted bean is well worth this extra effort. They are best lightly cooked when sprouted and added to

stir-fry vegetables or made into a delicious purée (see page 122 for recipe).

SPROUTING GRAINS

BARLEY
See page 82 for more information on barley. Buy pot barley not pearl barley for sprouting, as pearl barley is polished (processed). The sprouted seed is very chewy and best cooked. I toast the sprouted grain and use it in bread-making. The sprouted seeds contain vitamins C, B_1 and B_2.

BUCKWHEAT
For more information on buckwheat see page 81. Do not buy toasted buckwheat as it will not sprout. These sprouts need hulling before eating. To do this simply immerse the sprouted seeds in a bowl of cold water, stir carefully and the hulls will float to the surface. Tilt the bowl and pour off the floating hulls.

MILLET
For more information on millet, see page 81. This grain sprouts very easily and is chewy with a sweet taste. I use it in salads and in bread-making to sweeten the loaf. The sprouted seeds are high in protein with good amounts of the B-complex vitamins and calcium. They are often ready within 2 days so are well worth trying.

WHEAT
This seed is very easy to sprout and because of its sweetness it is good added to wholemeal flour when baking bread or added to salads to give a sweet taste. Do not over-sprout because they become too tough and are best harvested as soon as the sprout is the same length as the seed. Sprouted wheat contains approximately 14 per cent protein and is well supplied with the B-complex vitamins and vitamin E.

SPROUTING SEEDS

ALFALFA
The roots of this plant grow to about 12 metres/40 feet or deeper underground, while the plant itself only grows to about 90 cm/3 feet. Experts believe that when plants grow to such depths they gain more minerals from the soil than shallow-growing plants. This plant is regarded in America as a vitally important food supplement. The sprouted seeds contain 40 per cent protein, are rich in vitamins A, B, C, D, E and K and well supplied with calcium, iron, sodium, potassium, sulphur, phosphorous and magnesium. They also have the same amounts of carotene as carrots. The sprouts are very thin and curl around each other in a light bundle. They are excellent in sandwiches.

FENUGREEK
You can buy these seeds crushed for tea-making or whole, so make sure you buy the latter as the crushed ones will not sprout. These seeds, which are members of the pea family, have a spicy taste and are used extensively in the East in all manner of curry and rice dishes. In medicine, they are considered to be a good cleanser for the liver and kidneys. The leaf of the plant also has a most aromatic spicy taste and is sold as methi. The sprouted seeds contain 30 per cent protein, are rich in vitamin A and C and are a good source of iron.

SESAME SEEDS
For more information on sesame seeds see page 84. Buy the unhulled variety as the polished seeds will not sprout. The sprouted seeds are full of flavour and are well supplied with vitamins and minerals which include the B-complex and vitamin A, calcium, iron and phosphorous. The sprouts from these seeds are best eaten as soon as the shoots appear as they turn bitter very quickly as they grow.

SUNFLOWER SEEDS
For more information on sunflower seeds see page 84. Unlike most seeds you can sprout sunflower seeds in their unhulled state. These

are easily obtained from health food or wholefood shops. They should be sprouted in a warmish place.

HOW TO SPROUT BEANS, SEEDS AND GRAINS

You can buy seed sprouters which have three tiers and allow you to sprout individual seeds or beans separately and also ensure that your seeds and beans do not sit in stagnant water. You can however successfully sprout using a glass jar, a piece of muslin and an elastic band.

To start germinating, all beans and seeds need is the right temperature, water and air. Generally the temperature, which varies depending on the type of bean, grain or seed you wish to sprout, should be between 18° to 21°C/65° to 70°F. During the growing period, after the initial soaking, the beans or seeds need to be rinsed regularly but drained well or they will stagnate.

You might wonder, when you start to grow your own sprouts, why they are not long and straight like commercially bought ones. Well, roots grow downwards so the jar method of growing sprouts means each time the seeds are rinsed they are disturbed and the roots curl and twist about to find their way down. Commercially grown beansprouts are grown in huge containers and are never disturbed as they are rinsed by having water poured over the top and drained through tiny holes at the bottom of the containers. I will give you two methods of sprouting – the second one (particularly suitable for mung beans) will give you longer, straighter sprouts.

You will be amazed at the bulk of fresh produce you end up with after sprouting just a handful of seeds, grains or beans. Just 55g/ 2 oz of mung beans for instance will yield 225g/8 oz fresh bean sprouts.

METHOD 1

1. The first step in sprouting is to pick over the chosen beans, grains or seeds and take out any split or crinkled ones and of course remove any stones and bits of sticks. Approximately 55g/2 oz of beans, grains or seeds will produce approximately 225g/8 oz of sprouts. Wash the seeds, grains or beans by placing in a sieve and running cold water over them.

2. Soak the beans, grains or seeds in cold water. The soaking time differs depending on the type of seed you are sprouting so refer to the chart on page 144 which will give you the individual soaking times.

3. If using a seed sprouter follow the manufacturer's directions. If using a jar, drain the soaked beans, grains or seeds. Place in the clean jar and secure a piece of muslin over the top opening with an elastic band. Place the jar out of direct sunlight and in a temperature of between 18°–21°C/65°–70°F.

4. Germination will now begin and the beans, grains or seeds will need rinsing at least twice daily but refer to the chart on page 144 for more individual information. Rinse by gently pouring cold water through the muslin, then tipping it and draining all the liquid out again through the muslin. Avoid moving the jar too much as the sprouting beans, grains or seeds are quite delicate and may break and go bad.

5. Eat when ready – refer to chart on page 144.

METHOD 2 – SPROUTING LONG CHINESE-STYLE MUNG BEANS

I have already explained why the commercial mung bean sprouts are longer and straighter than the home-grown variety. Here is a method of achieving home-grown mung bean sprouts more like the commercial ones.

1. Follow directions 1 and 2 in Method 1 on page 143 for sprouting in a jar.
2. Prick holes with a fork in a good size polythene bag. Put soaked beans in the bag. Leave the top of the bag wide open and fit into a colander.
3. Dampen a tea towel, fold it and place it over the opening of the plastic bag.
4. Now put the colander over a bowl, so that it fits snugly on the rim of the bowl, making sure that there is a good drainage space underneath the colander.
5. Place all this in a dark place which has a temperature of around 21°–24°C/70°–75°F.
6. Water once every four hours. To do this just lift the colander out of the bowl and pour lukewarm water over the tea towel making sure that all the beans are fed and the water drains away through the holes in the bag and colander. If the beans are not rinsed frequently this method tends to dry them out more quickly. But if you water regularly for about 4–5 days you will end up with sprouts approximately 7.5 cm/3 inches long, straight and juicy.
7. To get rid of the green skins, just rinse the grown sprouts in a large bowl of cold water. Stir a few times and the skins will float to the surface. Pour these away. Drain the sprouts and refrigerate. Eat as soon as possible.

VARIETY TO BE SPROUTED	SOAKING TIME (HOURS)	NUMBER OF DAILY RINSES	SPROUTS READY TO EAT (DAYS)
Beans			
Aduki	12	3	5
Alphatoco	0	3	5
Chick Peas	15	4	4 to 5
Flageolet	12	3	4
Lentils	8	3	4
Mung Beans	12	3	4 to 5
Soya Beans	12	4	4 to 5
Grains			
Barley	12	3	3 to 4
Buckwheat	12	3	4 to 5
Millet	12	3	2 to 3
Wheat	12	3	3
Seeds			
Alfalfa	6	3	5 to 6
Fenugreek	12	3	4 to 5
Sesame	8	3	3 to 4
Sunflower	12	3	4

Sprouting Seeds – Soaking, Rinsing and Germination Times

LESSON 8

VEGETABLES AND FRUIT

This lesson not only includes a variety of fresh land vegetables and fruit, but also the much neglected sea vegetables which are now fortunately more easily available.

Fresh raw vegetables and fruit are one of the best aids to health we can treat ourselves to. They are rich in vitamins, minerals and fibre and should be a major part of your daily diet. You should try to eat at least one good salad a day, and I hope the recipes for the delicious salad dressings in this lesson (see pages 152 to 155) will encourage you to do so. If cooking vegetables or fruit, then lightly steam or briskly stir-fry to retain as many nutrients as possible.

The quality and food value of the vegetables and fruit you eat also depends on the way they are grown and stored. A 'quality' vegetable should be one that gives you the most nutritional value – it should not just be one that looks nice. Many of the beautifully polished, shiny, perfect specimens, arranged neatly in our greengrocers' shops and supermarkets are often sadly depleted in nutrients.

There is now growing evidence that organically grown produce is 'healthier' than that which is chemically grown and treated. Organically grown fruit and vegetables may not always look so perfect but they are far more nutritious and generally have a much better flavour – just try some and you will need no further persuasion. If organic produce is sometimes a little more expensive, then remember that is is much better value in terms of health. Try and buy it whenever you can. If your greengrocer or supermarket does not stock organic produce, pester them until they do. Remember they make money by

meeting your demands.

I have not included a shopping list in this lesson as it is best not to store fruit and vegetables for too long – try to buy and use them as you need them. Below I have given information on the various sea vegetables (sea weeds) which you might be unfamiliar with and on the less common land vegetables and fruit.

Keep your store cupboard well stocked with herbs, spices and good salad oils (see page 152) and buy the more unusual ingredients in this lesson as you need them.

SEA VEGETABLES (SEA WEEDS)

Edible sea weeds are highly nutritious as they are a rich source of vitamins, minerals and trace elements. Look out for them in wholefood and oriental food shops.

ARAME
This is a thin string-like weed, rich in vitamins including B_{12}, minerals and trace

elements. It has a mild nutty flavour and is good added to rice dishes (see page 88 for *Chinese rice with arame, almonds and peas*, stir-fry vegetables, soups and salads.

To prepare, soak in cold water for 15 minutes and squeeze dry. Lightly steam if adding to salads or fry for a few minutes with vegetables or add just as it is to soups. The soaking water is quite nutritious so also add it to soups.

DULSE OR DILLISK

This is one of my favourite sea weeds, as I was brought up on it on summer holidays in the west of Ireland. We used to have it in sandwiches.

Dulse is one of the richest organic sources of iron. It also contains calcium, iodine, potassium and magnesium in abundance. It is 25 per cent protein and has valuable amounts of vitamins A, C, E and the B complex. In the past it has been used as a tonic to help strengthen the blood, adrenal glands, kidneys and muscles. It was also used in the prevention of scurvy and herpes.

To prepare, simply wash well, pat dry, chop and add to salads.

HIZIKI

This is similar to the string-like arame but much stronger in flavour. You'll either love it or hate it, so buy a small amount to try out. It has the same vitamin and mineral content as arame.

To prepare, soak in cold water for 15 minutes, squeeze and add to stir-fry vegetables or soups. I think it is too strong in salads.

KOMBU

This is rich in vitamins and minerals and also contains natural sodium (salt) and glutamic acid (a flavour enhancer which is not unlike monosodium glutamate). It is used in Japan as the basis of dashi (basic stock) and in soups. It is also used as a softening agent when cooking beans.

Do not soak, but simply break up and add to the cooking broth. About one strip is sufficient for 850ml/1½ pints of liquid.

NORI

Pound for pound, nori contains more vitamin A than carrots, more protein than cheese, meat or soya beans and more calcium than milk. As if that were not enough, it is also rich in trace elements, helps to emulsify fats and aids digestion.

It comes in paper-thin sheets, which can be used in a variety of ways, from wrapping up various savoury fillings (see *Nori wrapped cocktail bites* – see page 165) to garnishing grain and vegetable dishes. To use as a garnish, toast in the oven on a moderate heat until crisp (do *not* grill, as packets of nori often suggest, as it will burn), then crumble up and sprinkle on salads or cooked vegetable dishes for extra flavour.

WAKAME

This is a long, feather-like, dark green, sea vegetable. It contains thirteen times more calcium than milk, which makes it a valuable food for growing children and pregnant women. It has an abundance of trace minerals, notably iodine, and is one of the rare vegetable sources of vitamin B_{12} (see page 13 for notes on B_{12}). It has a mild flavour and, like arame and nori, is recommended for those not yet familiar with the distinctive taste of sea vegetables.

Wakame also contains an acid called alginic acid which is known to help fight the ill-effects of heavy metals in the body. This action is enhanced when wakame is used with fermented foods like miso and shoyu or tamari.

To prepare soak for 10 minutes in cold water, chop finely and boil in the soaking water for 10 minutes. Drain and add to salads or stir-fry vegetables. For soups, simply soak for ten minutes, then chop and cook in the soup for the last ten minutes of cooking time.

LESS COMMON VEGETABLES

I have not used all of the vegetables and fruit listed below in recipes in the book. I have included them here so you will have some information about them and a few ideas on how to use them, just in case you feel like experimenting a little.

AUBERGINE

This delicious vegetable is still used only a few times a year by the majority of people in the British Isles, whereas it features widely in American, Asian, Middle Eastern and Mediterranean cookery. There is no need to peel the beautiful purple skin, but as it has a slightly bitter taste it is advisable to slice, sprinkle with a little salt and leave in a colander for 20 minutes to let the bitter juices drain off. Then rinse well, pat dry and use as directed in a recipe. Salting in this way does destroy some of the nutrients, so you can try slicing, placing in a colander, then covering with a plate with a heavy weight on top and leaving for thirty minutes. I find this takes enough bitter juices out for my taste. Try these aubergine slices dipped in batter for *Pakora* (see page 169) or in the recipe for *Red bean moussaka* (see page 108).

CELERIAC

This root vegetable is related to celery and has a similar flavour. I like to grate it finely with other vegetables – see page 158 for *Celeriac, courgette, carrot and fennel remoulade*. This is a very tasty salad and even better if allowed to marinate for a few hours before serving. Celeriac is also delicious added to soups and casseroles as you would other vegetables.

DANDELION

This free food contains a good supply of iron, calcium and protein as well as being rich in vitamins A, B and C. So instead of just regarding them as a nuisance in the garden, cultivate them for their nutritional value. They are delicious lightly steamed or chopped into salads.

EDDOES

This is a long brown rough and hairy root vegetable imported from the Caribbean. To prepare, peel thinly and cook in the same way as potatoes. It is very tasty steamed, mashed with a little butter, nutmeg and freshly ground black pepper.

FENNEL (FINNOCHIO OR FLORENCE FENNEL)

This variety of cultivated fennel is usually bought with the shoots cut off, which is a shame because they are good for flavouring soups, stews and sauces – if you can grow fennel use the long feathery shoots and delight your broths. The flavour is a mixture of celery, aniseed and dill. It can be eaten raw, grated into salads or braised in the oven with a tomato sauce.

KOHLRABI

This exotic looking purple-tinted vegetable is developed from the cabbage for its round swollen stem from which long thin-stemmed leaves shoot out. Its texture is similar to turnips but it has a much more delicate flavour. It is delicious thinly peeled, grated and dressed with a vinaigrette, chopped chives and fresh parsley (see page 158). You can also cook it in its skin, then serve the flesh with a sauce or simply a knob of butter and a little black pepper.

KUCHAI (CHINESE CHIVES)

Mostly obtainable in bundles from oriental grocers, a few supermarkets in large towns now stock these. They have white flowery heads and are thicker and much stronger in flavour than our own chives, with a pungent taste of garlic. Chop them into sauces, omelettes and salads.

LAND CRESS

Similar to watercress and, for vegetable growers, well worth giving a patch of garden to. I'm still picking mine after the frost in December. Rich source of vitamins particularly vitamin C, and minerals including iron. Try it in soups and chopped into salads. Watercress, which is sold everywhere, also grows in abundance throughout Britain in streams and ditches, but there is a danger that watercress, if growing near fields of sheep, could be infested with liver fluke which if eaten by humans can be fatal. If the watercress is cooked, in soup for example, then there is no danger. So stick to cooking wild watercress to be on the safe side.

LEMON GRASS
This delicate plant is available from oriental grocers and some supermarkets. It is sold in bundles and has a lemon flavour with a hint of ginger. It is used in south-east Asia to add flavour to a variety of dishes and is absolutely delicious in sauces and added to curries.

LOTUS ROOT
This underwater root is available fresh from Chinese grocers in summer. To prepare, peel and immediately immerse in cold water with a little lemon juice or it will become discoloured. Chop and add to curries or slice thinly and add to stir-fry dishes.

MUSHROOMS, FRESH AND DRIED
Most commonly available in Britain is the cultivated *field mushroom*. It is sold all year round either button size or large flat capped. Commercially force-grown mushrooms are not as flavoursome as the wild field mushrooms. Other types of mushroom that are becoming increasingly common in our shops include:

Chanterelle mushrooms (or gorolle). These are widely sold in continental Europe but only in a few select shops in the UK. Wild food gatherers will find them in woodlands, especially pine woods, from July until the first frosts. They are bright yellow, shaped like a fluted cap and have a faint smell of fresh peppery apricots. Use in stir-fries and omelettes and in the recipe for *Leeks with mushrooms and bean sprouts* (see page 162).

Oyster mushrooms (or pleurotte). These are pear-shaped delicate mushrooms widely used in continental Europe and now grown commercially in Britain. They vary in colour and can be cream, pink, fawn, light brown or yellow. To prepare discard the tough stalks, slice and add to stir-fry vegetables and herby fluffy omelettes.

Dried mushrooms. These are available from Chinese and Italian grocers. Usually imported from France, Germany, Italy and Japan, they are expensive but they are much stronger than fresh mushrooms and swell up a great deal when hydrated. To prepare wash well and soak in warm water for 30 minutes. Cut off woody stems and discard. You can cut them in

very thin slices and add to stir-fry dishes or to savoury stuffings with rice, onion and herbs. Also see *Nori wrapped cocktail bites* on page 165, *Aubergine, dried mushroom and sunflower seed dip* on page 160 and *Chinese vegetable spring rolls* on page 165 for special recipes which use these delicious preserved mushrooms.

NASTURTIUM
This plant is related to landcress (see page 147) and watercress and is just as nutritious. Leaves and flowers are edible. Pick young tender leaves and chop them into salads. Use the beautiful orange flowers for garnish.

NETTLES
Stinging nettles, another free food, are a good source of iron, folic acid, ammonia, silicic acid and histamine. These chemicals are known to assist the relief of rheumatism and other related ailments. They act as a purifying agent, increase the haemoglobin in the blood, improve circulation and generally tone the body. If that's not enough they also help lower blood pressure as well as sugar levels in the blood. Pick very young shoots before June. Any later and the leaves become tough and bitter tasting.

OKRA (OR LADIES FINGERS)
This member of the bean family has an unusual aromatic flavour and a sticky, glue-like centre. It originates from the Caribbean and is also used in South American, Middle Eastern and Indian cookery. I prefer to cook okra with the pods whole – 7 to 10 minutes' cooking time is adequate, otherwise you end up with a gluey mess. Try the recipe for

Spiced okra with mushrooms on page 167). When adding as an extra vegetable to curries or other dishes than add near the end of cooking time.

PAK CHOI

This is very similar to Chinese leaf in flavour but the stalks are long with fleshy leaves at the top. Pak choi is mild in flavour and can be eaten raw or lightly cooked. I chop the crisp stems and leaves for salads but I usually add watercress, land cress (see page 00) or a little rocket (see below), chopped spring onions or chives and herbs to give a delicious contrast in texture and flavour. The only way I cook pak choi is to chop and add to stir-fry vegetables 1 minute before the end of cooking time.

PUMPKIN

This beautiful-looking plant is much neglected in the British Isles but is widely featured in North American cookery. There it is most popular used in the traditional sweet pumpkin pie which I personally dislike. But I do think it makes the most delicious soups (try *Pumpkin soup* on page 171) and is great chopped with other vegetables in curry or spiced sauces. If you buy one in the autumn it will last, if uncut, for several months.

RADICCHIO (RED CHICORY)

This rich deep red plant looks more like a young cabbage in shape than the usual white chicory heads. It has a slightly bitter flavour like ordinary white chicory. I use it to add a contrast of colour in salads – see page 158 for *Papaya, avocado, mushroom and radicchio salad*. Generally I tend to use both varieties of chicory sparingly, as I find their bitter flavour overpowers other ingredients and tends to be popular with only a few people.

ROCKET

This delightful member of the watercress family has a very mild hot taste tinged with a toasted hazelnut flavour. It is a good source of iron and other minerals and vitamin C. Since we grew it in our garden last year I have added it to many salads. I am still picking the last few leaves from this year's crop and it is late December. It is well worth giving it a

small area of your garden. It is not new to Britain as it was first introduced here from southern Europe in the sixteenth century and for many years was used as a salad vegetable. Get planting and spread the taste around to your friends and local restaurants.

SALSIFY (OR VEGETABLE OYSTER)

This root plant can be black skinned or white. It has a delicate subtle flavour. To prepare, scrape off the skin, chop and immerse in cold water with a little lemon juice to stop discoloration. Cook in lightly salted water for 30 minutes, drain and serve with a knob of butter and sprinkle with a little chopped parsley. It cannot be eaten raw as it is too tough.

SHALLOTS

This plant is closer to garlic than onion in the way that is grows. The bulb divides itself into several large cloves and it does not produce seed like the onion. Shallots are milder in flavour than ordinary onions and more suitable for sauces.

To prepare, you should always mince or at least chop very finely. Never brown but gently cook or they will produce a bitter taste. Use instead of leeks in the *Leek and tarragon sauce* on page 173 or if raw onion is an ingredient in a salad then try shallots paper-thinly sliced instead.

SORREL

This grows wild in England but the wild variety is quite bitter. The French use a cultivated variety extensively in their cookery but unfortunately it is very rarely found in Britain (garden vegetable growers can easily grow this cultivated variety from seed). It is well worth seeking out or growing yourself because it has the highest potassium content of all green vegetables and is also rich in vitamin C. It has a slightly tangy flavour and a few chopped leaves will add a delicious zing to the salad bowl. It is also good chopped into sauces and soups near the end of cooking time. It shrinks like spinach so you would have to cook 225g/8 oz per person if you wanted to serve it as a side vegetable. Also try chopping some into omelettes or soufflés, pancake batters and quiches.

SQUASH

There are several varieties now available in the shops. Most popular is golden nugget squash and custard squash. These are both suitable for stuffing and baking as you would marrow (see page 136) or peeling and steaming until soft and served with a sauce. Butternut squash, which is pear-shaped, is best served with a sauce. My favourite is spaghetti squash which unfortunately is rarely seen in Britain. I love this stuffed (with the filling for *Stuffed marrow* on page 136) and baked. All you do is slice in half, scoop out the seeds and discard. Scoop out some of the string-like flesh, fry it with the filling and fill the slightly hollowed-out halves with this mixture. Top with plenty of grated cheese and bake in a moderate oven for 1 hour. You can also top with a few dollops of thick white sauce and cheese and then bake.

SWEET POTATOES

This plant was the first potato to arrive in the British Isles from South America and is often mentioned in sixteenth and seventeenth century cookery books. It is now imported from the Caribbean where it is sometimes used in sweet dishes as well as savoury. It is also used extensively in the southern states of North America and much liked all over the United States. Sweet potatoes take the place of ordinary potatoes in many tropical countries. They have pinky-red skins and pale pink to orange coloured flesh and have a delicious chestnut-like flavour. There is also a white sweet potato smaller than the red variety with yellow flesh. These are a bit drier and fluffier than the red variety. Like ordinary potatoes both varieties are rich in vitamin C. The sweet potato is often confused with yams (see below).

To prepare scrub well, leaving the skin on. Bake or steam as you would ordinary potatoes. To bake, rub the clean skins with a very little oil and bake in their jackets for 1 hour depending on their size (400°F/200°C/Gas Mark 6). Slit open and serve with butter and freshly ground black pepper or with cottage cheese or Greek yoghurt spooned on top. Also try the recipe for *Nutty stuffed sweet potatoes* on page 00. To steam, cut in chunks with the skins on. Steam until soft, then peel off skin and mash with butter, freshly ground black pepper and a little nutmeg. Sprinkle on a little chopped parsley and serve.

YAMS

These are related to sweet potatoes but are less sweet and more like ordinary potatoes in flavour. They vary enormously in shape and size, sometimes growing to 45Kg/100 lb in weight. The skin is very tough and has to be removed before cooking. The flesh can be either off-white, browny-pink or yellow.

To prepare, peel off the skin, chop and either steam until soft then mash and serve with knobs of butter and freshly ground black pepper, or roast with a little oil and herbs. You can simply add yam to soups and stews as you would ordinary potatoes.

LESS COMMON FRUITS

CRANBERRIES

Now easily available, this very popular North American fruit is rich in vitamin C. Long used by the North American Indians, before the first settlers arrived in the sixteenth century, both in their food and for dying rugs and blankets. They make lovely sauces and relishes and are delicious in pies and crumbles – see page 50 for *Cranberry and apple pie* and page 178 for *Brandied cranberry and apple sauce* (or relish).

KIWI FRUIT (OR CHINESE GOOSEBERRY)

This brown hairy egg-shaped fruit has a very high content of vitamin C. It grows in the

Yangtze valley in China but our supply comes from a cultivated variety grown in New Zealand. This cultivated variety is slightly larger than the Chinese variety. Kiwi fruit contains an enzyme, actinidin, which aids digestion and is used as a meat tenderizer. This same enzyme will also prevent jellies from setting unless the fruit is cooked so don't add raw Kiwi fruit to your fruit jellies. Kiwi fruit is delicious in ice cream, adds a zing to fruit salads and is good in fruit chutney.

LIMES
These are originally grown in south-east Asia but now are cultivated all over the sub-tropical world. The main supply comes from Mexico and the West Indies. Like lemons they have been used for centuries for medicinal purposes. Both are rich in vitamin C, limes containing one third more than lemons. Limes are also a little sweeter than lemons and have a more subtle flavour. Try using limes instead of lemons from time to time in recipes where lemons are an ingredient, such as salad dressings, soufflés or sorbet. The subtle difference is worth experiencing.

LYCHEES
Cultivated in China for over 2000 years, this exotic fruit is sweet with a delightful refreshing flavour and very juicy. If you have only eaten the canned variety, then you have a real treat in store when you taste lychees freshly peeled. They have a brown prickly nut-like skin with translucent pearl-like flesh. They are a rich source of vitamin C and have a high nutritional sugar content. The best way to eat lychee is on their own, but they are always lovely added to rice, salads and vegetable dishes.

MANGOES
These are one of my favourite fruits, the flavour of which resembles a mixture of peach and sweet melon with a very subtle hint of ginger. Mangos are a rich source of vitamin A and C. They are delicious served alone with a squeeze of lime and great as an addition to a fresh fruit salad. One mango goes a long way in mousses and ice creams. They are difficult to slice without making a mess if you want to use as a garnish. Use a very sharp vegetable knife, cut through the skin horizontally down to the stone, then gently saw off a quarter of the flesh at a time from the stone. All mangoes are green when unripe. On ripening the skin colour varies from green to a rich pink-orange. Try the delicious recipe for *Chilled mango cheese pie* on page 00.

Dried mango pieces are now easily available and far less expensive to use. When hydrated the flavour is amazingly like fresh mango. I soak them in apple juice and use them like fresh. Try *Dried mango, apple and ginger cake* on page 60 and *Sweet and sour mango and courgette chutney* on page 176, which will delight any curry.

PAPAYA (OR PAPAW)
The papaya tree is often called the medicine tree in the Caribbean and parts of Africa because of the curative powers of the fruit and leaves. The fruit is rich in vitamin A and C and contains an enzyme called papain. This is a protein-digesting enzyme and so is a helpful aid to the digestive system. The enzyme also has blood clotting properties. Papain is also used as a meat tenderizer. The seeds contain properties which are used to dispel flatulence and the seed juice is prescribed by naturopaths as a remedy for certain liver disorders and piles. The leaves contain carpaine, an alkaloid which is said to have the same effect on the heart as digitalis.

The fruit is yellow when ripe and the flesh peachy-pink. It has a sweet musky taste not unlike mango but smoother in texture. It is delicious in fruit salads or eaten alone sliced and sprinkled with lime juice.

PASSION FRUIT (OR GRENADILLA)
Claimed throughout history as a sedative, this wrinkled purplish-black skinned fruit has a refreshing tasting aromatic yellow pulp with seeds. It is delicious beaten into Greek yoghurt, ice cream or fruit sauces. Other varieties have orange and yellow skins but these are not often available in Britain.

DRIED FRUIT
All types of dried fruit are a marvellous stand-by and can be used in a huge variety of dishes

including salads, purées, fruit sauces and chutneys. They contain a wealth of vitamins and minerals. Unfortunately most are preserved with sulphur dioxide, so if not just adding to cakes or puddings but perhaps using as part of a fruit salad or in chutneys, then boil for 2 minutes, drain and soak overnight in fresh water (this process helps remove the sulphur dioxide). You can buy unsulphured, naturally sun-dried fruits, so get these whenever possible.

SALAD DRESSINGS

How many times have you said 'Oh, I can't be bothered to prepare a salad because it means messing about with a dressing'? Well the best way to encourage yourself to eat more salads is to mix up one or two jars of dressing a week and store in the fridge. Then all you have to do is chop a few vegetables, pour a little pre-prepared dressing over them and in two or three minutes you have a healthy bowlful.

Treble the recipe quantity of any of the following dressings will fill a 450g/1 lb jam or honey jar. Use natural cold-pressed oils for dressings whenever possible as the flavour and nutritional value is far superior to refined oils. Although I use a variety of vinegars including my own herb and fruit vinegars a note here about cider vinegar is important. Cider vinegar is rich in potassium and calcium and reputed to help in balancing the acids and alkalis in the body. It also contains a wealth of minerals.

You will find some of the dressings have silken tofu as an ingredient (see page 120 for more information on silken tofu). This is preferable to firm tofu in dressings as it blends in with other ingredients more easily. In any dressing which includes yoghurt you can use silken tofu as an alternative, but you might have to add a little more seasoning as tofu is very bland.

HERB VINEGAR AND OILS
Herb oils and vinegars are delicious in salad dressings and marinades. Choose tarragon, basil and dill for three beautiful herb-flavoured oils and vinegars.

To every 570ml/1 pint cold-pressed olive or sunflower oil or 570ml/1 pint light cider or wine vinegar add 3 heaped teaspoons of the slightly bruised leaves of only the herbs mentioned above. Stir, bottle and cork tightly. Let the oil and herb infuse for 2 to 3 weeks and the vinegar and herb for 1 week to 10 days. Shake from time to time. Strain and pour into clean bottles adding just 1 sprig of the chosen herb before corking very tightly.

You can freeze the oil with the bruised herb leaves in small containers without having to infuse or strain. When defrosted the flavour is superb and will excite any salad dressing.

FRUIT VINEGARS
For these you can use a good wine or light cider vinegar. They will be ready in 2 days and, after straining and bottling, will last for several months or longer. I have not used these vinegars extensively throughout the book, because there is nothing more irritating than wanting to do a recipe and finding one of the ingredients is not obtainable in the shops or you can't make it quickly. If you can spare the time, fruit vinegars are well worth making and storing for use in salads and marinades.

To every 570ml/1 pint white wine or light cider vinegar you will need 225g/8 oz soft fruit, such as raspberries, strawberries, ripe pears (chopped with the skin on), redcurrants (pressed very, very gently with a potato masher), chopped peaches, chopped apricots, or chopped mangoes. Put the washed and prepared fruit of your choice into a bowl. Pour on the wine or light cider vinegar. Stir well and cover with foil and a towel and leave for 2 days. Put the lot into a saucepan and bring to boiling point. Strain and pour the fruity vinegar into sterilized bottles. Cork or secure tightly with screw tops. Use as you would plain vinegar.

If making these fruit vinegars sounds all too time consuming, then simply cheat. Add a teaspoon of pure fruit juice concentrate to the *Basic oil and lemon, lime or vinegar dressing* recipe which follows and omit the honey.

BASIC OIL AND LEMON, LIME OR VINEGAR DRESSING

*3 tablespoons either virgin olive oil or cold-
   pressed safflower, sunflower or corn oil*
*1 tablespoon fresh lemon or lime juice or light
   cider or wine vinegar*
¼ teaspoon sea salt
¼ level teaspoon Dijon mustard
few twists freshly ground black pepper
½ level teaspoon clear honey (optional)
1 small clove garlic, crushed (optional)

1. Shake all the ingredients together in a screw top jar and keep in the fridge until needed.
2. Treble the recipe to fill a 450g/1 lb jar for storing and using on several salads. Always keep chilled.

FRUIT VINEGAR AND OIL DRESSING
Use 1 tablespoon fruit vinegar (see page 152) instead of the lemon juice, lime juice or plain vinegar in the previous recipe and omit the honey.

FRESH HERB DRESSING
You can include other fresh herbs in this recipe especially if you grow your own such as basil or marjoram. The ones in the recipe are usually more generally available and are a good combination.

*3 tablespoons either virgin olive oil or cold-
   pressed safflower, sunflower or corn oil*
*1 tablespoon fresh lemon or lime juice or light
   cider or wine vinegar*
¼ teaspoon sea salt
¼ teaspoon Dijon mustard
few twists freshly ground black pepper
½ level teaspoon clear honey
1 level dessertspoon fresh chopped parsley
1 teaspoon fresh chopped mint leaves
*1 level dessertspoon fresh chopped tarragon or
   ½ teapsoon dried*
1 level dessertspoon chopped chives

1. Mix all the ingredients together in a blender or food processor for ½ minute.
2. Store in a screw top jar in the fridge until needed. Treble the recipe quantity will fill

a 450g/1 lb jar, sufficient for storing and using on several salads. Always keep chilled.

TANGY CAPER VINAIGRETTE

*1 tablespoon tangerine juice or fresh orange
   juice*
1 tablespoon lime juice
5 tablespoons virgin olive oil or sesame seed oil
½ teaspoon Dijon mustard
*1 rounded teaspoon capers, rinsed and patted
   dry*
1 clove garlic, crushed

1. Blend all the ingredients well together in a liquidizer or food processor.
2. Store in a screw top jar in the fridge until needed.

RICH TARRAGON VINAIGRETTE
This is a favourite for any green salad mixture and superb used as a marinade for grated salads such as *Celeriac, courgette, carrot and fennel remoulade* (see page 158). It is also delicious on any tomato-based salad.

*5 tablespoons either virgin olive oil or cold
   pressed safflower, sunflower or corn oil*
1 tablespoon fresh lemon juice
*1 tablespoon light cider vinegar or wine
   vinegar*
1 rounded teaspoon vegetable bouillon powder
1 level teaspoon dried tarragon
¼ teaspoon freshly ground black pepper
½ teaspoon clear honey
½ level teaspoon Dijon mustard
1 good size clove garlic, crushed

1. Shake all the ingredients in a screw top jar.
2. Store in the fridge until needed.

RICH TARRAGON, AVOCADO AND YOGHURT DRESSING
Following the previous recipe, use 4 tablespoons of oil instead of 5, omit the vinegar and add 1 small or ½ large avocado, chopped, and 2 rounded tablespoons of Greek yoghurt. Mix the lot in a blender or food processor until smooth. Store in a screw top

153

jar in the fridge until needed (store for no more than 3 days). This is also delicious on lightly steamed vegetables such as broccoli, cauliflower or carrots.

RICH TARRAGON AND TOFU DRESSING

Omit the yoghurt from the *Rich tarragon vinaigrette* recipe on page 153, then use 2 tablespoons of lemon juice instead of one and add 110g/4 oz silken tofu (see page 120).

SLIMMER'S YOGHURT AND HERB DRESSING

If you have fresh basil then this recipe will be even more delicious.

150g/5 oz Greek yoghurt
1 tablespoon lemon juice
1 tablespoon virgin olive or cold pressed safflower or sunflower oil
1 clove garlic, crushed
1 level tablespoon finely chopped parsley
1 level tablespoon finely chopped fresh basil leaves or 1 scant teaspoon dried basil
½ level teaspoon dried tarragon
1 very level teaspoon vegetable bouillon powder
¼ teaspoon Dijon mustard
little freshly ground black pepper, to taste

1. Blend all the ingredients together in a liquidizer or food processor.
2. Store in a screw top jar in the fridge until needed.

SLIMMER'S TOFU AND HERB DRESSING

Omit the yoghurt from the previous recipe and use 150g/5 oz silken tofu (see page 120) instead.

SWEET AND SOUR DRESSING

This dressing is delicious on the *Sweet and sour bean sprout salad* (see page 156). It is also great on rice salads. Using some sesame oil in this recipe gives it an authentic Chinese flavour but you can use safflower, sunflower, corn or virgin olive oil. It will still taste good. Five spice is also worth adding.

3 tablespoons cold-pressed sesame oil
3 tablespoons sunflower oil
1½ tablespoons light cider vinegar
1½ tablespoons shoyu (naturally fermented soy sauce)
1 tablespoon dry sherry (optional)
1 teaspoon clear honey
¼ teaspoon dry mustard powder
good pinch five spice or allspice
1 heaped teaspoon fresh ginger root grated
1 large clove garlic, crushed

1. Put all the ingredients in a blender and process for 1 minute.
2. Store in a screw top jar in the fridge until needed.

BASIC MAYONNAISE

Your mayonnaise will never curdle if you add the lemon juice or light cider vinegar after all the other ingredients are well blended and thickened. With this method you don't have to add the oil drop by drop, a steady stream will still thicken the mixture. For a simple light-tasting mayonnaise use sunflower or corn oil.

Makes 285ml/½ pt.

1 large egg, room temperature
250ml/8 fl oz sunflower, corn or virgin olive oil
½ teaspoon dry mustard powder
¼ teaspoon black pepper, freshly ground
½ level teaspoon sea salt
2 tablespoons either light cider vinegar or 2 tablespoons lemon juice (or use half and half)

1. Put egg, 55ml/2 fl oz of the oil, mustard, pepper and salt in a liquidizer or food processor. Turn on low speed and blend well together.

2. Turn to high speed and pour in the rest of the oil in a slow steady stream, through the opening in the lid of the liquidizer or food processor. The mixture will thicken.
3. Finally, with the machine still running, pour in the vinegar or lemon juice or half and half vinegar and lemon juice.
4. Store in a screw top jar in the fridge until needed.

PIQUANT ITALIAN MAYONNAISE
Follow the recipe for *Basic mayonnaise* given above, but use virgin olive oil and mix in 2 crushed cloves of garlic and ½ level teaspoon each of sweet basil, oregano and tarragon with the vinegar or lemon juice.

PISTACHIO PESTO MAYONNAISE

1 recipe quantity Piquant Italian mayonnaise
110g/4 oz shelled pistachios, ground

1. Put all the ingredients in a blender (make sure the nuts are ground separately first) and process until thick and smooth.
2. Serve with crudités or as a sauce for light cooked vegetables or as a dressing for chunky salads.

TOFU PISTACHIO PESTO MAYONNAISE

110g/4 oz pistachios, ground
280g/10 oz silken tofu (see page 120)
2 cloves garlic, crushed
2 tablespoons lemon juice
½ teaspoon Dijon mustard
1 rounded teaspoon vegetable bouillon powder
¼ teaspoon freshly ground black pepper
½ teaspoon each basil, oregano and tarragon

1. Put all the ingredients in a liquidizer or food processor and blend until smooth.
2. Store in a screw top jar in the fridge until needed.

COLESLAW DRESSING
You can buy the grated horseradish root used in this recipe in jars.

4 rounded tablespoons Basic mayonnaise (see page 154)

2 rounded tablespoons Greek yoghurt
2 teaspoons grated horseradish root

1. Stir all the ingredients together well.
2. Chill for a few hours before using to let the flavour of the horseradish penetrate the mayonnaise and yoghurt.

SALADS

You can turn any mixture of raw vegetables into a delicious salad if you stir in or pour over a tasty dressing, but I would like to give you some ideas for extra special salads – some simple, some more exotic with flavours and textures which complement each other and delight the palate.

One very important point to remember when preparing any vegetables or fruit for salads is that you must pour on a dressing immediately these foods are cut. The reason for this is that the valuable vitamin C contained in fruit and vegetables is very quickly destroyed when exposed. So always have your dressing ready and prepare salads as near to serving time as possible.

SHADES OF SUMMER GREEN SALAD WITH TOASTED SHOYU SUNFLOWER SEEDS
You can choose from a huge variety of green salad vegetables, especially if you are fortunate enough to grow your own. Shredded rocket (see page 00) and nasturtium leaves for example would be a delicious addition, so include these if available.

Serves 4 to 6.

1 recipe quantity either Basic oil and lemon dressing (see page 153) or Rich tarragon vinaigrette (see page 153)
1 medium size iceberg, webb or cos lettuce
good handful young spinach leaves
1 bunch watercress (or nasturtium leaves)
½ large cucumber, cut in small chunks
1 small avocado, peeled, stoned, cut in small chunks and sprinkled with lemon juice
4 good size spring onions, or small bunch chives, finely chopped

1 dessertspoon fresh mint leaves, finely
    chopped
2 tablespoons parsley, finely chopped
3 rounded tablespoons Tamari sunflower seeds
    (see page 92)

1. Shred the lettuce, spinach leaves,
   watercress (or nasturtium leaves) and
   place in a serving bowl.
2. Stir in the cucumber chunks, spring
   onions, mint, parsley and tamari
   sunflower seeds.
3. Pour on the dressing of your choice and
   mix well in.

DULSE AND CHINESE LEAF SALAD

Chinese leaf varies enormously in size, so if
large then slice off 450g/1 lb lengthwise so
that you get some of the green leafy top as
well as the crisp base.

Serves 4 to 6.

1 recipe quantity Basic oil and lemon or
    vinegar dressing (see page 153)
handful dulse, washed and chopped
450g/1 lb Chinese leaf, shredded
1 punnet mustard, water or land cress, washed
    and chopped
1 good size red eating apple, cut in small
    chunks (leave skin on)
6 spring onions, finely chopped (use green ends
    as well)
1 medium size carrot, cut in paper-thin
    slanting ovals

1. Mix dulse, Chinese leaf, cress, apple,
   chopped spring onions and sliced carrots
   into a mixing bowl.
2. Stir in the dressing and serve.

DULSE SALAD WITH SWEET AND SOUR DRESSING

Serves 4 to 6.

Add 55g/2 oz thinly sliced button mushrooms
and 2 segmented seedless satsumas to the
previous recipe and use the *Sweet and sour
dressing* (see page 154) instead of the *Basic oil
and lemon dressing* for a more exotic looking
and tasting salad.

MEDITERRANEAN SALAD

This is delicious for a special meal or buffet
party.

Serves 4 to 6.

2 medium size potatoes, steamed, peeled and
    cubed
1 small green pepper, deseeded and chopped
1 small red pepper, deseeded and chopped
170g/6 oz Florence fennel, cut in very small
    pieces
2 medium size courgettes, cut into small pieces
1 small onion, very finely chopped
4 large tomatoes, peeled and cut into thin
    wedges
2 tablespoons fresh parsley, finely chopped
1 tablespoon fresh basil leaves, chopped (if
    available)
crisp lettuce leaves, to serve
3 hard boiled eggs
12 black olives, stoned and sliced in half
1 recipe quantity Rich tarragon vinaigrette (see
    page 153) but use raspberry vinegar (see
    page 152) instead of the lemon juice and
    cider vinegar and 1 extra clove garlic

1. Mix all the ingredients except the lettuce,
   eggs and half the olives in a mixing bowl,
   pour on two-thirds of the dressing, toss
   well and leave to marinate for 20 minutes.
2. When ready to serve arrange the lettuce
   leaves on a flat serving dish, spoon in the
   salad mixture, top with the egg and olives
   then spoon on the rest of the dressing.

SWEET AND SOUR BEAN SPROUT SALAD

A variety of your own home-grown bean or
seed sprouts would make this salad a real
treat (see page 143 on sprouting). You can use
commercial packs of bean sprouts and the
salad will still be delicious.

Serves 4 to 6.

½ recipe quantity Sweet and sour dressing (see
    page 154)
340g/12 oz bean sprouts
110g/4 oz small button mushrooms
1 small green pepper, deseeded and chopped
1 medium size carrot, cut in paper-thin
    slanting ovals

6 spring onions, very finely chopped (use green
    ends as well)
2 tablespoons either fresh or canned and
    drained pineapple, chopped

1.   Mix all the salad ingredients together.
2.   Stir in the dressing, mix well and serve.

ALFALFA, ORANGE, TOMATO AND ONION SALAD WITH TANGY CAPER VINAIGRETTE
Serves 4 to 6.

4 tablespoons Tangy caper vinaigrette (see page
    153, but omit the tangerine juice and use all
    lime juice)
170g/6 oz sprouted alfalfa seeds (see page 143
    on sprouting)
6 medium oranges, peeled and diagonally
    sliced in very thin wedges
2 onions the size of the oranges, cut in very
    thin rings
8 medium size tomatoes, cut in thin rings
2 tablespoons parsley, very finely chopped to
    garnish

1.   Arrange the alfalfa sprouts on a flat
    serving dish.
2.   Place orange, onion and tomato rings
    overlapping in circles on top, sprinkle on
    the parsley and then trickle over the
    dressing.

RAW BEETROOT, TOMATO AND MINT SALAD
Dried mint is not suitable for this delicious
refreshing salad.

Serves 4 to 6.

675g/1½ lb raw beetroot, thinly peeled and
    grated
6 medium size tomatoes, cut in thin wedges
½ large cucumber, cut in thin 2.5 cm/1 inch
    sticks
1 tablespoon fresh mint, finely chopped
1 recipe quantity Basic oil and lime dressing
    (see page 153)
2 tablespoons Greek yoghurt
sprig of mint to garnish

1.   Fork the tomatoes, cucumber and mint
    into the grated beetroot.
2.   Blend the dressing with the Greek
    yoghurt until well mixed.
3.   Stir this into the salad ingredients,
    garnish with a sprig of mint.
4.   Chill for 30 minutes before serving.

RED CABBAGE SALAD WITH PECAN NUTS
Serves 4 to 6.

1 recipe quantity Basic oil and lemon or
    vinegar dressing (see page 153)
675g/1½ lb red cabbage, finely shredded
2 green eating apples, chopped in small chunks
    (leave skins on)
little lemon juice
55g/2 oz raisins
2 tablespoons parsley, finely chopped
55g/2 oz pecan nuts, roughly chopped (leave a
    few halves to garnish)

1.   Place cabbage in a serving bowl.
2.   Sprinkle a little lemon juice over the
    chopped apple to stop it browning.
3.   Stir apple, raisins, parsley and chopped
    pecans into the shredded cabbage.
4.   Stir in the dressing and garnish with a
    few halves of pecan nuts.

COLESLAW
Serves 4 to 6.

1 recipe quantity Coleslaw dressing (see page
    155)
675g/1½ lb white cabbage, finely shredded
3 tender sticks celery (use inside sticks, not
    tough outer ones)
2 red eating apples, cut in small chunks (leave
    skins on)
1 good size carrot, grated
1 small onion, very finely chopped
55g/2 oz raisins or sultanas
55g/2 oz pecan nuts or walnuts
little parsley, finely chopped to garnish
    (optional)

1.   Put all the salad ingredients into a mixing
    bowl.
2.   Stir in the dressing.

3. Leave to stand to allow the flavours to blend for 1 hour before serving.

Note for vegans For the dressing use 1 quantity *Basic oil and lemon dressing* (see page 153). Blend this in a mixer with 110g/4 oz silken tofu (see page 120), one extra tablespoon lemon juice and 2 teaspoons grated horseradish root.

POTATO SALAD
Serves 4 to 6.

6 tablespoons Basic mayonnaise (see page 154)
½ medium red pepper, deseeded and chopped
1 medium pickled gherkin, finely chopped
1 level tablespoon capers, rinsed and patted dry
900g/2 lb potatoes, steamed, peeled and cubed
4 tender sticks celery, finely chopped
1 small onion, finely chopped
110g/4 oz frozen peas
110g/4 oz frozen sweet corn
1 tablespoons parsley, finely chopped

1. Mix all the vegetables, except the parsley in a serving bowl.
2. Carefully stir in the mayonnaise.
3. Garnish with parsley and serve.

POTATO SALAD WITH CHUTNEY
Serves 4 to 6.

Use the same salad ingredients as for the *Potato salad* above, but dress with 4 tablespoons *Basic mayonnaise* mixed with 3 tablespoons *Dried peach chutney* (see page 177).

CELERIAC, COURGETTE, CARROT AND FENNEL REMOULADE
This is one of my favourite salads. Allow the dressing to be absorbed and all the delicious flavours to blend for 1 hour before serving. If kohlrabi (see page 147) is available then add 1 grated tablespoon of it to the ingredients list.

Serves 4 to 6.

1 medium size celeriac, peeled and grated
2 medium size courgettes, grated
2 medium size carrots, scraped and grated
1 small bulb Florence fennel, grated

1 recipe quantity Rich tarragon vinaigrette (see page 153)
2 rounded tablespoons Greek yoghurt

1. Put all the grated vegetables in a serving bowl.
2. Blend the vinaigrette with the yoghurt and stir this into the grated vegetables.
3. Let stand in a cool place for 1 hour before serving.

Note: As an alternative, try using celeriac, carrot, chopped watercress or mustard cress and chopped tomatoes. Dress with the same dressing as above and you have another delicious, easy to chew salad.

KOHLRABI VINAIGRETTE
A simple and delicious salad.

Serves 4 to 6.

3 medium size kohlrabi, peeled and grated
1 small bunch chopped chives
2 tablespoons parsley, finely chopped
1 recipe quantity either Basic oil and lemon, lime or vinegar dressing (see page 153)

1. Mix all the ingredients together.
2. Leave to marinate for 30 minutes before serving.

Note: You can elaborate on this salad by adding chopped avocado, chopped papaya and chopped watercress. This adds an exotic flavour which is quite superb and great for a special occasion dinner party.

PAPAYA, AVOCADO, MUSHROOM AND RADICCHIO SALAD
This is an expensive salad, so make it for a special occasion only. The red radicchio leaves (see page 149) are left whole and the other ingredients are spooned into the centre in any artistic arrangement you feel like. It looks very colourful and tastes delicious. One of the home-made fruit vinegars, especially raspberry, would be ideal (see page 152 on how to make fruit vinegars) or you can add two teaspoons pure raspberry juice concentrate to the dressing as suggested in the recipe.

Serves 4 to 6.

1 good size papaya
1 avocado the same size as the papaya
little lemon juice, to stop fruit browning
6 radicchio leaves, left whole (or iceberg lettuce
 leaves)
170g/6 oz small button mushrooms, thinly
 sliced
chopped chives, to garnish
1 recipe quantity Basic oil and lemon dressing
 (without the honey – see page 153)
2 teaspoons pure raspberry juice concentrate

1. Peel the skin off the papaya, cut in half
    and scoop out the seeds. Cut in very thin
    wedges.
2. Slit the avocado in quarters, peel off the
    skin and take out the stone. Cut in thin
    wedges and sprinkle with lemon juice to
    stop browning.
3. Arrange the radicchio leaves in a flatish
    serving dish. Spoon equal amounts of
    sliced mushrooms into the centre of each
    leaf, then arrange the avocado and papaya
    slices slightly overlapping in a circle
    around each mound of mushrooms.
4. Mix the dressing with the raspberry juice
    concentrate (or use raspberry vinegar) and
    spoon this over each filled leaf.
5. Sprinkle on the chopped chives and let
    stand in a cool place for 30 minutes before
    serving.

CUCUMBER, YOGHURT AND MINT BOWL COOLER (RAITA)

This refreshing dish is a great complement to
any hot spicy meal. Instead of cucumber, you
can add other salad vegetables such as red
peppers and spring onions but this
combination is cooling and delicious.

Serves 4.

285ml/1/2 pt thick natural yoghurt
225g/8 oz cucumber, cut in small dice or grated
1 level teaspoon clear honey (more if you wish)
1 level tablespoon fresh mint, finely chopped
little sea salt and freshly ground black pepper
1 level teaspoon cumin seeds
sprig mint, to garnish

1. Mix all the ingredients, except the cumin
    seeds, in a bowl.
2. Dry roast the cumin seeds in a pan, then
    finely ground. Sprinkle this over the
    yoghurt mixture and garnish with a sprig
    of mint.

CUCUMBER, TOFU AND MINT BOWL COOLER (RAITA)
Serves 4.

Omit the yoghurt and salt from the previous
recipe and instead use 280g/10 oz silken tofu
(see page 120) and 2 tablespoons lemon juice.
Then season with vegetable bouillon powder to
your taste.

CHUNKY CHILLED AVOCADO PATE (QUACAMOLE)
This is delicious served with *Fried tortilla
fingers* (see page 78). Make this as near to
serving time as possible. If left to stand too
long, it starts to brown.

Serves 6.

3 medium size ripe avocados, peeled and
 stoned
2 tablespoons lemon juice
1 large clove garlic, peeled and crushed
1 green chilli, finely chopped
1/2 level teaspoon sea salt
1 medium size pepper, very finely chopped
1 small onion, peeled and very finely chopped
1/2 medium size cucumber, cut in small chunks

110g/4 oz firm, ripe tomatoes, skinned and
  chopped
6 black olives, stoned and cut in half (optional)
110g/4 oz sour cream or Greek yoghurt

1. Chop and mash the avocado, mixing in the
   lemon juice immediately to stop any
   browning.
2. In a pestle and mortar crush the garlic,
   chilli and salt into a paste-like mixture.
3. Stir into the avocado and lemon blending
   well together.
4. Stir in the chopped vegetables and finally
   the sour cream or yoghurt. Spoon into a
   serving bowl and chill.

LIGHT VEGETABLE DISHES

The following recipes make nourishing and
delicious side dishes for any meal. Some of the
recipes are a meal in themselves.

Cook vegetables by either blanching in
boiling water for a few minutes, stir-frying,
steaming or baking in their own juice to
retain as many nutrients as possible. Boiling
vegetables for more than a few minutes is fine
when they are in stews and soups where you
eat all the goodness in the cooking liquid, but
simply boiling then throwing away the
cooking water means that most of the
nourishment goes down the sink.

AUBERGINE, DRIED MUSHROOM AND SUNFLOWER SEED DIP

This delicious dip can be garnished with thin
onion rings and stoned and halved black
olives.

Serves 4.

6 dried mushrooms
a little sunflower or corn oil
2 medium aubergines
2 cloves garlic, crushed
1 level teaspoon coriander seeds, ground
2 rounded tablespoons sunflower seed spread
2 tablespoons lemon juice (more if you wish)
2 tablespoons fresh parsley, chopped
little sea salt and freshly ground black pepper,
  to taste

1. Wash the mushrooms well then soak in
   hot water for 15 minutes. Cut off woody
   stems and chop very finely.
2. Rub the aubergines in a little oil and bake
   at 350°F/180°C/Gas Mark 4 for 1 hour.
   Place under a cold tap to cool, then peel
   the skins off.
3. Sauté the chopped mushrooms in a very
   little oil with the garlic and coriander for
   7 minutes. Put the sautéed mushrooms in
   a blender and process until well minced.
4. Add the aubergine pulp, sunflower seed
   spread, lemon juice and parsley and blend
   until smooth. Taste and add sea salt and
   black pepper to your liking.

BAKED LEMON CARROTS

These are great with nut or bean roasts or
rissoles.

Serves 4.

900g/2 lb carrots, scraped
1 tablespoon shoyu (naturally fermented soy
  sauce)
2 tablespoons lemon juice
2 tablespoons water
few knobs polyunsaturated margarine or butter

1. Cut the carrots lengthwise in four if thick
   and two if thin, then in half widthwise so
   that you have approximately 5 cm/2 inch
   sticks.
2. Spread the carrots over a large sheet of
   cooking foil and sprinkle on the shoyu,
   lemon juice and water. Dot with the
   margarine or butter.
3. Bring the sides of the foil up to the centre
   to form a loose parcel. Place in a shallow
   baking tin and bake in the oven 375°F/
   190°C/Gas Mark 5 for 40 to 45 minutes.

Note: The delicious juice from these can be
added to a gravy or sauce if the meal includes
one.

SAUTEED RED CABBAGE WITH CORIANDER

Serves 4.

160

675g/1½ lb red cabbage
1 medium size onion
3 tablespoons virgin olive or sunflower oil
1 rounded teaspoon coriander seeds, freshly
ground
little sea salt and freshly ground black pepper
1 tablespoon lemon juice

1. Cut the cabbage in half, remove the stalk
   and shred (not too finely).
2. Sauté the onion in the oil until soft. Push
   the onion to the side and fry the ground
   coriander for 1 minute.
3. Add the cabbage and stir-fry for 5 minutes
   on moderate heat until lightly cooked but
   still crisp.
4. Season with a little sea salt and freshly
   ground black pepper and the lemon juice.

CELERY WITH TOMATO AND THYME
Serves 4.

2 plump heads celery with good hearts
1 medium onion, finely chopped
225ml/8 fl oz tomato juice
sea salt and freshly ground black pepper
little dried or chopped fresh thyme

1. Take off the outer tough stalks of the
   celery and save for soups. Cut the celery
   into 2.5 cm/1 inch lengths and steam for 7
   minutes.
2. Sauté the onion in the oil until soft. Add
   the celery and fry briskly for 5 minutes.
3. Add the tomato juice, a little sea salt and
   freshly ground black pepper and the
   thyme.
4. Cook with the lid on the pan for a few
   minutes more.

STIR-FRY COURGETTES WITH MUSHROOMS, GARLIC AND HERBS
Fresh herbs are best in this recipe but dried
will do.

Serves 4.

4 medium size courgettes
1 large clove garlic
3 tablespoons virgin olive or sunflower oil

110g/4 oz button or chanterelle mushrooms (see
page 148), sliced
1 dessertspoon either fresh chopped basil or 1
very level teaspoon dried
1 level teaspoon dried tarragon
1 tablespoon fresh chopped parsley
1 level teaspoon vegetable bouillon powder
little freshly ground black pepper, to taste
1 tablespoon lime juice

1. Cut the courgettes in either thinnish
   rounds or 2.5 cm/1 inch thinnish sticks.
2. Sauté the garlic in the oil for 1 minute on
   moderate heat, then stir-fry the courgettes
   and mushrooms briskly for 4 minutes.
3. Add the herbs, vegetable bouillon powder,
   the black pepper and lemon juice and stir-
   fry briskly for 1 minute more.

COURGETTES WITH TOMATOES, ONION AND GARLIC
This is good enough to spoon on pasta with a
sprinkling of Pecarino or Parmesan cheese on
top and serve as a light main meal. When
fresh tomatoes are in season and cheap, then
use these instead of canned.

Serves 4.

900g/2 lb courgettes, cut in 2.5 cm/1 inch
rounds
1 medium onion, chopped
2 cloves garlic, crushed
3 tablespoons virgin olive or sunflower oil
1 large bay leaf
1 level teaspoon dried basil
½ teaspoon dried oregano
½ teaspoon dried tarragon
1 tablespoon parsley, chopped
450g/1 lb ripe skinned tomatoes (400g/14 oz
can will do), chopped
little sea salt and freshly ground black pepper,
to taste

1. Heat the oil in a wide pan with a lid and
   add the onion, garlic and courgettes and
   cook gently with the lid on for 7 minutes.
2. Take off lid, turn up heat and very lightly
   brown.
3. Turn down heat and add the rest of the
   ingredients and cook for 5 minutes more
   on moderate heat, stirring a few times.

LEEKS WITH MUSHROOMS AND BEAN SPROUTS
Serves 4.

2 tablespoons virgin olive or sunflower oil
1 large leek, trimmed and cut in thin rings
170g/6 oz button or chanterelle mushrooms (see
  page 148), sliced
225g/8 oz bean sprouts
little freshly ground black pepper
2 teaspoons lemon juice
sprinkling of shoyu (naturally fermented soy
  sauce)
2 tablespoons parsley, finely chopped

1. Sauté the chopped leeks in the oil for 4 minutes.
2. Add the mushrooms and fry for 3 minutes more.
3. Finally add the bean sprouts, parsley, lemon juice, a light sprinkling of shoyu and a little black pepper. Heat through for 30 seconds and serve immediately.

BAKED AUBERGINE AND TOMATO
This is delicious served with lentil, bean or nut rissoles (see pages 93, 105 and 111).

Serves 4.

2 large aubergines
450g/1 lb fresh ripe tomatoes, skinned and
  sliced
2 large cloves garlic, crushed
55g/2 oz wholemeal breadcrumbs
grated rind of 1 lemon
55g/2 oz Parmesan or Pecarino cheese, finely
  grated
little virgin olive oil

1. Slice the aubergines and sprinkle with a little sea salt. Leave for 20 minutes, rinse and pat dry on absorbent kitchen paper.
2. Mix the garlic with the breadcrumbs and lemon rind.
3. Pour a little olive oil in the bottom of a shallow ovenproof dish.
4. Layer the bottom with aubergine slices, then a layer of tomatoes. Sprinkle on a little of the breadcrumb mixture.

5. Repeat this ending with a layer of aubergine slices. Press gently down with a potato masher.
6. Sprinkle the grated cheese on top and bake in the oven 425°F/220°C/Gas Mark 7 for 30 minutes.

FILLING FOR STUFFED VEGETABLES
The following filling is suitable for stuffing aubergines, courgettes, red and green peppers, marrows and other varieties of squash. You can make the filling the day before and keep in the fridge.

400g/14 oz can tomatoes, mashed (take out ½
  tea cup of the juice and reserve)
3 tablespoons either virgin olive oil or
  sunflower oil
225g/8 oz onion, finely chopped
2 large juicy cloves garlic
110g/4 oz mushrooms, chopped
1 teaspoon dried basil
1 large bay leaf
1 level teaspoon ground coriander
2 tablespoons parsley, finely chopped
110g/4 oz pine kernels
1 rounded tablespoon tomato purée
1 tablespoon lemon juice
1 dessertspoon Worcester sauce
little sea salt, to taste
freshly ground black pepper, to taste
225g/8 oz dry weight short grain brown rice,
  cooked for 30 minutes only (see page 80)

1. Sauté the onion and garlic in the oil for 10 minutes with the lid on.
2. Add the mushrooms and cook for 3 minutes.
3. Add basil, bay leaf, ground coriander, parsley and pine kernels and cook for 1 minute.
4. Add mashed tomatoes, tomato purée, lemon juice and Worcester sauce and cook for 2 minutes more. Taste and season with a little sea salt and freshly ground black pepper.
5. Stir in the cooked and well drained rice.

STUFFED AUBERGINES

Serves 6.

1 recipe quantity of Filling for stuffed
  vegetables (see page 162)
6 medium aubergines
little sea salt
1 tablespoon oil to fry pulp
1 rounded tablespoon tomato purée
reserved ½ teacup of tomato juice from making
  the filling (see page 162)
½ teacup hot water

1. Trim the aubergines, slice in half
   lengthwise and sprinkle a little sea salt on
   the flesh. Leave to stand for 30 minutes to
   get rid of the bitter juices.
2. Rinse well and pat dry.
3. Cut out the flesh leaving 1 cm/½ inch still
   on the skins. Chop this flesh in small
   pieces and sauté in the oil for a few
   minutes until soft.
4. Mix this with the filling and spoon the
   mixture into the aubergine skins. Place in
   a baking dish.
5. Mix tomato purée with the reserved
   tomato juice and the water and pour this
   into the baking dish.
6. Cover the dish with foil or a lid and bake
   in the oven 350°F/180°C/Gas Mark 4 for 45
   minutes until the shells of the vegetables
   are soft.
7. Garnish with a few pine nuts and fresh
   chopped parsley just before serving.

STUFFED COURGETTES
Serves 4.

1 recipe quantity Filling for stuffed vegetables
  (see page 162)
8 medium size courgettes
1 tablespoon oil to fry the flesh
1 rounded tablespoon tomato purée
reserved ½ teacup of tomato juice from making
  the filling (see page 162)
½ teacup hot water

1. Cut courgettes in half lengthwise and cut
   out shallow grooves from each half. Chop
   the cut out flesh in small pieces and fry
   for a few minutes until soft. Add this to
   the filling.
2. Spoon the filling into the courgette cases
   and place in a baking dish.
3. Mix tomato purée, tomato juice and water
   together and pour this into the baking
   dish.
4. Cover with foil or a lid and bake in the
   oven at 350°F/180°C/Gas Mark 4 for 45
   minutes.
5. Garnish with a few pine nuts and fresh
   parsley just before serving.

STUFFED PEPPERS
Choose young medium to small red and green
peppers for this recipe.

Serves 4.

1 recipe quantity Filling for stuffed vegetables
  (see page 162)
10 medium to small red and green peppers
1 rounded tablespoon tomato purée
reserved ½ cup tomato juice from making the
  filling (see page 162)
½ teacup hot water

1. Cut a slice off the stalk ends and pull out
   the core. Wash out the seeds and place the
   peppers in a baking dish.
2. Spoon the filling into the peppers.
3. Mix the tomato purée, tomato juice and
   water together and pour into the baking
   dish.
4. Cover with foil and bake in the oven at
   350°F/180°C/Gas Mark 4 for 45 minutes.
5. Garnish with a few pine nuts and fresh
   chopped parsley just before serving.

NUTTY STUFFED SWEET POTATOES
Serves 4.

4 good size sweet potatoes
2 rounded tablespoons Greek yoghurt
1 rounded tablespoon polyunsaturated
  margarine or butter
¼ level teaspoon black pepper, finely ground
½ level teaspoon nutmeg

1 medium onion, very finely chopped
85g/3 oz mixed sunflower seeds and almonds,
    medium finely ground
3 tablespoons parsley, finely chopped
little sea salt, to taste
85g/3 oz Cheddar cheese, grated

1. Rub the scrubbed potatoes with a little oil
    and a very little sea salt. Bake in their
    jackets at 400°F/200°C/Gas Mark 6 for 1 to
    1½ hours depending on their size (test for
    softness after 1 hour by piercing through
    to the centre with a steel knitting needle
    or skewer).
2. Cut in half and scoop out the flesh.
3. Mash this with all the other ingredients
    except the cheese. Spoon the mashed
    mixture into the potato skins and sprinkle
    on the grated cheese.
4. Put back in the oven and bake for 15
    minutes (if not browned then grill for 2
    minutes under moderate heat but do not
    leave the potatoes in the oven more than
    the 15 minutes).

TOMATOES STUFFED WITH SWEETCORN

These are great as an appetizer or for a buffet
party. Fresh herbs make this dish into a
beautiful and delicious delicacy. One good size
stuffed tomato is sufficient for each person. If
you cannot obtain fresh coriander leaves then
double the amount of parsley.

Makes 12.

12 medium to large tomatoes
280g/10 oz fresh sweetcorn, scraped off the cob
    or frozen
1 large clove garlic, peeled and crushed
1 tablespoon fresh chopped parsley
1 tablespoon fresh chopped coriander leaves
1 tablespoon fresh chopped basil or 1 level
    teaspoon dried
1 tablespoon fresh chopped oregano or
    marjoram, or 1 level teaspoon dried
1 rounded tablespoon chopped chives
1 teaspoon vegetable bouillon powder
225g/8 oz either fromage blanc, quark or goat's
    curd cheese
freshly ground black pepper
good pinch cayenne pepper

1. Slice a piece off the top of each tomato and
    scoop out the middle leaving just enough
    pulp attached to the skin so that it
    remains firm.
2. Cook the sweetcorn in a little salted water
    for 3 minutes only, drain well and cool.
3. In a mixing bowl put all the other
    ingredients and mix with a fork, then stir
    in the cold sweetcorn. Chop the tomato
    pulp and stir into the corn mixture.
4. Fill the tomato cases to slightly
    overflowing. Pop the caps sideways on top
    and stick a tiny sprig of any fresh herb
    you have available by the side of the cap.

GRATED POTATO PANCAKES

Children love these. They are like having egg
and chips all in one with less fat and less
bother.

Makes 12.

450g/1 lb potatoes, scrubbed
3 eggs
3 level tablespoons either 100% wholewheat or
    81% brown wholemeal flour
good pinch grated nutmeg
1 medium onion, peeled
½ teaspoon sea salt
little freshly ground black pepper
little soya oil for frying

1. Coarsely grate the potatoes and put into a
    mixing bowl.
2. Coarsely grate the onion and add to the
    potatoes.
3. Beat the eggs in another bowl.
4. Add the flour, nutmeg, salt and black
    pepper to the beaten eggs and pour this
    into the potato and onion mixture. Mix
    well.
5. Heat enough oil in a large frying pan to
    just cover the bottom.
6. Drop tablespoons of the mixture into the
    pan and fry on moderately high heat on
    both sides until golden brown.
7. Drain on absorbent kitchen paper and
    serve piping hot with cottage cheese and a
    salad.

Note: You can add other grated vegetables.

For example, use half the potatoes mixed with equal amounts of grated carrot or very finely chopped red and green peppers or a mixture of vegetables, but keep the same total weight of vegetables as in the list of ingredients. You can also add spices and herbs to give a variety of flavours.

MEXICAN SPICED SWEET POTATO CAKE
Makes 12.

900g/2 lb sweet potatoes
little oil and sea salt for rubbing potatoes
1 rounded teaspoon garam masala
1 very level teaspoon cayenne pepper
1 medium onion, peeled and very finely
  chopped
1 tablespoon each of sweet red and green
  peppers
2 tablespoons either chopped coriander or
  parsley
1 large egg
little sea salt to taste
soya oil for frying

1. Scrub the sweet potatoes and steam until soft but not mushy, peel and mash.
2. Add all the other ingredients while the potatoes are still hot.
3. Form into about 12 rounds, 0.75 cm/ ⅓ inch thick.
4. Heat a little soya oil in a frying pan and fry the sweet potato cakes until crisp and golden on both sides.
5. Serve immediately.

CHINESE VEGETABLE SPRING ROLLS
You can buy the wrappers for these delicious deep-fried rolls. They are made from tofu (soya bean curd) and called bean curd sheets or spring roll wrappers. Follow the directions on the packet.

Makes 16.

8 dried mushrooms (see page 148)
2 tablespoons cold-pressed sunflower or sesame
  oil
8 small courgettes
2 good size spring onions, finely chopped
225g/8 oz bean sprouts

1 tablespoon shoyu
2 tablespoons dry sherry (optional but
  delicious)
1 level teaspoon freshly grated ginger
freshly ground black pepper
16 bean curd sheets (see note above)
soya oil for deep-frying
few spring onions to garnish

1. Soak the mushrooms in hot water for 15 minutes. Cut off woody stalks and discard. Cut mushrooms into tiny strips.
2. Wash and wipe the courgettes, slice lengthwise into six then chop into tiny chunks.
3. Heat oil in a wok or large heavy-based frying pan. On a high heat cook the courgettes for half a minute stirring constantly, then add the bean sprouts and spring onions and continue to fry for 1 minute.
4. Add shoyu, sherry, ginger and a few twists of black pepper. Cook on lower heat for just 20 seconds stirring constantly.
5. Allow to cool slightly then using a slotted spoon place 1 generous tablespoon of the mixture in the middle of each bean curd sheet. Form rolls by folding the bottom edge of the sheet over the filling first, the left and right edges over and roll the lot towards the top. Seal as directed on the packet.
6. Heat oil in a deep frier or heavy-based frying pan to 350°F/180°C and fry the rolls for just 1½ minutes until golden brown. Drain on absorbent kitchen paper. Serve immediately.

NORI WRAPPED COCKTAIL BITES
For more information on nori, a seaweed vegetable, see page 146. I have chosen a filling of aubergines, dried mushrooms and garlic, but for meat eaters you can try a mixture of minced sea food, avocado, red and green peppers and chives with a touch of lemon and soya sauce to season. Also try curried rice or mashed beans or lentils with a touch of lime juice.

The quantity is ideal for a buffet party but if you want to serve as an appetizer, for say a dinner party for four, then halve the recipe.

Makes 40.

2 large aubergines
55g/2 oz dried mushrooms, washed and soaked
*   in hot water for 30 minutes*
1 tablespoon sunflower oil or virgin olive oil
110g/4 oz onion, very finely chopped
1 large juicy clove garlic, crushed
1 level teaspoon ground coriander
1 rounded tablespoon parsley, finely chopped
1 very level tablespoon tomato purée
1 tablespoon lemon juice
1 rounded tablespoon ground almonds or
*   Parmesan cheese*
little sea salt and freshly ground black pepper,
*   to taste*
10 sheets of nori

1. Preheat the oven to 375°F/190°C/Gas Mark 5.
2. Lightly oil the aubergines and bake in the oven for 40 minutes.
3. Soak the mushrooms while aubergines are baking.
4. Cut the baked aubergines in half and scoop out the flesh, put into a mixing bowl and mash.
5. Sauté the onion and garlic in the oil for 10 minutes with the lid on (do not burn).
6. Cut stems off the mushrooms, discard these, squeeze out any moisture from the mushroom caps and chop these very finely.
7. Add chopped mushrooms, coriander and parsley to the onion and fry gently for 5 minutes.
8. Mince this mixture or process in a blender then mix it with the aubergine pulp, tomato purée, lemon juice and ground almonds or cheese.
9. Season with a little sea salt and freshly ground black pepper. The mixture should be firm and stick together (if too soft then add a little toasted wholemeal breadcrumbs).
10. Cut the nori sheets in four with a pair of scissors, dampen each piece and put a heaped teaspoon of the filling mixture in the centre. Then fold the edges over the filling, securing the folds at the top with a cocktail stick (damp nori sticks together well).
11. Store in the fridge until ready to serve. Garnish the serving dish with a few sprigs of watercress or flat-leafed parsley.

CURRIED VEGETABLE DISHES

Here are just a few of my favourite vegetable-based recipes using a variety of spices mainly found in Indian cookery. All have been tried and tested on students, customers in my shop and friends, and have been enjoyed even by those who aren't too keen on spicy food.

Buy all spices in small quantities and store in airtight jars away from direct sunlight. A good commercial curry powder mixture is great if you are in a hurry, but you can't beat using a variety of fresh spices to achieve an authentic Indian flavour. So make the effort and experiment with these lovely spices.

Most of the spices will be familiar to you but below I give a little information about a few ingredients with which you might be less familiar.

SOME UNUSUAL INGREDIENTS
Chapati flour. See page 17 for information on this and pages 28 and 29 for information on *Chapatis, Puris* and *Samosas.*

Ghee. This is clarified butter and is often an ingredient in Indian cookery. To make ghee, you just heat butter (you can use margarine) in a thick saucepan and simmer for 1 hour. Strain through muslin and store in a jar. I still prefer, however, to use sunflower or safflower oil in curry recipes.

Gram flour (chick pea flour or besan). This is ground chick peas and is marvellous for *Pakora* (see page 169) and *Tempura* (see page 126). Other bean flours are also used in Indian cookery, such as mung bean and pea flours. All are full of protein and have many variable uses, including thickening sauces and soups.

Tamarind. This is the fruit of the tamarind tree. It is very tart with a sharp citrus-like taste. The fruit is dried and pressed and looks like a block of dried dates. To prepare, soak the required amount in enough hot water to just cover for 1 hour. Then press the lot through a sieve. You will have a tangy, thickish liquid. Use as directed in the recipes. Lemon, lime or vinegar is sometimes used as an alternative.

MIXED VEGETABLE CURRY

This rich flavoursome curry is a great success with all who sample it and I haven't altered the ingredients since the first time I made it 15 years ago.

Serves 6.
You will need a very large heavy-based saucepan with a tight lid.

*2 medium size potatoes, scrubbed and cut into
    2 cm/¾ inch cubes*
*55g/2 oz tamarind, soaked (see above for
    information)*
1 level dessertspoon turmeric
1 level dessertspoon ground cumin
1 level dessertspoon ground coriander
1 very level teaspoon cayenne or chilli powder
4 cardamom pods, crushed
¼ teaspoon clove powder
2.5 cm/1 inch knob fresh ginger, grated
4 tablespoons sunflower or safflower oil
340g/12 oz onion, chopped
3 good size cloves garlic, crushed
1 level teaspoon black mustard seeds
*2 medium carrots, scraped and cut into 2.5 cm/
    1 inch sticks*
3 sticks celery, chopped
½ medium cauliflower, broken into florets
*1 good size green pepper, deseeded and
    chopped*
*1 medium size cooking apple, chopped (leave
    skin on)*
1 rounded tablespoon gram flour (see page 166)
*either 6 good size tomatoes, skinned and
    minced or 400g/14 oz can*

1 rounded tablespoon tomato purée
285ml/½ pt hot water
1 cinnamon stick
little sea salt
1 rounded teaspoon methi (fenugreek leaf)
107g/6 oz French beans, fresh or frozen

1. Steam the cubed potatoes for 5 minutes only.
2. Press the soaked tamarind through a sieve. Mix the tamarind juice with the turmeric, cumin, coriander, cayenne or chilli powder, crushed cardamom pods, clove powder and ginger to a smooth paste. Add a little water if too stiff.
3. Sauté the onion, garlic, mustard seeds, carrots and potatoes for 5 minutes in 3 tablespoons of the oil.
4. Add the celery, cauliflower, green pepper and apple and fry for 3 minutes more.
5. Make a space in the centre, add the remaining 1 tablespoon of oil then the tamarind mixture and heat through.
6. Stir this around the vegetables, coating them well.
7. Stir in the gram flour and cook on gentle heat stirring constantly for ½ minute.
8. Add tomatoes, tomato purée and hot water, still stirring constantly.
9. Bring to boil and add a little sea salt, the cinnamon stick and the methi. Stir well, cover and let simmer gently for 30 minutes.
10. Let stand for 30 minutes then add the French beans and simmer for 5 minutes or until the beans are cooked.
11. Serve with brown rice and *Cucumber and yoghurt and mint bowl cooler* (see page 159). You could also accompany this curry with a *Dhal* (see page 112) and *Coconut and onion relish* (see page 178) for a truly delicious and entertaining meal.

SPICED OKRA WITH MUSHROOMS
Serves 6 as a side dish.

1 rounded tablespoon desiccated coconut
140ml/¼ pt hot water
1 rounded teaspoon ground coriander
1 level teaspoon ground cumin
½ level teaspoon turmeric

½ level teaspoon cayenne or chilli powder
3 tablespoons lemon or lime juice
3 cardamom pods, crushed
4 tablespoons sunflower or safflower oil
½ teaspoon black mustard seeds
2 large cloves garlic, crushed
1 dessertspoon curry leaves or 2 bay leaves
170g/6 oz button mushrooms
340g/12 oz young okra
sea salt to taste

1. Mix the coconut with the water and leave to stand while you prepare the other ingredients.
2. Mix the coriander, cumin, turmeric, cayenne or chilli powder, lemon or lime juice and crushed cardamom seeds together.
3. Heat the oil in a large pan and gently fry the mustard seeds with the garlic for 1 minute.
4. Add curry leaves or bay leaves and mushrooms and cook for 2 minutes.
5. Stir in the lemon or lime spice mixture. Fry for 1 minute on very gentle heat stirring constantly.
6. Add the okra and the coconut and water mixture plus a little sea salt to taste. Bring to boil turn down to simmer and cook for 10 minutes only with a tight lid on the pan.

SPICED GINGER AND SESAME POTATOES
This dish was inspired by Madhur Jaffrey, a very wonderful writer and cook. It is strong and spicy.

Serves 6 as a side dish.

900g/2 lb potatoes, scrubbed
1 rounded tablespoon fresh ginger, grated
2 large juicy cloves garlic, crushed
1 level tablespoon tahini (sesame seed paste)
2 tablespoons water
just under 1 teaspoon turmeric
½ level teaspoon cayenne pepper
just under 1 level teaspoon sea salt
6 tablespoons sunflower or safflower oil
1 level teaspoon whole fennel seeds

1. Cut the potatoes in 2 cm/¾ inch cubes (leave skins on) and steam until cooked but not mushy (if you boil most of the flavour goes). This takes about 15 minutes but test after 10 minutes.
2. Put ginger, garlic, tahini, tumeric, cayenne, salt and water into a blender and process until thick and smooth.
3. Heat the oil in a large heavy-based frying pan to hot then throw in the fennel seeds. Cook on a high heat for only a few seconds.
4. Turn down heat to moderate and fry the tahini paste for 2 minutes. Keep stirring and do not burn.
5. Add the potatoes and stir-fry for 6 minutes over moderate heat until golden brown.

SPICED GINGER AND SESAME CAULIFLOWER OR BROCCOLI FLORETS
Serves 6 as a side dish.

Follow the ingredients list and method for the previous recipe, but use 675g/1½ lb cauliflower or broccoli florets instead of the potatoes. Steam the florets for 5 minutes before frying in the spices.

LIMED HOT ONION RINGS WITH STIR-FRY CABBAGE
This dish is delicious hot or cold and a great accompaniment to any bean or lentil bake, rissoles or curry dishes. Prepare at least an hour before needed.

Serves 6 as a side dish.

2 medium onions, cut in thin rings
4 tablespoons lime juice
1 very level teaspoon chilli or hot red pepper
  sauce or ½ teaspoon cayenne pepper
675g/1½ lb white or red cabbage, roughly
  shredded
2 tablespoons sunflower or corn oil
1 teaspoon coriander seeds, finely ground

1. Put onion rings in a bowl and cover with boiling water. Leave for 5 minutes to soften. Rinse in very cold water and pat dry.

2. Mix the lime juice with the chilli sauce or cayenne pepper.

3. Put the onions back in the bowl and let marinate in the lime mixture for 1 hour.

4. Pour boiling water over the cabbage, drain and immediately plunge in cold water. Drain in a colander.

5. Heat the oil in a heavy-based frying pan or wok and fry the coriander for ½ minute.

6. Add the well drained cabbage and stir-fry for 2 minutes only.

7. Top with the limed onion rings and serve.

PAKORA (INDIAN DEEP-FRIED BATTERED VEGETABLES)

These are battered vegetables and are delicious as a snack or as an accompaniment to a main meal.

Serves 6 as a side dish.

55g/2 oz gram flour (chick pea flour)
55g/2 oz soya flour
55g/2 oz brown rice flour
55g/2 oz unbleached white flour
¾ level teaspoon cayenne pepper
¾ level teaspoon ground coriander
¾ level teaspoon sea salt
1 level teaspoon baking powder
1 egg
285ml/½ pt water
225g/8 oz prepared vegetables (see method below)

1. Sieve the flours into a mixing bowl with the spices, salt and baking powder.

2. Beat the egg with the water and gradually add the liquid to the flours to form a smooth creamy batter. Or process the lot in a blender for a few seconds.

3. Let batter stand for 1 hour (important because the mixture takes on a more gluey thicker consistency and achieves a much crisper coating). Stir well before using.

4. The vegetables are a matter of choice. My favourites are onion rings, small cauliflower or broccoli florets, whole small button mushrooms, sliced courgettes, aubergines and potatoes (with skins on).

Sprigs of parsley and other herbs are also delicious.

5. Dip prepared vegetables individually into the batter and deep-fry in hot soya oil (as you would chips but do not use a chip basket or the batter will stick to it) until golden.

SOUPS

There are several soup recipes in Lessons 5 and 6, but here are a few of my favourite fresh vegetable-based soups for you to try.

The first recipes in this section on soups are for a vegetable stock and gravy. After tasting the gravy I don't think you will miss any meat flavour. It is delicious and well worth making in bulk ready to serve with rissoles, bean and nut roasts.

BASIC VEGETABLE STOCK

This stock is delicious for making gravy and sauces and for using in any recipe where chicken stock is called for. Make the stock with left-over vegetables, such as odds and ends of peppers, softish carrots, tough outside sticks of celery, outside leaves of lettuce, tough tops of fennel, squashy tomatoes, in fact any vegetables going spare. The flavour will differ according to the vegetables and herbs you use. Summer is a good time for making stock, as more fresh vegetables are available and cheaper. Fresh herbs are a wonderful addition but the parsley and bay leaves in the basic recipe are usually available.

Makes about 1 litre 700 ml/3 pt.

2 tablespoons sunflower or corn oil
1 very large onion, chopped
2 large cloves garlic, crushed
4 good size carrots, scrubbed and chopped
4 large sticks celery, chopped
green ends of leeks (even tough parts), chopped
bits of red or green peppers, chopped
squashy tomatoes
2 generous tablespoons tomato purée
2 bay leaves
4 tablespoons parsley, chopped
1 level teaspoon fennel seeds
8 black peppercorns, roughly crushed
2 rounded tablespoons vegetable bouillon
   powder
2 litres/3½ pt hot water

1. Heat the oil in a large heavy-based
    saucepan and stir-fry all the vegetables
    except for the tomatoes for 2 minutes.
2. Add all the other ingredients. Bring to
    boil, turn down to simmer and cook gently
    with the lid on for at least 1 hour.
3. Strain through a colander, mashing the
    vegetables with a potato masher to extract
    as much stock juice as possible. The liquid
    will be a rich brown and is now ready to
    use. It will be fine in the fridge for 3 days
    or freeze it in 570ml/1 pt containers.

VEGETABLE GRAVY

Makes 570ml/1 pt.

570ml/1 pt Basic vegetable stock (see above)
1 level tablespoon plain unbleached white or
   wholemeal flour
2 teaspoons shoyu (naturally fermented soy
   sauce)

1. Blend the flour to a smooth paste with the
    shoyu and a little cold stock.
2. Heat the stock, blend a little of the hot
    stock into the flour mixture, then pour
    this into the rest of the stock.
3. Bring to boil stirring constantly, then
    simmer for 5 minutes. The gravy will
    thicken slightly.

4. You can add 2 tablespoons red wine to
    each 570ml/1 pt stock for a richer festive
    gravy.

BEETROOT AND RED CABBAGE SOUP
This is based on the traditional Russian recipe
called bortsch. It is very tasty served with
either Greek yoghurt or sour cream. It freezes
well.

Serves 4 to 6.

3 tablespoons sunflower or corn oil
2 medium onions, chopped
675g/1½ lb red cabbage, shredded
1 level tablespoon dried dill (fresh is superb
   but use double the quantity)
½ teaspoon caraway seeds
2 bay leaves
6 medium size beetroots, peeled and grated
1 rounded teaspoon clear honey
3 tablespoons lemon juice
1 teaspoon cider vinegar
2 litres/3½ pt hot water
2 rounded tablespoons vegetable bouillon
   powder
Greek yoghurt or sour cream, to serve
little fresh chopped parsley or fresh chopped
   dill (not dried), to garnish

1. Stir-fry the onion and cabbage for 3
    minutes.
2. Add dill, caraway seeds, bay leaves,
    beetroot, honey, lemon juice and vinegar
    merging the ingredients well together.
3. Pour in the hot water with the vegetable
    bouillon powder or stock cubes.

4. Add a little freshly ground black pepper and bring to boil. Turn down to simmer and let cook gently with the lid on for 20 minutes only.
5. Take out the bay leaves. You can liquidize or serve as it is with dollops of the Greek yoghurt or sour cream. One level tablespoon of either can be dropped into the centre of each serving and topped with either the chopped parsley or dill.

CARROT COOLER
This chilled soup is absolutely delicious and very simple to prepare. Best with young home grown or new season carrots.

Serves 6.

1 medium onion, chopped
2 tablespoons sunflower or safflower oil
675g/1½ lb carrots, scrubbed or scraped and
*   chopped*
1 level teaspoon dried tarragon
850ml/1½ pt water
1½ tablespoons vegetable bouillon powder or
*   1½ vegetable stock cubes*
110g/4 oz Greek yoghurt
freshly ground black pepper
55g/2 oz shelled pistachio nuts, ground, to
*   garnish*
little parsley, finely chopped, to garnish

1. Sauté the onion and carrots in the oil for 7 minutes on low heat with the lid on.
2. Add the tarragon, water and vegetable bouillon powder.
3. Bring to boil turn down to simmer and cook with the lid on for 20 minutes.
4. Liquidize in a blender until smooth.
5. Blend a little with the yoghurt then stir in the lot together. Season with a little black pepper and chill well.
6. Just before serving sprinkle on the ground pistachio nuts, the parsley and a few more twists of black pepper.

PUMPKIN SOUP
This is one of my favourite soups and is delicious with or without the curry powder in the recipe.

Serves 6.

900g/2 lb pumpkin (weight after peeling),
*   roughly chopped*
3 large cloves garlic, crushed
2 tablespoons sunflower or safflower oil
1 rounded teaspoon curry powder (optional)
1 level teaspoon aniseed, crushed
2 tablespoons parsley, chopped
400g/14 oz can tomatoes, or even better, 450g/
*   1 lb fresh, skinned and chopped*
570ml/1 pt hot water
sea salt and freshly ground pepper, to taste

1. Stir-fry the pumpkin and garlic in the oil for 3 minutes.
2. Fry the aniseed and curry powder in a space in the centre for 1 minute.
3. Add parsley, chopped tomatoes, water and sea salt and black pepper to your taste.
4. Bring to boil then simmer with the lid on for 20 minutes. Liquidize until completely smooth.

SPANISH SALAD SOUP
Exciting and different, this is a must for days when lunch is eaten in the garden. It is served chilled with a choice of garnishes, including chopped vegetables, olives and croûtons. Granary bread and a choice of cheeses turns this lovely soup into a main meal.

Serves 4.

4 thick slices wholemeal bread, crumbled
1 large Spanish onion, peeled and chopped
2 cloves garlic, peeled and crushed
3 tablespoons olive oil
1 small red pepper, deseeded and chopped
1 small green pepper, deseeded and chopped
2 medium courgettes, chopped
450g/1 lb ripe tomatoes, skinned and chopped
2 tablespoons tomato purée
3 tablespoons mayonnaise
approximately 425ml/¾ pt iced water
1 teaspoon of either marjoram or basil or if
*   using fresh herbs 1 tablespoon of either herb*
sea salt and freshly ground black pepper to
taste

1. Put breadcrumbs into a large mixing bowl.
2. Sauté the onion, garlic, peppers and courgettes for 7 minutes with the lid on.

3. Scoop out and add to breadcrumbs.
4. Purée the skinned tomatoes, tomato purée, marjoram or basil with 285ml/½ pt of the iced water.
5. Pour this over the breadcrumbs and vegetable mixture. Mix well together.
6. Now purée this mixture half at a time, and blend until smooth.
7. Place in a serving bowl, stir in the mayonnaise and enough iced water to give the consistency of a thin batter or light single cream.
8. Season well with freshly ground black pepper and sea salt.
9. Serve with garnishes arranged in separate bowls, to be spooned into individual portions of the soup when ready to eat. I suggest small bowls of onion rings, chopped cucumber, lightly cooked French beans, stoned olives and croûtons.

POT BARLEY AND TOMATO BROTH
This is a very simple and tasty soup which is delicious for children if liquidized. The recipe makes lots so freeze what you don't eat.

Serves 8.

110g/4 oz pot barley, washed well and soaked
    in 1 litre 140 ml/2 pt water overnight
3 tablespoons sunflower oil
1 large onion, chopped
2 cloves garlic, crushed
4 medium carrots, scraped and chopped
2 medium potatoes, scrubbed and chopped
4 sticks celery, chopped
2 tablespoons parsley, finely chopped
2 level teaspoons mixed herbs
790g/1 lb 12 oz can tomatoes, well chopped
1 rounded tablespoon vegetable bouillon
    powder
½ teaspoon black pepper, freshly ground
little shoyu (naturally fermented soy sauce), to
    taste

1. Drain the barley, reserving the water. Measure the water in a jug and add more water to bring the level up to 1 litre 140 ml/2 pt.
2. Heat the oil in a very large heavy-based saucepan and fry the onion, garlic, carrots, potatoes, celery and drained barley for 3

minutes only. Stir well as they fry over moderate heat.
3. Add the herbs, tomatoes, vegetable bouillon powder, black pepper and reserved barley water.
4. Bring to boil, turn down to simmer and cook with the lid on for 20 minutes only.
5. Finally taste and add shoyu to your own liking.

SAUCES

How many times have you thought, 'I won't do that recipe because it entails making a sauce'? Well, I hope my recipes for simple sauces and more exotic sauces for special occasions will encourage you to think differently. Sauces can make very simple meals into a delight to the taste buds. Once you get the knack of preparing a few basic sauces the variations with the addition of vegetables, spices and herbs are endless.

BASIC WHITE SAUCE
As I don't like the flavour of white sauces made with wholewheat flour, I use a mixture of unbleached white flour and soya flour with excellent creamy results. Non-stick saucepans are easiest for this sauce.

Makes 570ml/1 pt.

40g/1½ oz unbleached white flour
28g/1 oz soya flour
570 ml/1 pt milk (either cow's, goat's or soya)
½ level teaspoon ground mace
just under ½ teaspoon mustard powder
1 large bay leaf
sea salt and freshly ground black pepper, to taste
1 knob of polyunsaturated margarine or butter

1. Mix the flours with 140 ml/¼ pt of the milk, the mace and mustard powder to form a smooth paste.
2. Heat the rest of the milk with the bay leaf to boiling.
3. Take off heat and blend a little of the hot milk into the flour mixture. Then pour this back into the rest of the milk. Stir well.

4. Return to low heat and stirring constantly slowly bring to boil. Keep stirring until the sauce thickens.

5. Turn down to simmer, add a little sea salt and freshly ground black pepper and the margarine or butter. Stir once more and let simmer for 3 minutes. Remove the bay leaf.

Note: If using a food processor or liquidizer, then simply blend flours, mace, mustard and 140 ml/¼ pt milk until smooth. Heat the rest of the milk to boiling and gradually add this to the other ingredients while the machine is still on. Blend until smooth. Pour this plus the bay leaf, a little sea salt, black pepper and the margarine or butter back into the saucepan. Bring slowly to the boil stirring constantly and keep stirring until the sauce thickens. Simmer for 3 minutes. Remove the bay leaf.

YOGHURT CHEESE SAUCE
Makes 570ml/1 pt.

Makes the *Basic white sauce* above with 140 ml/¼ pt less milk. Take off heat and while still hot add 110g/4 oz thick Greek yoghurt and 140g/5 oz either grated Farmhouse Cheddar or crumbled Lancashire Farmhouse cheese. Whisk in well.

ONION SAUCE
Makes 570ml/1 pt.

Simmer 2 medium size onions, finely chopped, in just enough slightly salted water to cover, for 10 minutes until soft. Drain saving the cooking liquid. Then make the *Basic white sauce* (see page 172) but use the onion cooking water and milk to make up 570ml/1 pt liquid in all. Omit the mace and use 1 very level teaspoon allspice instead. When sauce is thick, add the onion and 2 tablespoons chopped parsley and let simmer gently for 3 minutes.

MUSHROOM SAUCE
Makes 570ml/1 pt.

Sauté 1 medium size onion, very finely chopped, in a little oil for 3 minutes, add 170g/ 6 oz sliced mushrooms and fry for 3 minutes

more. Stir in 2 tablespoons lemon juice and 1 level teaspoon dried oregano or marjoram. Stir this mixture into the cooked hot *Basic white sauce* (see page 172) just before serving.

LEEK AND TARRAGON SAUCE
Makes 570ml/1 pt.

Trim and slice 2 good size leeks in thin rings and sauté in 2 tablespoons sunflower oil for 6 minutes. Stir in 1 rounded teaspoon dried tarragon. Add this to the *Basic white sauce* (see page 172) when the sauce first thickens then simmer the sauce for 3 minutes.

LEMON DILL SAUCE
Makes 570ml/1 pt.

Omit the bay leaf, mace and mustard from the *Basic white sauce* (see page 172) and when the sauce begins to thicken add 3 tablespoons lemon juice, 1 teaspoon very finely grated lemon peel and 2 tablespoons fresh chopped dill or 1 rounded tablespoon dried dill. Simmer the sauce for 3 minutes.

THINNER WHITE SAUCE
Makes 610ml/1¼ pt.

This is ideal for dishes like *Lasagne* (see page 136) where you are adding a sauce to a pasta dish. Simply make the *Basic white sauce* on page 172, but add 140ml/¼ pt more milk. Add a little more seasoning to your taste.

TOMATO SAUCE
Makes 1 litre/1¾ pt.

3 tablespoons virgin olive oil
1 large onion, finely chopped
2 large cloves garlic, crushed
1 teaspoon celery seeds, crushed
1 medium size green pepper, deseeded and
*   chopped*
2 bay leaves
2 tablespoons parsley, chopped
1 heaped teaspoon dried basil, or generous
*   tablespoon fresh, chopped*
1 level teaspoon dried oregano
1 level teaspoon clear honey (optional)
1 tablespoon lemon juice

794g/1 lb 12 oz canned tomatoes, chopped
2 rounded tablespoons tomato purée
1 tablespoon shoyu (naturally fermented soy
  sauce)
freshly ground black pepper, to taste

1. Sauté the onion and the garlic in the oil with the lid on the pan for 7 minutes.
2. Add the crushed celery seeds and green pepper and fry for 3 minutes more.
3. Stir in the bay leaves, parsley, basil, oregano, honey, lemon juice, tomatoes and purée. Stir well and cook on gentle heat with the lid on for 20 minutes. Take the lid off and continue to cook for 10 minutes more until the sauce thickens.
4. Add the shoyu and a little black pepper to taste.
5. Liquidize the sauce and reheat, but do not boil, just before serving.

PIQUANT CHILLI TOMATO SAUCE
Makes 1 litre/1¾ pt.

Add 1 generous teaspoon ground coriander and 1 slightly rounded teaspoon cayenne or chilli powder to the previous recipe when you are adding the celery seeds. After liquidizing stir in 4 tablespoons Greek yoghurt or sour cream. Delicious hot or cold. If reheating do not boil.

HUNGARIAN PAPRIKA SAUCE
Makes 1 litre/1¾ pt.

Paprika is not hot. It has a very high vitamin C content if not stored too long. Add 2 tablespoons paprika to the *Tomato sauce* (see page 173) when you add the tomatoes. You can leave this sauce chunky or liquidize it. Stir in 4 tablespoons Greek yoghurt or sour cream just before serving.

BARBECUE SAUCE
This sauce keeps well for 10 days in the fridge or freeze what you don't need.

Makes 570ml/1 pt.

½ recipe quantity Tomato sauce (see page 173)
1 tablespoon tomato purée
1 tablespoon cider vinegar
1 very level tablespoon molasses
1 very level tablespoon cayenne pepper
1 rounded teaspoon paprika
1 level teaspoon mustard (dry or Dijon)

1. Blend the purée, vinegar and molasses together until smooth.
2. Add the spices then stir into the tomato sauce.

BASIC CURRY SAUCE
Make this in bulk and store pots of it in the freezer. It is a great stand-by when you fancy a curry but the rest of the family don't. Simply pour over boiled eggs, mix into rice and vegetables or add cooked beans to make simple curry dishes in minutes. If you want it hotter simply add a little more cayenne or chilli powder.

Makes 1 litre/1¾ pt.

1 large onion, finely chopped
2 large cloves garlic
3 tablespoons sesame, safflower or sunflower
  oil
1 teaspoon mustard seeds
1 level teaspoon ground coriander
1 level teaspoon cumin
1 level teaspoon turmeric
1 level teaspoons cayenne or chilli pepper
¼ level teaspoon clove powder
1 cinnamon stick
3 cardamom pods
1 heaped teaspoon methi (fenugreek leaf) or 2
  large bay leaves
1 heaped teaspoon fresh ginger, grated
1 teaspoon honey (optional)
170 ml/6 fl oz water
1 small cooking apple, peeled and grated
1 rounded tablespoon tomato purée

*40g/1½ oz tamarind, soaked in ½ cup hot
water for 30 minutes or 2 tablespoons lemon
or lime juice and a curl of the rind*

1. Sauté the onion and garlic in the oil for 7
   minutes with the lid off on moderate heat.
   Let it brown very slightly.
2. Make a space in the centre and fry the
   mustard seeds for a few seconds. Take off
   heat.
3. Mix the dry spices with a little water to
   make a thinnish paste and fry this gently
   with the onion for 1 minute.
4. Add the cinnamon stick, cardamom pods,
   methi, ginger, honey, the water, cooking
   apple and tomato purée. Stir well and
   start to cook on gentle heat.
5. Press the tamarind and soaking water
   through a sieve and add the resulting
   syrupy liquid to the curry. Stir well and
   continue to simmer for 30 minutes.
6. This sauce improves if left to stand for at
   least 2 hours before serving. Take out
   cinnamon stick, bay leaf (if using) and
   cardamom pods. You can leave the sauce
   slightly chunky or liquidize depending on
   what you are using it for.

MOLEE CURRY SAUCE (LIGHT COCONUT MILK CURRY)

This is another curry sauce which can be the
basis of very simple curry dishes. It is used in
vegetable, fish or meat curries. Start making
the day before you wish to use it or use ready-
made coconut milk which can be bought in
cans.

Makes 1 litre/1¾ pt.

225g/8 oz desiccated or fresh grated coconut
850ml/1½ pt boiling water
3 tablespoons sunflower or corn oil
2 medium onions, chopped
3 cloves garlic, crushed
1 level teaspoon black mustard seeds
1 level teaspoon fennel seeds, crushed
4 cardamom pods, crushed
*2 tablespoons gram flour (chick pea flour, see
    page 166)*
1 level teaspoon turmeric
1 rounded teaspoon ground coriander

1 level teaspoon ground cumin
1 level teaspoon cayenne pepper
good pinch clove powder
2 tablespoons lemon juice

1. Pour the boiling water over the coconut,
   cover and leave to stand overnight.
2. Liquidize, then strain through a muslin-
   lined colander, squeezing out as much
   liquid as possible. You should get about
   800ml/1¼ pt thickish coconut milk.
3. Sauté the onion and the garlic in oil for 5
   minutes until soft.
4. Make a space in the centre and fry the
   mustard seeds for a few seconds until they
   pop.
5. Mix all the other ingredients with a little
   of the coconut milk to form a thickish
   paste. Fry this with the onion on gentle
   heat for half a minute.
6. Gradually add the rest of the coconut milk
   and keep stirring as you bring to the boil.
7. Turn down to simmer and cook gently
   with the lid on for 10 minutes.

Note: If adding vegetables then sauté chunks
of these for a few minutes in the oil just before
adding the spices and milk. You will have to
lightly steam those vegetables, such as
potatoes and other root vegetables, which take
a long time to cook. A good one to try in this
sauce is pumpkin. Just steam cubed pumpkin
pieces for 10 minutes then sauté with the
onion.

HOT 'N' SPICY 'CHOCOLATE' SAUCE (SULSA MOLE)

I use carob powder (see page 58 for more
information on carob) instead of cocoa in this
Mexican sauce (sulsa mole) which
traditionally includes meat. The traditional
recipe also includes sugar but as carob is
naturally sweet (whereas cocoa is very bitter)
added sugar is not necessary. I have also used
sunflower seed spread or hazelnut spread
instead of peanuts or peanut butter and I
think the results are even better than the
original classic recipe. You can serve this
sauce with beans and a rice and vegetable
dish. You can cut down on the chillies if you
want a milder sauce. If using the sauce with

beans then 340g/12 oz (dry weight) beans will be sufficient. Red kidney beans go very well with this sauce (see page 100 on how to cook these).

Makes 1 litre/1¾ pt.

2 tablespoons sesame seeds
2 level tablespoons hazelnut or sunflower seed
  spread
3 level tablespoons tomato purée
1 rounded teaspoon clear honey
½ teaspoon ground cumin
½ teaspoon ground coriander
½ teaspoon anise or fennel seeds, ground
pinch clove powder
¼ teaspoon ground cinnamon
2 teaspoons paprika
2 tablespoons cold pressed sunflower or olive
  oil
275g/10 oz onion, very finely chopped
1 large clove garlic, peeled and chopped
1 red fresh chilli
1 green fresh chilli
1 level tablespoon carob powder
1 tablespoon lime juice (lemon will do)
3 tablespoons raisins
330 to 385 ml/12 to 14 fl oz boiling water
1 level tablespoon vegetable bouillon powder
1 teaspoon oregano (or marjoram)

1. In a heavy-based frying pan toast the sesame seeds on a moderate heat, stirring constantly until they are lightly browned and popping.
2. Transfer to a mixing bowl, reserving 1 tablespoon of seeds for garnishing.
3. Blend the sunflower seed or hazelnut spread with the tomato purée, honey and spices until smooth and well mixed.
4. Stir this into the sesame seeds.
5. In a small bowl blend the carob powder with the lime juice until a smooth paste is achieved.
6. Heat the oil in a heavy-based frying pan and sauté the onion, garlic and chillies for 5 minutes with the lid on.
7. Make a well in the centre and spoon in the hazelnut and spice mixture, fry on gentle heat for 3 minutes.
8. Mix together and spoon into a liquidizer or food processor with the carob, lime juice and raisins. Blend, adding a little of the hot water as you process to make a smooth, runny purée.
9. Now put this purée with the remaining boiling water, vegetable bouillon powder and oregano into a saucepan, stir well and if too thick add a little more water. You should have the consistency of unwhipped double cream.
10. Bring to boil slowly, turn down to simmer and cook with the lid on for 10 minutes. Allow the sauce to stand for at least 1 hour to let the full flavour develop.

CHUTNEYS AND RELISHES

Here are just a few choice recipes which are firm favourites with those I have cooked for and taught.

SWEET AND SOUR MANGO AND COURGETTE CHUTNEY
Make 2 weeks before needed. This is my favourite chutney. It is equally delicious with spiced dishes as it is in sandwiches. Try a few dollops in potato salad.

I use dried mango in this recipe and after soaking you can really taste that lovely fresh mango flavour.

Makes 4 x 450g/1 lb jars.

225g/8 oz dried mango pieces
55g/2 oz tamarind (see page 166)
295 ml/½ pt cider vinegar
170g/6 oz demerara sugar
2 medium size courgettes, cut in 1 cm/½ inch
  cubes
2 level teaspoons black mustard seeds
1 large green pepper, deseeded and chopped
1 medium red pepper, deseeded and chopped
3 large cloves garlic, crushed
2 medium size cooking apples, cored and
  chopped (leave skins on)
170g/6 oz sultanas
1 level tablespoon fresh ginger, grated
1 rounded teaspoon ground coriander

1 rounded teaspoon cayenne pepper
2 cinnamon sticks, broken up
4 star anise (aniseed)
8 cloves
1 rounded teaspoon fennel seeds

1. Soak the tamarind in 1 cup boiling water for 30 minutes. Press through a sieve getting as much pulp out as possible. You will have a very runny brown liquid. Soak the mango in this liquid with the cider vinegar and sugar overnight.
2. Heat a large saucepan and dry roast the mustard seeds for a few seconds until they pop. Add all the other ingredients except the cinnamon sticks, star anise, cloves and fennel seeds.
3. Tie cinnamon sticks, star anise, cloves and fennel seeds in a piece of muslin and drop this into the rest of the ingredients.
4. Bring to boil, turn down to simmer, cover and cook gently for 20 minutes only.
5. Take out the muslin bag and discard.
6. Spoon the chutney into sterilized screw-top jars.
7. The chutney will store well for at least 6 months, but it won't last that long if you don't hide it!

DRIED PEACH CHUTNEY
You can use fresh peaches instead of dried, but you will need three times the quantity. The chutney will keep well for at least 6 months.

Makes 6 x 450g/1 lb jars.

450g/1 lb dried peaches, washed and soaked for 24 hours
425ml/³⁄₄ pt cider vinegar
340g/12 oz demerara sugar
1 large green pepper, deseeded and chopped
1 medium red pepper, deseeded and chopped
3 large cooking apples, thinly peeled, cored and chopped
170g/6 oz raisins or sultanas
1 level tablespoon cayenne pepper
2 tablespoons fresh ginger, grated
1 dessertspoon ground coriander
¹⁄₄ teaspoon clove powder

1 tablespoon white and black mustard seeds mixed
6 large cloves garlic, crushed

1. Drain and chop the soaked peaches.
2. Put the vinegar and sugar in a large saucepan and heat slowly until the sugar dissolves.
3. Add all the other ingredients and bring to boil. Turn down to simmer. Stir well, cover and simmer for 30 minutes.
4. Spoon into sterilized screw-top jars.

Note: The flavour is at its best after 2 weeks and surprisingly, even with all that cayenne pepper, it is not hot but just subtly warm and spicy. It is delicious with curries and in cheese and salad sandwiches.

ASIAN SPICED COCONUT AND SUMMER FRUIT RELISH
This unusual and delightful relish is not for long storing, but it will keep in the fridge for 10 days if kept in screw-top jars.

Makes 2 x 450g/1 lb jars.

85g/3 oz desiccated coconut
170 ml/6 fl oz water
1 very level teaspoon sea salt
85 ml/3 fl oz lime juice (lemon will do)
675g/1¹⁄₂ lb mixed fruit (choose some of these – peaches, apricots, mango, papaya, ripe pears, pineapple)
2 tablespoons fresh ginger, finely grated
1 level teaspoon cayenne pepper (more if you wish)
¹⁄₄ teaspoon ground clove powder
1 rounded teaspoon turmeric
3 tablespoons clear honey
1 level tablespoon coriander seeds

1. Purée the coconut, water, salt and lime juice in a blender until smooth. Stop the machine a few times and then blend again. Scoop out.
2. Prepare the fruit, washing and peeling if necessary. Chop as small as possible then mash this with the ginger, cayenne, clove powder, turmeric and honey.

3. Dry roast the coriander seeds in a pan over moderate heat until they start popping. Grind to a powder and add this to the fruit mixture.
4. Now combine the coconut mixture with the fruit mixture and mash together.
5. Let the flavours merge for a few hours before serving.

COCONUT AND ONION RELISH

This is a very simple recipe, but does not keep well. Use immediately served with curries and other spicy Asian dishes.

110g/4 oz desiccated coconut
¾ teaspoon cayenne pepper or 2 small fresh green chillies, deseeded and minced
2 rounded tablespoons very finely chopped onion
4 tablespoons lemon juice (or lime, even better)
good pinch paprika

1. Mix all the ingredients together in a bowl except for the paprika. Squeeze well together then loosen with a fork.
2. Sprinkle on the paprika and leave to stand for 1 hour before serving.

BRANDIED CRANBERRY AND APPLE SAUCE (OR RELISH)

This sauce is great served with *Nut, seed and bulgur roast* (see page 93) and many other savoury dishes. It keeps for 2 months if kept in the fridge.

Makes 2 x 450g/1 lb jars.

280g/10 oz packet cranberries
280g/10 oz tart cooking apples, thinly peeled, cored and chopped
140 ml/¼ pt apple juice concentrate
juice of 1 large orange
grated rind of 1 orange
1 level tablespoon clear honey (optional)
3 tablespoons cherry brandy

1. Put cranberries, apples, apple juice concentrate, honey (if using), orange juice and peel in a saucepan and cook on very low heat for 20 minutes.
2. Add the cherry brandy and cook for ½ minute only.
3. Spoon into sterilized screw-top jars and store in the fridge.

LESSON 9

MAKING SIMPLE DAIRY PRODUCE

This lesson includes making yoghurt and light low-fat cheeses, which are very simple to produce from either cow's, goat's or sheep's milk

You need no specialist equipment except for a dairy thermometer and some muslin. A small cheese press is only necessary if you want to make *Sally Hughes' pressed soft cheese* on page 183.

A *starter culture* is necessary in most cheese-making except for *Quark* (see page 181) and *Fromage blanc* (see page 182). Although milk has to be heat-treated to eliminate undesirable bacteria, this process destroys the cheese-making properties in untreated milk. A starter culture reintroduces these, ensuring a healthy ripening of the curd. The starter is milk containing a special bacterial culture which produces acid during the process of cheese-making. This bacteria feeds on the milk sugar, lactose, changing it to lactic acid. Wholefood shops and some chemists often sell starter culture.

Rennet is also an ingredient in most cheeses. You can use junket rennet but it is not as efficient as cheese-making rennet which is stronger. Rennet is an enzyme which comes from the stomach lining of a suckling animal and coagulates the milk. The discovery of rennet probably dates back to the time when milk was carried in bags made from calves' stomachs, where the enzyme was still alive and coagulated the milk as it travelled. You can use vegetable rennet with equal success. This is produced from a non-animal enzyme.

Most of the cheeses in this lesson are now widely available in shops, so even if you haven't the time or the inclination to make your own the following information will at least tell you a bit more about dairy foods and what goes into some of the huge variety of products available.

After reading the information about milk which is to follow you will understand why I suggest you try to obtain goat's or sheep's milk rather than cow's milk for making your own dairy produce.

ABOUT MILK

COW'S MILK

Recent medical research suggests that approximately 70 per cent of the world's population are most probably experiencing detrimental effects from over-eating cow's milk and cow's milk products. Also there is a great deal of evidence pointing to a strong connection between the over-consumption of these foods and heart disease. Furthermore, there is also evidence which associates cow's milk intolerance with conditions such as hyperactivity, hay-fever, asthma, migraine, eczema, aches in the joints, recurrent infections and diseases of the blood and kidneys.

The reason that such a high percentage of people have some difficulty in tolerating cow's milk and its products is because a significant number of us have a deficiency in the intestinal tract of an enzyme called lactase, which breaks down the lactose (a milk sugar) present in large amounts in cow's milk. This does not mean that you have to cut out cow's milk and its products altogether (unless you have been diagnosed as lactose intolerant). It simply means that these foods should be eaten

179

in moderation as part of a balanced healthy diet. Also if you have any of the symptoms listed above it does not necessarily mean that they are directly connected to consuming cow's milk, but you would be well advised to find out the cause.

Another important point to be aware of and that is that most of our cow's milk and its products are produced from livestock injected with growth-promoting hormones and fed on manufactured foodstuffs. The result is that much of the produce from these animals contains residual antibiotics. The true, short- or long-term effects upon the human body of consuming these residues has not yet been revealed, but why wait for them to show. Simply keep on asking for free-range produce. Fortunately, as the demand for produce from free-range animals grows, so does the supply. This year three local butchers' shops in our small town in Devon started selling free-range meat. It's about time!

GOAT'S MILK
Unlike most cows today, goats are free-range, that is they live naturally and feed on wild herbage from various grasses to beet leaves, nettles and thistles. Goats produce a milk richer in vitamins and minerals than cow's milk. It is also more digestible, and contains no allergy-producing proteins. A growing number of doctors now recommend using goat's milk and its produce as an alternative to dairy produce from the cow, because findings have shown that certain allergic reactions (see notes on cow's milk on page 179) have often been alleviated after eliminating cow's dairy produce from their diet.

This does not mean that a cure of these illnesses can be solely attributed to changing from cow's milk produce to goat's milk and its produce. All it means is that goat's milk produce seems to be easier on the human digestive system and is less likely to cause allergic conditions. Again I will stress that the whole of one's diet is important to maintaining health and to curing any illness. No one food can be a miracle cure for ailments of the body.

Goats are highly unlikely to catch tuberculosis, brucellosis or meleteuses, whereas cows not only can catch these diseases but can transmit them through their milk to humans. For this reason, cow's milk has to be pasteurized which destroys valuable nutrients and enzymes. Goat's milk can be drunk fresh with all its nourishing properties intact. It is now advocated that goat's milk is preferable to cow's milk for weaning babies. Goat's milk has better keeping properties than cow's milk and because of its molecular structure, it freezes well, though it is not advisable to store it frozen for longer than three months.

Taking all these factors into consideration, I think the hardy goat deserves to be more widely recognized and bred for its nutritionally valuable produce.

SHEEP'S MILK
This delicious milk is much thicker than either cow's or goat's milk. Like goat's milk, it has none of the allergy-forming proteins present in cow's milk and contains twice as many minerals, like calcium, phosphorous and zinc, and all the important B group vitamins. It also makes beautiful yoghurt and cheese.

Pecarino cheese from Italy is often mentioned in the book as an alternative to Parmesan. This is made from sheep's milk and matured in the same way as Parmesan, but it is half the price of Parmesan and I think it has a far better flavour. Some types of strained Greek yoghurt are also made with sheep's milk.

YOGHURT AND SOFT CHEESE

YOGHURT
Yoghurt must be 'live' to be of any use to the body. Live natural yoghurt contains two beneficial complementary bacteria – *Lactobacillus bulguricus* and *Streptococcus thermophilius*. If stabilizers and sweeteners are listed on a carton of shop-bought yoghurt, then it is not live.

Scientific research has shown that the bacteria in live yoghurt kill harmful bacteria in the large intestine by turning lactose milk sugar into lactic acid. Harmful bacteria cannot live in lactic acid. It has also been found that the bacteria in live yoghurt manufactures B vitamins in the intestine. So those who are taking antibiotics, which are known to cause vitamin deficiency, would be well advised to eat live yoghurt regularly.

You can make yoghurt with cow's, goat's, sheep's (ewe's) or soya milk (for soya milk yoghurt, see page 118) and either a dried starter culture or a few spoonfuls of live natural yoghurt. These are, however, some important points to remember. If the developing yoghurt is exposed to too high a heat it will separate and turn sour or bitter. If cheesy in taste, then it may have stray bacteria in it, so be sure to sterilize all utensils. The perfect temperature is around 43°C/110°F, because at 49°C/120°F the bacteria will die and under 35°C/95°F they become inactive. You can buy various yoghurt-making gadgets or use a wide-necked vacuum flask which keeps a constant temperature. You can also make very successful yoghurt in any deep plastic or stainless steel container with a lid. Wrap the container in a thick warm towel and leave it in a warm place such as an airing cupboard or alongside a radiator.

Makes 1 litre 140 ml/2 pt.

1 litre 140 ml/2 pt goat's, sheep's (ewe's) or skimmed cow's milk
dried yoghurt culture or 2 rounded tablespoons live natural yoghurt

1. Boil the milk until it reaches 88°C/190°F (test with a dairy thermometer).
2. Now put a lid on the saucepan to stop a hard skin forming and place the saucepan in a sink or large bowl of cold water to cool as quickly as possible to approximately 46°C/115°F (again test with a dairy thermometer).
3. Pour into a large sterilized jug and stir in either the dried culture (follow directions on packet for adding) or the 2 tablespoons of natural yoghurt. Stir well with a plastic spatula or a long plastic spoon.
4. Pour into the container of your choice (see notes above). Keep the developing yoghurt at as constant a temperature as possible by placing in a warm place. Leave to set –

it will take about six hours. When set refrigerate immediately.

THICK NATURAL YOGHURT
You can thicken your yoghurt either by maintaining the milk at simmering point for 15 minutes (before cooling to 46°C/115°F) which concentrates it or by adding four level tablespoons dried skimmed milk powder before adding the culture. Both will achieve a rich thick consistency.

STRAINED YOGHURT OR YOGHURT CHEESE
All you need is a piece of muslin and some cord to tie the dripping yoghurt up with. Spread the muslin over a colander, pour the fresh yoghurt into this, twist and tie the edges of the muslin with the cord. Hang over a pot and let drip for 4 to 8 hours. The longer you let it drip the thicker the cheese will be.

GREEK STRAINED YOGHURT
This is strained yoghurt where most of the whey is removed. You can buy cow's milk Greek strained yoghurt which is very creamy and ideal for making ice cream (see page 184). It contains 10 per cent fat which is more than most yoghurts. If you crave double cream and are on a diet then use this as an alternative. There is also a sheep's (ewe's) milk Greek strained yoghurt which is much lower in fat but still creamy and delicious.

QUARK
This is a low-fat soft cheese which is now widely available. It is very similar to paneer (Indian lemon cheese) and made either with

whole or skimmed milk. If using cow's milk then use skimmed but if using either goat's or sheep's milk then use whole milk. The only curdling agent is lemon juice so it is one of the simplest cheeses to make.

Makes approximately 225g/8 oz.

1 litre 140 ml/2 pt goat's, skimmed cow's milk or sheep's milk
4 tablespoons fresh lemon juice

1. Bring the milk to boil, take off heat and stir in the lemon juice.
2. Leave to stand for 10 minutes, bring the mixture to boil again then take off heat immediately.
3. Line a colander with a double thick sheet of muslin (large enough to hang well over the sides of the colander) and pour in the curdled mixture. Let most of the whey run through the muslin into the centre and tie up the overhanging ends of the muslin with string (do not squeeze). Suspend this over a bowl and let the rest of the whey drip slowly out for 1½ hours.
4. Open the muslin and scrape off the curds. Chill before using. Keeps for 2 to 3 days in the fridge.

FROMAGE BLANC
This soft French cheese was traditionally made with single cream or full-fat milk, but it is now commercially made with skimmed milk. It is similar to quark but instead of lemon juice, rennet is used as a curdling agent (see note on rennet in the introduction to this lesson, page 179).

Makes approximately 280g/10 oz.

1 litre 140 ml/2 pt goat's, skimmed cow's or whole sheep's milk
5 drops vegetable rennet

1. Heat the milk to 43°C/110°F (test with a dairy thermometer). Remove from heat and stir in the rennet.
2. Cover and leave to stand for 24 hours at an average temperature of 15°C/60°F (a warm room should be all right).

3. When set line a colander with a double thickness of muslin, pour in the mixture, bunch up the edges of the muslin and tie together (do not squeeze). Suspend and leave to drip slowly for 1 hour.
4. Open the muslin and scrape off the soft curds. Chill before using. Keeps for 2 to 3 days in the fridge.

LACTIC CURD CHEESE
This cheese is easily digestible and a good food for infants and invalids. It does not require rennet, but needs a starter to sour the milk (see introductory notes to this lesson for information on starter culture). The process in making is very simple, but it takes three days to make the cheese because of the long hanging time.

Makes 450g/1 lb.

2.2 litres/4 pt goat's milk
1 tablespoon starter culture
sea salt (optional)

1. Heat milk to 71°C/160°F and cool quickly to 32°C/90°F (test with a dairy thermometer) by placing saucepan in a sink of cold water.
2. Stir in the starter, mix well for approximately 1 minute.
3. Cover and leave in the airing cupboard for 24 hours. Heat gently to 38°C/100°F and leave for 30 minutes.
4. Turn this onto a large square of cotton sheeting, tie edges and hang to drain for 24 hours.
5. Open the cotton sheeting, add a little sea salt to the curds if you wish to, then turn in curds onto a large square of muslin. Tie edges and hang for a further 24 hours.
6. Chill before using. This cheese freezes well, and is good in both savoury and sweet dishes.

SALLY HUGHES' SOFT CHEESE
Absolutely delicious and very simple to make. Sally uses only 1 tablespoon starter and 4 drops of rennet when making double this quantity, with equal success.

Makes 450g/1 lb.

2.2 litres/4 pt goat's milk
1 tablespoon starter culture
4 drops vegetable rennet

1. Heat milk to boiling point (just beginning to rise up the pan).
2. Cool quickly, by placing the saucepan in a sink of cold water, to 32°C/90:F (test with a dairy thermometer) and pour into a scalded bowl.
3. Stir in 1 tablespoon starter and three drops of rennet.
4. Mix well for 1 minute. Cover and place in the airing cupboard for 15 to 18 hours. By then you will have a fairly solid mass.
5. Drape a large piece of muslin over a scalded colander.
6. Carefully ladle the curds into the muslin. Gather up the edges of the muslin, tie muslin and hang to drip in a fairly cool place for 18 hours.
7. When the cheese has drained enough, remove from the muslin, place in a dish, cover and refrigerate until needed. It will keep for at least a week in the refrigerator.

Note: There is no need to salt the cheese but you can if you wish. A good idea is to put some of the cheese into individual containers and flavour these little cheeses with either fresh chopped herbs, chopped chives, garlic and chopped parsley, nuts and raisins, celery seeds, green and red peppers, fresh chopped pineapple or mandarin oranges.

SALLY HUGHES' PRESSED SOFT CHEESE

Taking Sally's previous recipe for soft cheese, but doubling up on the ingredients, you can make a firmer cheese, either plain or flavoured, by pressing in a cheese press for about 12 hours.

If you have not got a cheese press you can improvise. Use a small 15 cm/6 inch cake tin or a large, cleaned and sterilized can (about 790g/1 lb 12 oz capacity) with holes drilled in the sides. You will also need a round, smooth, well-seasoned piece of wood (called a follower) which is just smaller than the cake tin or can in diameter and about 3.2 kg/7 lb in weight.

Makes 450g/1 lb.

4.41 litres/8 pt Sally Hughes' soft cheese (see page 182)
1 tablespoon finely chopped parsley (optional)
1 teaspoon minced garlic (optional)

1. Line your scalded cheese press, cake tin or can with a damp piece of butter muslin and pack in the soft cheese. If using parsley and garlic, mix with the cheese before packing into the press.
2. Fold the muslin over the cheese, place the wooden follower on top and then the weight. Let stand for 12 hours. You will only get a little whey so place the press, cake tin or can in a shallow dish while the cheese is firming. When pressed enough, remove the muslin, place cheese in a polythene bag and refrigerate. It will keep for 1 week. Try roughly ground black pepper pressed around the edge of this cheese, toasted crushed almonds, or walnut halves, for a change in flavour.

LESSON 10
HEALTHY DESSERTS

Traditional desserts are invariably packed with rich ingredients, such as cream, sugar, eggs and chocolate, which bump up the calories and, if taken in excess, can be detrimental to our health. I think a little of what you fancy does you good, but you don't have to overload the system for the sake of a 'naughty' indulgence when you can treat yourself without doing any harm or feeling too guilty. You can make superb sweet dishes using only the minimum amount (if any) of the ingredients mentioned above. For example, I tend to use Greek strained yoghurt where more traditional dessert recipes would use double cream.

There is no need for a shopping list in this lesson as most of the ingredients will have to be bought when needed. There are however a few ingredients which I will discuss in case some of you are not familiar with them.

SOME UNUSUAL INGREDIENTS

AGAR AGAR
This is a gelling agent which is 100 per cent vegetable in origin. It is produced from strong-tasting seaweeds but ends up as neutral-tasting powdery granules or flakes. It is great for making aspics, jellies and many delicious desserts. The quantity used varies depending on how firm the finished product is to be. Read the instructions on the packet but a good guide for ordinary fruit jellies is 1 slightly rounded teaspoon agar agar powder to 285 ml/ ½ pt liquid. It will not set in the presence of oxalic acid – found in wine, distilled vinegars, chocolate, spinach and tomatoes.

MAPLE SYRUP
Many so-called maple syrups are artificially flavoured and are in fact sugar-based. Always buy *pure* maple syrup which has no additives. It is dearer but has a much better flavour. So look carefully at the label.

FRUIT JUICE CONCENTRATES
These are made with 100 per cent concentrated fruit juice and contain no sugar. All varieties are naturally sweetened with apple juice concentrate which does not take away from the flavour of the other juices. The concentrates are evaporated by a low temperature centrifugal process that preserves the nutritional value of the fruit (high temperature processing destroys nutrients). The varieties available include strawberry, raspberry, blackcurrant, cherry and exotic fruit. I use these in making ice cream (see below) and jellies (see page 187). I also use them to make delicious fizzy drinks by adding 1 tablespoon to a glass of sparkling mineral water. Children love these.

ICE CREAM

Ice cream made with Greek strained yoghurt (see page 181) is very simple to prepare and makes a delicious dessert or, popped in a cone, a healthy wonderful treat for children. It is important to blend the ingredients twice during the freezing process as this breaks up the ice particles and results in a much creamier texture. The higher the fat content in ice cream, the more creamy the texture and although my ice cream recipes have a lower fat content than is traditional, they are deliciously creamy.

You can use either cow's milk Greek strained yoghurt or sheep's (ewe's) milk Greek strained yoghurt. Both give excellent results. You can also make ice cream using all yoghurt instead of the cream and yoghurt mix used in the following recipes. The ice cream will be a little icy but still very tasty.

STRAWBERRY ICE CREAM
Makes 800g/1 lb 12 oz.

225g/8 oz strawberries, washed
5 tablespoons strawberry juice concentrate
450g/1 lb either cow's or sheep's (ewe's) milk
  Greek strained yoghurt
1 small carton double cream
2 large free range egg yolks (fresh as possible)
1 teaspoon natural vanilla essence

1. Heat the strawberries with the strawberry juice concentrate on a very low heat until warmed through (do not boil).
2. Press through a sieve to get as much pulp as possible, then cool.
3. Put the cooled strawberry pulp and all the other ingredients in a blender and process until smooth and creamy.
4. Put in a plastic container with a tight lid and freeze for about 1½ to 2 hours until the edges are firming but the centre still softish.
5. Scoop out and blend again until smooth and all the lumps gone.
6. Return to freezer for another hour. It should still be softish in the middle.
7. Blend once more until completely smooth, then freeze until needed.
8. Before serving defrost for about 20 minutes in the kitchen until scoopable.

Note: In winter, when strawberries are either scarce or expensive, you can omit the strawberry pulp and make this ice cream using just the strawberry juice concentrate and a few drops of natural red food colouring. Blend all the ingredients together and freeze as before.

RASPBERRY ICE CREAM

Makes 800g/1 lb 12 oz.

Follow the recipe for *Strawberry ice cream* above, but use raspberries and raspberry juice concentrate (or just raspberry juice concentrate and natural red food colouring). Frozen raspberries are fine for this recipe.

CHERRY ICE CREAM
Makes 800g/1 lb 12 oz.

Follow the recipe for *Strawberry ice cream* opposite, but use cherries and cherry juice concentrate (or just cherry juice concentrate and natural red food colouring).

BLACKCURRANT ICE CREAM
Makes 800g/1 lb 12 oz.

Follow the recipe for *Strawberry ice cream* opposite, but use fresh or frozen blackcurrants and blackcurrant juice concentrate (or just blackcurrant juice concentrate and natural red food colouring). Add 1 tablespoon clear honey if not sweet enough.

APRICOT ICE CREAM
Makes 800g/1 lb 12 oz.

Follow the recipe for *Strawberry ice cream* (see opposite) but use exotic fruit concentrate and 225g/8 oz of ripe fresh apricots instead of the strawberry juice concentrate and strawberries. Stone the apricots and cook on very gentle heat with the juice concentrate until soft. Press the lot through a sieve and cool. Then blend with the other ingredients and freeze in the usual way.

MAPLE AND TOASTED HAZELNUT ICE CREAM
Makes 800g/1 lb 12 oz.

450g/1 lb either cow's or sheep's (ewe's) milk
  Greek strained yoghurt
1 small carton double cream
2 large egg yolks
1 teaspoon natural vanilla essence
5 tablespoons pure maple syrup
55g/2 oz toasted hazelnuts, roughly ground

1. Put all the ingredients in a blender except the hazelnuts and process until smooth.
2. Stir in the hazelnuts and freeze and reblend twice as for *Strawberry ice cream* (see opposite).

3. To serve trickle a little more maple syrup on top if you wish.

COFFEE, MAPLE AND TOASTED HAZELNUT ICE CREAM
Makes 800g/1 lb 12 oz.

Simply add 2 to 3 level teaspoons decaffeinated coffee instant granules dissolved in a tablespoon of warm water to the previous recipe. Blend and freeze in the usual way.

MELON AND GINGER ICE CREAM
This is very refreshing and great to serve with an Indian meal.

Makes 800g/1 lb 12 oz.

40g/1½ oz fresh ginger, grated
4 tablespoons warm water
1 good size Ogen melon
110g/4 oz fruit sugar
3 large egg yolks
340g/12 oz Greek strained yoghurt
1 small carton double cream
1 tablespoon lemon juice

1. Soak the ginger in the water for 10 minutes then press through a sieve or squeeze out the juice by placing the water and the ginger in a piece of muslin.
2. Cut off the top of the melon, scoop out the seeds and fibres.
3. Scoop out the rest of the melon pulp into a heavy-based saucepan.
4. Add the fruit sugar and cook on low heat until the pulp is soft. Mash with a potato masher and take off heat.
5. Whisk the egg yolks until a thin creamy consistency is achieved. Pour this into the melon pulp, put back on very gentle heat and whisk hard until a thin creamy consistency is achieved. Remove from heat and let cool in the fridge.
6. Whisk the cream then fold in the yoghurt.
7. When the melon mixture has cooled stir in the ginger syrup then fold the lot into the cream and yoghurt.
8. Spoon into a plastic container with a lid and freeze for 2½ hours. Remove from the freezer and blend until completely smooth,

then refreeze for a further 40 minutes. Blend again until smooth, then freeze for 40 minutes, then blend again and freeze until needed.

9. Leave to stand in the kitchen for 20 minutes until scoopable before serving. Meanwhile gently heat together 2 tablespoons maple syrup, ½ teaspoon grated ginger and 1 tablespoon brandy for a few seconds. Pour this over each serving of the ice cream.

FRUIT SORBET

APPLE AND MINT SORBET
Makes 800g/1 lb 12 oz.

450g/1 lb dessert apples, thinly peeled, cored and diced
200 ml/7 fl oz apple juice concentrate
2 tablespoons lemon or lime juice
1 large sprig fresh mint

1. Heat the apple juice concentrate, lemon or lime juice and the mint in a saucepan.
2. When hot add the chopped apples and cook on very low heat until softish for about 5 minutes only.
3. Let cool with the mint sprig still in, then take it out and liquidize the mixture until smooth.
4. Put into a shallow plastic container with a lid and freeze for 3 hours. Put into the chilled bowl of a blender and process for a few seconds until smooth but still frozen.

5. Spoon into the freezer container, cover and freeze until firm. Leave at room temperature for 10 to 15 minutes before serving.

PEACH, NECTARINE OR APRICOT SORBET

Choose ripe fruit and skin by blanching in boiling water for a few minutes. The skins will peel off quite easily.

Makes 800g/1 lb 12 oz.

450g/1 lb either peaches, nectarines or apricots or a mixture of all three, skinned and chopped
200 ml/7 fl oz exotic fruit juice concentrate
3 tablespoons lemon juice
2 tablespoons peach brandy (optional)

1. Follow the method as for *Apple and mint sorbet* above and add the peach brandy (if using) when liquidizing the mixture.
2. Freeze, beat and refreeze as in the previous recipe.

STRAWBERRY SORBET

Makes 800g/1 lb 12 oz.

1. Follow the method as for *Apple and mint sorbet* and freeze, beat and refreeze in the same way.
2. You can add the juice of one large orange and 2 tablespoons of curaçao if this is for a special occasion.

450g/1 lb ripe strawberries
200 ml/7 fl oz strawberry juice concentrate
4 tablespoons lemon juice

REAL FRUIT JELLIES

Forget those packets of jelly with artificial colourings and flavourings and make real fruit jellies very simply with pure fruit juice concentrates either with or without extra fruit.

SIMPLE FRUIT JELLY

850 ml/1½ pt water
170g/6 fl oz pure juice concentrate, either strawberry, raspberry, cherry, blackcurrant or exotic fruit
4 slightly rounded teaspoons agar agar granules or 28g/1 oz agar agar flakes

1. Warm the water with the juice concentrate.
2. Add the agar agar, stir well and continuously as you bring to boil. Boil until the agar agar is dissolved. Takes a few minutes only.
3. Pour into a jelly mould (children love animal shaped moulds) and let stand in a cool place until cold, then chill in the fridge.

EXTRA FRUITY JELLY

225g/8 oz fresh or frozen strawberries, blackcurrants, raspberries or apricots
850 ml/1½ pt water
170g/6 fl oz pure juice concentrate, either strawberry, blackcurrant, raspberry or exotic fruit, depending on the fruit used
4 slightly rounded teaspoons agar agar granules or 28g/1 oz agar agar flakes

1. Cook fruit in the water and the fruit juice concentrate for 5 minutes only on very low heat.
2. Strain through a sieve pressing as much pulp out as possible.
3. Return the strained juice and pulp to the saucepan. Heat to warm, stir in the agar agar, and keep stirring as you bring to boil. Simmer, still stirring, until the agar agar has completely dissolved.
4. Pour into a serving bowl or jelly mould and cool in a cool place then chill in the fridge.

CREAMY JELLY

Prepare either the *Simple fruit jelly* (see page 187) or the *Extra fruity jelly* (see page 187) but use 700 ml/1¼ pt water instead of the 850 ml/ 1½ pt. Let the jelly cool but do not set and whisk in 225g/8 oz Greek strained yoghurt. Chill in the fridge until set (you can use milk instead of the yoghurt – add in the same way).

CUSTARDS AND MOUSSES

FRESH APRICOT AND GINGER MOUSSE
This is a very simple and delicious uncooked mousse which can be made with a variety of fruits such as ripe peaches, pears, nectarines, mango and papaya. You can alter the flavour by using cinnamon or vanilla essence instead of the ginger and for a special dinner party dessert stir in a little brandy.

Serves 4.

450g/1 lb ripe apricots
1 tablespoon lemon juice
1 tablespoon clear honey
1 tablespoon maple syrup
1 heaped teaspoon fresh ginger, grated
110g/4 oz Fromage blanc (see page 182) or use
*   Quark instead (see page 181)*
1 large free range egg white

1. Blanch the apricots in boiling water for a few minutes. Peel skins off then cut in half and stone. Save 4 halves to garnish if you wish.
2. Purée the rest in a blender. Scoop out.
3. Stir in the honey and maple syrup.
4. Put the ginger in a piece of muslin and squeeze out as much juice as you can. Stir this into the apricot mixture and then mix in the fromage blanc or quark.
5. Whisk the egg white until stiff peaks form. Fold this gently into the fruit mixture.
6. Spoon into individual glass bowls and chill for 30 minutes.
7. Slice the remaining apricot halves into thin wedges and decorate the tops with these.

EGGLESS ALMOND CUSTARD
Serves 4.

110g/4 oz ground almonds
850 ml/1½ pt either cow's, goat's or soya milk
knob of polyunsaturated margarine
2 tablespoons clear honey or 2 rounded
*   tablespoons fruit sugar*
3 slightly rounded teaspoons agar-agar
few drops natural almond essence
a little grated nutmeg

1. Liquidize the ground almonds with 285 ml/½ pint of the milk for 1 minute.
2. Rub a heavy-based saucepan with the knob of margarine.
3. Pour the almonds with most of the remaining milk (save a little to blend with the agar-agar later) into the saucepan.
4. Bring slowly to a simmer then let simmer gently for 20 minutes.
5. Drape a double thickness of muslin over a colander (which you have placed over a bowl) and pour the almond mixture into the muslin.
6. Pour the liquid which has drained through into the bowl back into the saucepan. Add the honey and the almond essence and put back on low heat.
7. Blend the agar-agar with the remaining milk until smooth. Pour this into the almond milk, stirring vigorously.
8. Let simmer for 3 minutes still stirring. Pour into individual serving bowls or 1 large bowl and grate a little nutmeg on top.
9. Let cool then chill before serving.

CAROB BAKED CUSTARD CREAM POTS
This is a very rich egg custard with a chocolate flavour. You can use plain chocolate but carob (see page 58) is a healthier alternative.

Serves 6.

585 ml/1 pt milk
½ teaspoon natural vanilla essence
225g/8 oz plain carob bar, broken
3 rounded tablespoons fruit or raw cane castor
*   sugar*

½ teaspoon ground cinnamon
1 tablespoon + 1 teaspoon rum
4 large egg yolks
2 tablespoons flaked almonds

1. Preheat the oven to 325°F/160°C/Gas Mark 3.
2. Warm the milk and vanilla essence in a non-stick pan over very gentle heat.
3. Melt the carob in a good size bowl over a pan of hot water.
4. When melted stir in the sugar, cinnamon and rum, then whisk in the egg yolks one at a time.
5. Gradually add the warm (not hot) milk, stirring constantly.
6. Strain this into 6 individual ramekin dishes. Place these in a roasting tin with 2.5 cm/1 inch of water in it. Sprinkle a few flaked almonds on top of each dish and bake in the centre of the oven for 40 minutes or until a knife inserted in the centre comes out clean.

Note: In summer serve with *Strawberry yoghurt cream* (see page 191).

MISCELLANEOUS DESSERTS

CHILLED MANGO CHEESE PIE

No cooking is required for the filling but this pie takes 24 hours to set, so it is best to prepare it the day before it is needed. You can use 8 ripe apricots or 2 good size ripe peaches instead of the mango, but blanch them in boiling water first then skin them.

Serves 6.
You will need a 23 cm/9 inch loose-bottomed cake tin.

170g/6 oz wholewheat digestive biscuits
55g/2 oz sesame seeds
½ level teaspoon ground cinnamon
85g/3 oz polyunsaturated margarine, melted
225g/8 oz ricotta cheese, crumbled
170g/6 oz Greek yoghurt
3 tablespoons clear honey
1 teaspoon vanilla essence

finely grated rind of ½ lemon
1 large ripe mango
28g/1 oz flaked almonds

1. Preheat the oven to 300°F/150°C/Gas Mark 2.
2. Put the biscuits, sesame seeds, cinnamon and margarine in a food processor and process for a few seconds.
3. Press into the base and sides of the cake tin and bake in the preheated oven for 5 minutes only.
4. Cool (leave in tin) completely in the fridge before filling.
5. Put cheese, yoghurt, honey, vanilla and lemon rind into a blender and process until smooth.
6. Peel mango and cut into thin slices. Save 5 thin wedges for garnish and chop the rest of the mango into small pieces and stir into the cheese mixture.
7. Spoon this into the biscuit case and chill for 24 hours. Ease pie from cake tin.
8. Arrange the reserved thin mango wedges in the centre of the pie in a star shape.
9. Toast the almonds under a moderate grill until golden and sprinkle on top.

TIPSY FRUIT CHEESE PIE
Serves 6.

Follow the previous recipe for *Chilled mango cheese pie* (again you can use either mango, ripe apricots or peaches), but before adding the chopped fruit to the filling (remember to slice off a few thin wedges for garnish), make a marinade of 4 tablespoons exotic fruit juice concentrate (see page 184), 2 tablespoons brandy and a little grated fresh ginger. Stir this lot together and pour over the chopped fruit. Let stand for a few hours then drain and reserve the marinade. Stir the chopped fruit into the cheese mixture and continue as directed in the recipe.

When ready to serve decorate the top with the reserved fruit slices and put the marinade juice in a small bowl to spoon onto individual servings.

AUTUMN FRUIT COMPOTE

This is a lightly spiced mixture of fresh and dried fruit and is delicious as a dessert or spooned on top of breakfast cereal. You will have to soak the dried fruit overnight.

Serves 6.

170g/6 oz large stoned dried prunes, washed
170g/6 oz dried apricots, washed
1 litre/1¾ pt pineapple juice
2 each medium size ripe apples and pears,
*   peeled, cored and chopped*
170g/6 oz blackberries
2 tablespoons clear honey
2 tablespoons lemon juice
4 cloves
1 cinnamon stick, broken
1 level tablespoon arrowroot

1. Soak the dried fruit overnight in the pineapple juice.
2. Put the soaked fruit and the juice into a large saucepan. Add the rest of the fruit, the honey, lemon juice and the cloves and cinnamon stick tied in a piece of muslin.
3. Bring to boil, turn down to very low heat and simmer for about 15 minutes.
4. Mix the arrowroot with 140 ml/¼ pt cold water. Stir this into the fruit mixture and cook, stirring several times, for another 5 minutes. The mixture will thicken. Take out the muslin bag of spices.
5. Cool then chill in the fridge before serving, topped with *Vanilla yoghurt cream* (see page 191).

MINCEMEAT STUFFED APPLES
Serves 4.

110g/4 oz raisins, sultanas, currants, mixed
2 tablespoons lemon juice
1 rounded tablespoon honey or 2 tablespoons
*   maple syrup*
grated rind of ½ orange
2 tablespoons chopped almonds
½ level teaspoon mixed spice
4 good size Bramley cooking apples
knob of polyunsaturated margarine, to top

1. Mix all the ingredients, except for the margarine and apples, together and let marinate for a few hours. Chop in a food processor until almost minced.
2. Core the apples with an apple corer or a sharp knife.
3. Place apples in a baking dish.
4. Fill the hollow in the centre of each apple with the stuffing mixture.
5. Mix 1 rounded tablespoon honey (or 2 tablespoons maple syrup) with 110 ml/4 fl oz warm water and pour over the apples. Dot top of fillings with margarine.
6. Bake at 350°F/180°C/Gas Mark 4 for 45 minutes to 1 hour (depending on the size of the apples).

APRICOT AND WALNUT OR PECAN NUT STUFFED APPLES
Serves 4.

110g/4 oz dried apricot pieces
285ml/½ pt apple juice
1 rounded tablespoon clear honey
1 tablespoon lemon juice
½ teaspoon ground cinnamon
¼ teaspoon fresh grated nutmeg
pinch ground ginger (optional)
55g/2 oz chopped walnuts or pecan nuts
4 good size Bramley cooking apples
knob of polyunsaturated margarine, to top

1. Soak all the ingredients, except for the nuts, apples and margarine, for 4 hours.
2. Drain off soaking juices into a measuring jug (don't press the juices out – just drop out what will flow easily, leaving the fruit a bit moist).

3. Chop the fruit in a processor until nearly minced but not too mushy. Stir in the chopped nuts.
4. Core the apples and place in a baking dish, as in the previous recipe.
5. Spoon in the filling into the centre of each apple and dot tops with a little margarine.
6. Bring the soaking liquid in the jug up to the level of 140 ml/¼ pt and pour this over the apples.
7. Bake 350°F/180°C/Gas Mark 4 for 45 minutes to 1 hour.

VANILLA YOGHURT CREAM

If you have a passion for double cream but would like to cut down its consumption then here is a recipe to help you.

3 tablespoons double cream
225g/8 oz Greek strained yoghurt
few drops of vanilla essence
1 level teaspoon clear honey, to sweeten slightly

1. Whisk the cream in a small bowl until fluffy.
2. Fold in the yoghurt, vanilla and honey.

STRAWBERRY YOGHURT CREAM

Use 1 level tablespoon instead of 1 teaspoon honey in the *Vanilla yoghurt cream* above and stir in 225g/8 oz ripe strawberries, thinly sliced.

This is great with the *Carob baked custard cream pots* (see page 188).

ABOUT THE AUTHOR

EVELYN FINDLATER's interest in wholefood cookery began 13 years ago, when she was trying to incorporate more natural, healthy foods into her family's diet. She then progressed to running a wholefood shop and restaurant for four years, giving cookery courses and writing her first book, at the instigation of a local publisher.

She has now written and published ten books, is a regular contributor to several magazines and has appeared on radio and television. She also lectures and runs courses on wholefood cookery.

Evelyn lives near Bideford in north Devon, where she is just about to open her own cookery school and health centre.